# PORTRAITS OF AMERICAN CONTINENTAL PHILOSOPHERS

EDITED WITH PHOTOGRAPHS BY
## JAMES R. WATSON

**INDIANA UNIVERSITY PRESS**
*Bloomington and Indianapolis*

This book is a publication of

Indiana University Press
601 North Morton Street
Bloomington, Indiana 47404-3797 USA

www.indiana.edu/~iupress

*Telephone orders* 800-842-6796
*Fax orders* 812-855-7931
*Orders by e-mail* iuporder@indiana.edu

The paper used in this publication meets the minimum requirements
of American National Standard for Information Sciences—Perma-
nence of Paper for Printed Library Materials, ANSI Z39.48-1984.

Manufactured in the United States of America

Library of Congress Cataloging-in-Publication Data

Portraits of American continental philosophers / edited with photo-
   graphs by James R. Watson
      p. cm. — (Studies in Continental thought)
   Includes bibliographical references.
      ISBN 0-253-33593-0 (cl. : alk. paper). — ISBN 0-253-21337-1
(pbk. : alk. paper)
      1. Philosophers—United States. 2. Philosophy, European.  I.
Watson, James R.   II. Series.
B935.P66   1999
191—dc21
[B]                                                        99-35079

1 2 3 4 5  04 03 02 01 00 99

To the memory of
REINER SCHÜRMANN

*"The praxis that leaves things an open field can only
be polymorphous doing. . . ."*

# CONTENTS

# PREFACE

In autobiographical essays and photographs, *Portraits of American Continental Philosophers* presents a selection of contemporary American philosophers whose work falls within the distinctively American definition of "Continental Philosophy." Choosing the twenty-two individuals included in *Portraits* was a difficult task. Although I consulted and took into account the recommendations of colleagues, the selections were ultimately my own. I aimed to assemble a group of philosophers whose collected works demonstrate the nonhierarchical diversity and richness of continental philosophy in the United States. The only aspect of hierarchy reflected in this book is that the philosophers chosen represent more senior members of the profession. The years of experience and substantial contributions reflected in their essays provide a vibrant overview of the multiplicity and open-ended nature of continental philosophy in America.

Historically, continental philosophers in the United States have not been regarded as part of the philosophical mainstream. Although pluralism has become a watchword in the profession in recent years, the technical nature of much of the philosophy taught in American universities continues to limit the philosophical horizons of today's students. The American continental philosophers whose voices are heard in this volume have contributed immeasurably to the enrichment and broadening of our discipline. Working with each of the philosophers included in *Portraits* has been a wonderfully provocative experience. Their thoughts, writings, teaching, and professional dedication have made and will continue to make philosophy intellectually exciting for generations of American students.

This volume would have been greatly enriched by the inclusion of a contribution by Reiner Schürmann, late professor of philosophy at the New School for Social Research. Already gravely ill when I invited him to contribute to the book, Reiner was loathe to engage in any form of what might be perceived as self-display. Such was not his way. Had he lived, I hope that I could have persuaded him that his contribution would in no way be seen as self-display but as part of a many-sided celebration of what lies beyond the modernist and humanist encapsulation called the ego-self. It is vital to our field to keep the memory of Reiner and his crucial work alive. In this spirit of appreciation and remembrance, *Portraits* is dedicated to Reiner Schürmann.

# PORTRAITS
## OF
## AMERICAN
## CONTINENTAL
## PHILOSOPHERS

L‖

# ONE

# I Never Imagined Myself a Philosopher

## DEBRA BERGOFFEN

I never imagined myself a philosopher. An archaeologist or anthropologist perhaps, never a philosopher. But those were the days when American university women assumed they would marry and that their lives would follow their husbands'. Hardly compatible with wandering off on one's own. And then there was the question of finding my way in the world. A sense of direction was never one of my strong points. As I imagined myself an anthropologist I also imagined myself never finding the people I set out to study. A journalist perhaps? Same desires. Same problems. And so it went as I took the courses required of all Syracuse University students and searched for a suitable major. My first philosophy course barely caught my attention. If not for a certain weariness and impatience I never would have wandered over to the shortest registration line or allowed a certain Fernando Molina to convince me that a second philosophy course was essential.

Kant and I share the same alarm clock—David Hume. What do you mean, the sun might not rise tomorrow? My sophomoric head snapped. My imagination raced. My mind discovered high gear. My first experience of intellectual passion. If adventures in the material world seemed impractical, explorations in the world of ideas were possible. A young woman's version of the mind-body divide.

My apprenticeship in femininity was less than complete. It schooled me for marriage without teaching me that intellectual exercise would ruin my feminine figure. I was expected to think, to exert intellectual effort, to excel academically. When I announced my love for philosophy my parents were indulgent. Were I a son there might have been objections. Philosophy was not one of those professions considered practical for a son. But I was a daughter and could afford to be impractical. Ambiguous situations, chance openings—the incomplete feminine in a pre-feminist world steps through the looking glass.

Other passions led to marriage, to following a husband, and to children. The place and times of graduate school followed the laws of chance. Again there were odd openings. Washington, D.C., my new home, was the long-time home of Georgetown University, a fertile place in which to cultivate my interests in continental philosophy. A Jesuit institution accustomed to intellectual women in habits was welcoming to those in ordinary dress. A Jesuit institution that believed that marriage was a family institution could hardly discipline a married woman for conceiving. Allowances were made. Wilfrid Desan was crucial. He rejected my conventional wisdom—children now, philosophy later. Philosophus interruptus (master's degree now, doctoral degree later) he insisted would bear no fruit. And so I continued. Making time to take leave of children. Taking leave to make time for children. The rhythm method for philosophers.

Though my apprenticeship with Hume was brief, its effects were long lasting. His lessons in skepticism prepared me for Nietzsche's teachings in perspectivism. Hearing Nietzsche with Hume's ears, I did not hear the requiem for God as a prelude to nihilism. This is not to say that I gave up the idea of TRUTH easily. A sister to the Madman, I sought TRUTH. Following the madman in the company of Freud and Lacan, however, I have come to call TRUTH an imaginary object. As imaginary, TRUTH is the always already lost object whose loss either frees us for truths or lures us to nostalgic dogmatisms. It is both a promissory note (whose promise is always deferred) that enlists, sustains, and cultivates our desire and a nostalgic image whose lure alienates us in the *meconnaissance* of the fetish. Refusing melancholic nostalgia we elude the ascetic ideal and avoid the fate of those who either do not know that truth is a woman or who, like Bacon, prefer rape to flirtation, love, or friendship.

First lesson from Nietzsche: no philosopher wants disciples, no philosopher can be a follower. Second lesson from Nietzsche: we are all inheritors destined to take up the legacies of our genealogies. Third lesson from Nietzsche: we only belatedly, if ever, discern the lines of our inheritance; it is often only by chance that we arrive at the place we already were. I first applied these lessons to the constellation of issues that gathered around the names Sartre, Nietzsche, Freud, and Lacan. Later they informed my reading of Beauvoir.

In the beginning I read Nietzsche alongside (first) Freud and (then) Lacan. I now read these thinkers with and through each other. Nietzsche's eternal recurrence and supposing truth is a woman serve as koans for these readings. His themes of perspectivism, the abyss, and genealogy are threaded throughout. The idea of desire prevails. Taking up Nietzsche's charge that as heirs of the ascetic ideal we are the sick animal, I've explored the relationship between Nietzsche's diagnosis of our illness and the teachings of psychoanalysis. Over time, a feminist eye became essential to these readings. This eye sees that Nietzsche's genealogy (the genealogy of the ascetic ideal) and Freud's and Lacan's genealogies (the genealogies of Oedipus) are also the genealogies of patriarchy. As feminist my eye sees that the perversions of these genealogies feed on each other. I call the inheritor/perpetuator of these genealogies Oedipal man and see the symptoms of his (or her) disease in his (or her) image of woman, in his (or her) demand for TRUTH, and in his (or her) endorsement of the logic of sacrifice.

Neither Nietzsche, Freud, nor Lacan see his critique of the modern subject of Western culture as a critique of patriarchy. Nietzsche was no feminist. Freud said he never understood women. Lacan was content to mark her impossibility. Chewing on their writings, however, I find that they testify against themselves. Oedipal man will not be overcome without attention to the ways in which the desire of/for woman is figured and the desire for truth is lived. Nietzsche's idea of the eternal recurrence is a warning as well as a promise. The return (as in the psychoanalytic cure) may enact an overcoming. It may also produce a repetition of the same. Nietzsche and the psychoanalysts would have us overcome the illness of Oedipal man by returning to the Greeks. They may be duped by the idea of origins or they may be right. A cultural enactment of the psychoanalytic scene may be in order. This return, however, will be a mere repetition if it does not recover the repressed genealogies of the mothers and daughters, for it is in these genealogies of gifts and bonds that we find antidotes to the Oedipal legacy of sacrifice, violation, and destruction.

There are also resources for overcoming Oedipal man in the much-maligned humanist tradition. In calling himself an heir of Erasmus, Nietzsche directed us to them. In telling the story of humanism we have produced a monolithic narrative inspired by the names Moore, Bacon, and Descartes—modern epiphanies of the Oedipal ascetic desire. The name Erasmus has all but disappeared. *In Praise of Folly* has no place in this humanist line. In calling truth a woman, Nietzsche retrieves Erasmus's woman Folly without leading us to Erasmus's sustaining faith. Our affirmation of life's joys in the face of the abyss will need other hopes. Nietzsche offers us the eternal recurrence and the quarrel between the women life and truth. The quarrel is over a man, Zarathustra. It still speaks the logic of sacrifice. It is part of the Oedipal scene. Turning to other Greeks, I look beyond this quarrel. I ask what Demeter and Diana might teach us about returning and overcoming. The point of calling up/on these other genealogies is not to replace the destiny of Oedipal man with a destiny of woman but to learn to play the game of difference according to the rules of the *différance*. This is the game of the moment where the now is the when of the gap—the time of the *différance* of the before and the after—the time of the gift of deferral that defines us as finite, marks our passion, and opens us to the other.

Reading Sartre I struggled with the question of truth in terms of the questions of authenticity and alienation. The question of woman entered this reading only after I turned my attention to Simone de Beauvoir. *Being and Nothingness* was one of my formative texts. It introduced me to a philosophical subject, whose experience included feelings, whose moods carried philosophical currency, whose identity was fragile, vulnerable, unstable, and who was expert in the art of bad faith. Sartre's descriptions of the vulnerabilities, deceptions, and antisocial sociability of the *pour soi* rang true. I accepted the idea of the look, that there is no given "we," that violence is inherent in the human condition/situation, without giving up on the possibility of a "we."

Though I was prepared to accept Sartre's account of the ways in which political associations based on trust, friendship, and common commitments were unsustainable, I was troubled by his accounts of the body and sexual passion. At the time, my quarrel with the way in which Sartre inscribed lovers in the structure of the look seemed tangential to the important business of philosophy. Rather than focusing on the possibilities of the caress, my utopian desires turned to the possibilities of good faith, to Roquentin's hope at the end of *Nausea,* and to the secret of the "we" at the end of *No Exit.*

I determined that Sartre's *Critique of Dialectical Reason* sacrificed the insights of *Being and Nothingness* to Marxism as soon as it granted the Marxist the political premise of natural scarcity. At the time I noted, but did not probe, the implications of this tension in Sartre's thought. Now, thinking through the implications of Beauvoir's thought, I see it as indicative of the tensions between the ethical and political and see Sartre's failure to write the promised ethical sequel to *Being and Nothingness* in terms of his failure to extract the erotic from the violations of the look.

Our intellectual lives are no more autonomous than our "real" lives. That I spent part of my early school days crouched under a desk waiting for the bomb drill to end (or the bomb to fall) and most of my life in the shadow of the Final Solution cannot be segregated from my concern with the question of the "we." That the George Mason University philosophy faculty was absent a theorist to work with the university's emerging women's studies program was crucial for my feminist turn.

I came to *The Second Sex* late. Like many others I had heard so much about it I assumed there was no need to read it. Circumstances intervened. I agreed to teach our Women's Studies theory course, and found myself saying, "Well of course we will have to read *The Second Sex,*" which meant, of course, that I would have to read *The Second Sex*. Talk about being unprepared. The English translation may be problematic, the Sartrean overlay may seem obvious, Marxist social/economic categories may prevail, but for me, coming with ears tuned by Nietzsche, Freud, and Lacan, *The Second Sex* sounded different from the usual humanist, existential arguments for equality. Further, coming from a grounding in phenomenology and existentialism where the names Husserl and Merleau-Ponty are at least as important as the name Sartre, *The Second Sex* did not read as a text written by Sartre's invisible hand. My ears heard a distinct philosophical voice. To them Beauvoir's feminist breakthrough sounded like a unique ethical event. As a feminist breakthrough *The Second Sex* had clearly arrived. As an ethical event, however, it was invisible.

Taking my ruminations on Nietzsche, Freud, and Lacan into account, my reaction to *The Second Sex* now appears inevitable. That is not how it felt at the time. I seemed to be hearing voices. Beauvoir herself seemed to accuse me of hallucinating. I tested my readings at the Simone de Beauvoir and the Sartre Societies. Hazel Barnes was critical but supportive. Margaret Simons cheered me on. Jeffner Allen honed my reading. *The Philosophy of Simone de Beauvoir: Gendered Phenomenologies, Erotic Generosities* went to press.

I viewed the book as something of a reclamation project. Beauvoir by neither her nor anyone else's account was considered a philosopher. Whatever her personal reasons might have been for insisting that Sartre, not she, was the theorist, or that her ideas only echoed Sartre's, they failed to carry philosophical weight. There were texts that were clearly philosophical and these texts did not carry Sartre's signature. Ambiguity is one of Merleau-Ponty's categories, not Sartre's. Joy is not one of Sartre's definitive philosophical moods. Sartre's erotic, corrupted by the look, carries no ethical import. Most importantly, Beauvoir's analysis of intentionality was absolutely unique. There was nothing else like it in the existential-phenomenological corpus.

It was unavoidable: Beauvoir was a philosopher with a distinct philosophical voice. Like Sartre and Merleau-Ponty, she took up the legacies of the modern and phenomenological traditions. Unlike them, however, she attended to the phenomenological implications of ambiguity by developing the category of the erotic. Further, for her, the first philosophical questions concern the ethical relationship. Calling Beauvoir a philosopher, I hear her engaged in conversations with Sartre and Merleau-Ponty and speaking in two philosophical voices: a dominant voice that speaks of the situated, existential subject and advocates an ethic of liberation projects, and a muted voice that speaks of the flesh, the erotic, risk and vulnerability. This muted voice introduces us to an ethic of generosity and the gift and to the possibilities of a politics of the "we." It directs us to the ethical possibilities of the erotic event. It is more postmodern than modern with echoes of Bataille, Lacan (acknowledged), and Irigaray (refused).

In attending to Beauvoir's unique voice I hoped to grant her philosophical independence. In attending to her muted voice I hoped to find her a place in contemporary feminist and philosophical discussions. In the body of the book I see myself as a reader/interpreter heir of Beauvoir. In the epilogue I take up the role of heir differently. There I position myself as taking up Beauvoir's legacy by developing the implications of the erotic route to the "we."

Currently I find myself thinking through the possibilities of an ethics and politics guided by the principles of the erotic. This thinking is concerned to maintain the distinction and tension between the ethical and the political by attending to the difference between the gift, the mark of the first intentional moment, and the project, the second intentional moment's signature. It is attentive to the logic of ambiguity which I read as a logic of the "and" rather than as a logic of the "either/or," and which I see as a logic of finitude, failure, vulnerability, and risk. It is also attentive to the patriarchal situation.

In a world that reflected the life of consciousness we would each understand ourselves as the site of an intentional ambiguity. The desires of open generosity would be recognized as the ground of all values. In our world, the ambiguous human subject is gendered as either male or female and the contest between the desires of the first and second moments of intentionality becomes the war of the sexes. Further, as the desires of the first intentional moment are named woman and feminized and the desires of the second intentional moment are named man and valorized, the value of open generosity is "othered" and we "forget" its privileged ethical place. Given our current situation, I see the first task of ethics as that of exposing the perversions engendered by this "forgetfulness." Prompted by Beauvoir's "Must We Burn Sade?" and The Second Sex, I find that the disaster of the patriarchal perversion is clearest at the site of the erotically fleshed body and find the passions and vulnerabilities of this body recalling us to an ethic of generosity that challenges the concept of the modern subject and clears a space for a politics of the "we."

I see an ethics and politics guided by the principles of the erotic carrying two injunctions. First, I am enjoined to assume/accept the tensions of my ambiguity. Second, I am enjoined not to violate the other's vulnerability. Together, these injunctions create the opening for a meeting between us— an opening that we might call the space of generous intersubjectivity—the space of the "we."

This ethic of generosity and space of the "we" is an impossible ethic and place for both men and women who adopt the gendering of patriarchy. An ethic of generosity cannot find a place among those who prefer the securities of inequality to the risks of mutual vulnerability. It is, however, a possible ethic and place for those men and women who understand that it is neither as man nor as woman, but as sexed, ambiguous, fleshed and vulnerable beings that they occupy the site of their desires. Guided by the passions and generosities of the erotic event, they take up the risks of the gift and the bond. They bear witness against the politics that refuses to validate the original generosity that marks us as human.

My thinking again seems to be traveling along parallel paths. These paths are clearly self-referential if not autobiographical, but whether they will actually intersect in other ways I cannot say. On the face of it, thinking through the disaster of the Final Solution and thinking through the legacy of Beauvoir's ethics have little in common. Seen more closely, it may be that feminist questions and the question of the Final Solution cross on the body and intersect at the ethical and political. It may be that they share the responsibility of naming injustice and of witnessing. At the moment, saying this sounds too easy and too superficial. Better for now to keep these reflections separate and let them set their own courses.

Until very recently, I, like most, called the Nazi extermination project the Holocaust. I now find this name almost offensive. A holocaust presumes the existence of God. It recalls the story of Isaac. It promises redemption. What occurred in twentieth-century Europe was no holocaust. It was what the Nazis said it was—the Final Solution. We will only understand the Nazi legacy if we reflect on how it came to pass that political projects could be formulated and legitimated in terms of final solutions. We will not understand the implications of this legacy if we do not critically examine the ways in which we have, to date, chosen to name the disaster and to remember/ represent the monster in the public spaces of the monument and museum.

Immediately after the war the role of the witness was documentary. Today the role of the witness is more ambiguous and more complex. We were not there. For us the issue is not an issue of credibility but of propriety. It happened. It must be remembered. How can it be properly remembered? This, it seems to me, is the crucial question for our generation. This question is not entirely foreign to the questions of genealogy and the fate of Oedipal man.

My paper "Improper Sites" begins my philosophical confrontation with the Final Solution. It proposes that our witnessing be guided by two principles: one, the principle of the improper site, and two, the principle of uselessness. The second principle states that all witnessing to/of the Final Solution protests the politics of the look/teleology by insisting that no use be made of the Final Solution (e.g., that it not be made a case history for the teaching of tolerance and that the results of the "medical experiments" be destroyed). The first principle provides that memorials to/of the Final Solution not become proper (teleologically useful) sacred or secular places but be identified as improper sites—wasted places where only the monster speaks.

In thinking through the responsibilities of the witness I am trying to think through the secrets of the body and the ways in which these secrets were used to destroy the humanity of those who suffered at the limits of the degraded, tortured, and tormented body. I am also trying to understand why, despite the fact that the deportations and the policies of degradation were matters of public record, and despite the fact that hundreds of people helped the trains deliver the goods, only a few were informed of the policy of the Final Solution. I am trying to understand why these selected few were compelled to take death oaths of secrecy as they were accorded the highest praise for being chosen for this most honorable task, and why the millions selected for extermination were also forbidden to write or speak of their fate when victim and executioner agreed that no one would believe them. I think that thinking through the questions of finality, solutions, the body, and the secret may teach us how to remember those who were haunted (destroyed?) by the thought that there would be no one left to recite their names. Caught by this call to remember, this philosophical project feels weightier than my others. I think it will move more slowly than the others. It is, as they say, on its way.

I never imagined myself a philosopher. I now have the good fortune of being identified as one. I have the luxury of students and colleagues who encourage and challenge my thinking. I am given time and space to work. I have the privilege of not having to know where my thinking will lead. Certain responsibilities come with these luxuries and privileges: the responsibility to call students to the obligations of careful and complex thinking, to teach them to be suspicious of their assumptions and to encourage them to play/experiment with ideas; the responsibility to think as rigorously and honestly as possible; and the responsibility to speak of things that matter in ways that are accessible to those who care.

## Selected Bibliography

1978 "The Transcendence of the Ego: A Methodological Reading." *Philosophy Today* 22 (3/4).
1979 "Jean Paul Sartre's *Nausea:* Roquentin as Phenomenologist and Author." *The Personalist* 60 (1).

1982 "Sartre and the Myth of Natural Scarcity." *Journal of the British Society for Phenomenology* 13 (1).

1983a "The Eternal Recurrence Again." *International Studies in Philosophy* 15 (2).

1983b "Why a Genealogy of Morals?" *Man and World* 16 (Fall).

1984 "Sartre: From Touch to Truth." *Alaska Quarterly Review* 3 (1).

1986 "Sophocles' *Antigone* and Freud's *Civilization and Its Discontents.*" *American Imago* 43 (2).

1987 "Seducing Historicism." *International Studies in Philosophy* 19 (2).

1989 "On the Advantage and Disadvantage of Nietzsche for Women." In *The Question of the Other: Essays in Contemporary Continental Philosophy,* ed. Arleen B. Dallery and Charles E. Scott. Albany: State University of New York Press.

1990a "Being Philosophical about Sexual Harassment." *Women and Language* 15 (2).

1990b "Casting Shadows: The Body in Descartes, Sartre, de Beauvoir and Lacan." *Bulletin de la Société Américaine de Philosophie de Langue Française* 4 (2-3).

1990c "Nietzsche's Madman: Perspectivism without Nihilism." In *Nietzsche as Postmodernist,* ed. Clayton Koelb. Albany: State University of New York Press.

1990d "Posthumous Popularity: Reading, Privileging, Politicizing Nietzsche." *Soundings* 73 (1).

1990e "Simone de Beauvoir: Cartesian Legacies." *Simone de Beauvoir Studies* 7.

1990f "Toward a Feminist Ethics: First Steps." *Simone de Beauvoir Studies* 8.

1990g "The Body Politic: Democratic Metaphors, Totalitarian Practices, Erotic Rebellions." *Philosophy and Social Criticism* 16 (2).

1990h "The Look as Bad Faith." *Philosophy Today* 36 (3–4).

1990i "The Task of Becoming a Subject: Lacan's Rereading of Freud." In *Reconsidering Psychology: Perspectives for Continental Philosophy,* ed. J. Faulconer and R. Williams. Pittsburgh: Duquesne University Press.

1990j "Violence against Women." *So To Speak* 1 (2).

1993 "Feminism, Women's Studies, and the Media." *Matrix* 3 (1).

1994 "Nietzsche Was No Feminist. . . ." *International Studies in Philosophy* 26 (3).

1995a "Coveting a Body of Knowledge: Science and the Desires of Truth." In *Continental and Postmodern Perspectives in the Philosophy of Science,* ed. Babette Babich, Debra Bergoffen, and Simon Glynn. Aldershot: Avebury Press.

1995b "Out from Under: Beauvoir's Philosophy of the Erotic." In *Feminist Interpretations of Simone de Beauvoir,* ed. Margaret A. Simons. University Park: Pennsylvania State University Press.

1995c "The Science Thing." In *From Phenomenology to Thought, Errancy, and Desire,* ed. Babette E. Babich. Dordrecht: Kluwer.

1995d *Continental and Postmodern Perspectives in the Philosophy of Science,* ed. with Babette E. Babich and Simon E. Glynn. Aldershot: Avebury Press.

1996a "Contesting Intentional Anxieties." In *Phenomenology Past and Future.* Pittsburgh: Duquesne University, Simon Silverman Phenomenology Center.

1996b "From Husserl to Beauvoir: Gendering the Perceiving Subject." *Metaphilosophy* 27 (1–2).

1996c "Nietzsche's Women." *Journal of Nietzsche Studies* 12.

1996d "Queering the Phallus." In *Disseminating Lacan,* ed. David Pettigrew and François Raffoul. Albany: State University of New York Press.

1997a "Intentionale Angste bekampfen." In *Phänomenologie und Geschlechterdifferenz,* ed.Silvia Stoner and Helmuth Vetter. Vienna: WUV-Universitäts Verlag.

1997b *The Philosophy of Simone de Beauvoir: Gendered Phenomenologies, Erotic Generosities.* Albany: State University of New York Press.

1997c *Other Openings: Selected Studies in Phenomenology and Existential Philosophy,* vol. 22, ed. with John Caputo. *Philosophy Today* 41 (1/4).

1998a "Lacan's Hamlet." In *Cultural Semiosis: Tracing the Signifier.* Continental Philosophy Series, ed. Hugh J. Silverman, vol. 7. New York: Routledge.

1998b *Remembrance and Responsibility: Selected Studies in Phenomenology and Existential Philosophy, vol. 23,* ed. with Linda Alcoff and Merold Westphal. *Philosophy Today* 41 Supplement.

1998c "Nietzsche Was No Feminist. . . ." In *Feminist Interpretations of Friedrich Nietzsche,* ed. Kelly Oliver and Marilyn Pearsall. University Park: Pennsylvania State University Press.

1999a "Between the Ethical and the Political: Phenomenological Ambiguities." In *The Existential Phenomenology of Simone de Beauvoir,* ed. Lester Embree and Dorothy Leland. Dordrecht: Kluwer, forthcoming.

1999b "Buffoonery." In *Representation and the Unrepresentable,* ed. Thomas Brockelman, Hugh Silverman, and Wilhelm Wurzer. Evanston: Northwestern University Press, forthcoming.

1999c "Improper Sites." In *Contemporary Portrayals of Auschwitz and Genocide: Philosophical Challenges,* ed. Alan Rosenberg and James R. Watson. Atlantic Highlands, N.J.: Humanities Press, forthcoming.

1999d "Why Nietzsche Still." In *Nietzsche/Drama/Culture,* ed. Alan Schrift. Berkeley: University of California Press, forthcoming.

1999e "Simone de Beauvoir: Disrupting the Metonomy of Gender." In *Feminist Enactments,* ed. Dorothea Olkowski. Ithaca: Cornell University Press, forthcoming.

1999f "Marriage, Autonomy and the Feminine Protest." *Hypatia,* ed. Margaret A. Simons, forthcoming.

# TWO

## Expecting the Unexpected

⊑

# ROBERT BERNASCONI

It was not (to start again)
what one had expected. —*East Coker*

We do not know what the future will bring. That is why we must expect the unexpected, an attitude which, paradoxically, makes even the most predictable outcome surprising. If we keep the future open in this way, the past also becomes less certain. Insofar as my present projects are clearly defined, and so long as I am committed to them in their present form, it is a relatively easy task to map those events in my past that contributed to their formation. But if I am open to change and to possibilities that would never occur to me on my own, then I cannot be attached to a self-portrait that gives the impression that everything was already set from the beginning and that the point I have now arrived at was inevitable.

When James Watson invited me to present a self-portrait for a volume of American Continental philosophers, I was surprised. It was a pleasant surprise, but I could not shake the feeling that I did not belong in that category, even after ten years in the United States. I am certainly not—or, more cautiously, I am not yet and do not anticipate becoming—American. I still think of myself as English. And I have, in fact, increasingly come to dislike the label "Continental Philosophy," not least for its presumption that one can say "Continental" and mean "European," as we used to do without a second thought in Britain. Of course, philosophers from the European mainland are not likely to call what they do "Continental Philosophy" or even "European Philosophy." But Continental Philosophy is what I used to call the kind of philosophy I did and to a large extent continue to do, and insofar as the United States of America is where I do it, the label applies. It also fits insofar as I came to think differently of Continental Philosophy, not only after coming to America, but as a result of doing so.

I never expected to leave Britain for the United States, and when in 1988 I did make the move to Memphis, I was mistaken as to what I would find there. I moved for the department and the music, and both were even better than I had anticipated. But even though the PBS series on the civil rights movement, *Eyes on the Prize,* was shown on British television between the time I accepted the position and the time I arrived, I was totally unprepared for a society where anti-Black racism is not only outspoken but blatantly institutionalized, even as it is strenuously denied. Indeed, it took me a year or two to recognize its pervasiveness and the remorseless process by which I was being assimilated into an economic and social system whose consequences were unconscionable. In *The Colonizer and the Colonized,* Albert Memmi describes a similar process, albeit in a different context, undergone by those who come from elsewhere but are marked from the outset as beneficiaries of the system. So-called post-colonialism has not changed its basic structure. In today's global economy, the rich countries rely on the cheap labor of the so-called third world, even while they try to maintain low wages at home by keeping a portion of the labor force unemployed and in poverty. This means that I could have had a similar experience elsewhere—in Britain, for example, where the standard of living and social privileges I enjoyed were also paid for by others whose work still left them below the poverty line. It is well-known that the British, and especially the English, have their own forms of racism and xenophobia. But coming from England into a society where the gulf between rich and poor was so visible, there was no possibility of evading it. For how long, though, would my sense of outrage persist? And to what purpose would I maintain it?

I have said that I think of myself as English. The United States government classifies me as a resident alien. But in Memphis I am white. This is more than a question of other people's perceptions of me. However I may work to slow the process of assimilation by keeping my accent and my manners, it happens against my will. In a society organized around color, where long-standing white opposition to integration of the schools and of housing persists, my own attempt to resist integration is futile. The issues transcend the personal and invite a reflection on the relation of the ethical and the political. They provide the present context for my philosophizing.

It was Memphis, and the shock of a racially segregated society marked by so much indifference, that woke me from the dogmatic slumber into which I had slipped. It is possible that I would not have become quite so obsessed by the pervasiveness of American racism if at the same time I had not from the outset been so readily drawn to the culture developed by African Americans, partly in response to white hatred. Living in Memphis made certain aspects of this culture readily accessible to me, for example in the churches and the blues clubs. In any case, Memphis led me to investigate the roots of the racism pervading this society of which I, too, was now a part and in which I was therefore implicated.

In general, my philosophical questioning, such as it is, is inspired less by wonder than by puzzlement. I am not searching for answers, but for a little illumination. It is hard to know why what seems to illuminate does so. What is it about tracing a history, sketching a narrative, referring a concept to an experience and its context, that makes us think we are making sense of something? In offering some account of the hitherto largely unexplained, is one simply reducing the unexpected to something that might have been expected? Within a narrative, everything is accommodated; the unexpected happens but, once incorporated, tends to be dissolved as such. It is difficult to maintain a sense of contingency. Otherwise said, there is a task here for phenomenology, with its sensitivity to questions of access.

Philosophy in this mode begins in the experience of being at a loss. That includes being at a loss for words, as, for example, I was when a stranger, upon hearing that I was a philosopher, asked me, "Why do white people hate black people?" This is not a problem to be solved. The investigation of racism, the task of tracking it down and exposing its logic, should not attempt to offer an explanation of racism if that means to explain it away. Racism is not to be normalized, however normal it may have become. I cannot say for certain where my current research is leading. In addition to examining the contemporary discourse on race and racism, I am working on the history of the concept of race in Buffon, Kant, and Blumenbach, as well as its subsequent use in philosophies of history, where narratives, much like those we impose on others and on ourselves, are applied to world history, much to the advantage of the West. It is important to recognize the racism in Kant and Hegel, for example, but not so as to find an excuse for not reading them. The challenge is to chart the complexity of racist ways of thinking and to illustrate the ease with which prejudice infects even the most rigorous and reflective thinkers. There is a lesson to be learned about the difficulty of avoiding racism and the first task is to understand better the logic of racism.

I will soon finish a manuscript, *Boxes,* which deals with the invention of the confessional box, the poor box, the ballot box, the ghetto, and the suburb. My genealogical investigations show the unexpected effects of political and social planning. The intentions of those who invented these instruments were thwarted, producing something other than what was intended. My interest in these boxes arose out of an attempt to understand what seemed paradoxical in daily life: Why the obsession with confession and introspection in a church that preaches that the left hand should not know what the right hand is doing? Why do I feel guilty when I give to so-called panhandlers on the street and also when I do not give? Why do politicians appeal to the self-interest of isolated groups of voters and then believe that the results of the election will reflect the interests of the country as a whole? Why did anyone think that, by ghettoizing a class of people with whom they did not want to live, they would make that population disappear, when in fact the ghetto just prevents their assimilation? What underlies the abandonment of the cities by suburbanites and what are its effects?

I developed much of the work for *Boxes* in the context of the Taniguchi symposium on eco-ethics held in Japan under the inspiration of Tomonobu Imamichi. Each year Imamichi invites a handful of philosophers from around the world and by the strength of his example encourages us to rethink what we are doing philosophically with an eye to the new ethical problems posed by a world that traditional ethics were unable to anticipate. Imamichi, who is as well versed in Western philosophy as he is in Chinese and Japanese philosophy, is foremost among those who have helped me to understand, in a concrete way, what so many of us in Europe and North America have deprived ourselves of by restricting ourselves to the tradition of so-called Western metaphysics. Thanks in part to Imamichi's example, in addition to investigating individual racism and the structures of institutional racism, I have inevitably become concerned with racism in philosophy as well.

It seems to me that the refusal of Western philosophers to entertain the wisdom of, for example, Africa, India, and China as genuine philosophy will one day be seen to be as scandalous and as incomprehensible as the earlier failure of Westerners to recognize the genuineness of the art and religion of those countries. I have chosen that way of putting it to emphasize how readily and how recklessly an idiom leads one to look to the future to validate conclusions reached today. I have no idea what will happen, other than the unexpected, but in order to help provide the context in which the unexpected will happen, I have been examining the history of the history of philosophy in the eighteenth and early nineteenth centuries. It was only then that a consensus was formed in Western Europe to restrict philosophy to a linear tradition beginning in Greece. It is clear that this is an artificial construction and, having examined the evidence and heard in the churches of Memphis the complaints about the exclusion of Egyptian philosophy, I do not doubt that this construction should be discarded. It was, however, an assumption I did not question in my early publications. For example, my doctoral thesis with Rickie Damman at Sussex University, which became my first book, *The Question of Language and Heidegger's History of Being,* was concerned in its first chapter with the similarity, but especially with the differences, between Heidegger's account of the history of philosophy and Hegel's. Although I still, by and large, stand by the interpretation presented there, I no longer view the story about the unity of the history of Western metaphysics as the great truth that I once thought it to be. This change of view has also had an impact on how I now regard the early works of Derrida, whose overall effect, perhaps in spite of his intentions, has unfortunately been to reinforce a sense of the unity of Western philosophy.

Although much of my work over the past twenty-five years or so has been concerned with Heidegger's account of the overcoming of metaphysics, and with Derrida's transformation of Heidegger's account in the shape of deconstruction, it has always been with the larger aim of juxtaposing Derrida with Levinas as ways of thinking after Heidegger. I came across Levinas's *Totality and Infinity* (in Al Lingis's translation) in Compendium, a bookshop in Camden Town that was the main resource for those of us in Britain who had turned our backs on Anglo-American philosophy. That was in 1972, a year before John Mepham at Sussex told me about the work of Jacques Derrida, and it was not until 1979 that, under the auspices of David Wood at Warwick University, I first met any real Heidegger scholars with whom I could discuss questions of interpretation. It was not until 1981 that I began my long association with the Collegium Phaenomenologicum, held annually in Perugia, Italy, which put me in touch with a community of like-minded philosophers based mainly in France, Belgium, Germany, and North America. The friendships I made there provided the context for most of my early work, including both books on Heidegger. What I dislike most about what I have written here is my failure to mention the names of many of the people with and from whom I have learned, people by whom I have been inspired, including especially some who were at one time my students. There are books that I cannot reread without recalling them. If I do not list names, perhaps it is because of the classic problem at the heart of Levinas's thought: attention to one is violence to another. Or perhaps it is because I am still English enough to want not to embarrass anyone who might come across this piece and be taken by surprise.

In those early years I was drawn to Levinas because he seemed to provide some of what I was unable to find in Heidegger. In 1972 my expectations of philosophers were formed by my passion for Buber's *I and Thou,* Arendt's *Between Past and Future,* Jürgen Moltmann's *Theology of Hope,* and Scheler's *The Nature of Sympathy.* At that time, my thought was determined by experience, and the decisive experiences for me then were of love, beauty, and the holy. I first read Heidegger early in 1970 when, picking up on an endnote in Arendt, I turned to *Platons Lehre von der Wahrheit* to help me write an essay on Plato's *Republic* for my first philosophy course. I was a history major, and at the start of the term Terry Diffey gave us a choice between Plato and Ayer's *Language, Truth and Logic,* a book I had already tried to read without much success; this iconoclastic text literally put me to sleep every time I picked it up. Ayer was standard fare in British universities at the time. In 1976, when I moved to Essex University, it was the first book all students had to read and so the first book I had to teach there. I provide these details to emphasize not just the contingency of my path to philosophy, let alone my staying on that path, but also the arbitrariness with which I now reconstruct it. I could, after all, just as well include among the books that captivated me in the late '60s such works as Teilhard de Chardin's *Le milieu divin,* Dostoevsky's *Brothers Karamazov,* Fanon's *The Wretched of the Earth,* and Walter Ullman's *Individual and Society in the Middle Ages.* The wonder is that I became a philosopher in Britain at all —one of my teachers, after a Heideggerian moment in an essay on Leibniz, specifically told me that I never would—and as a graduate student there was no expectation, either on my part or anyone else's that I recall, that I would ever get a job.

I was drawn to Levinas because I was looking for an account of sociality, even though I now recognize that his intention was somewhat different. Today I am drawn to him in my desire to develop an account of the relationship between the political and the ethical, a relationship about which he is extraordinarily reticent. More specifically, I am looking for an account in which one cannot evade responsibility for a system which one did not create, but which one simply inherits. The new focus of my philosophical interests, which has led me to alter my take on both Heidegger and Derrida, has also complicated my response to Levinas. This new complexity, together with the fact that Derrida seems always to have something new to say about Levinas, and also the research on race and racism I mentioned earlier, have delayed completion of my long-announced book *Between Levinas and Derrida.* I thought it important to keep my new interests in touch with the old, not because I was worried about consistency or continuity as such, but because it seemed I had a responsibility to do so. In any case the book, virtually complete in 1988, is now nearing completion again. More precisely, I expect to complete it soon, but always with the foreboding that the unexpected might again take over.

Rewriting is what I do, partly because I never seem to get it right. *The Question of Language* was not only about Heidegger. It was about experience, especially the experience of the loss of language. The book was to have been called *Where Words Break,* with its echoes of Stefan George and T. S. Eliot, until the publishers insisted otherwise. Eliot wrote:

Words strain,
Crack and sometimes break, under the burden,
Under the tension, slip, slide, perish,
Decay with impression, will not stay in place,
Will not stay still.
—*Burnt Norton*

It is tempting to construct a text that is in pieces, discontinuous, self-interruptive, or in two columns, like Derrida's *Glas,* but it always seems to me that my texts fall apart of their own accord. It is more difficult, for me at least, to write a text that sustains a sense of the unexpected. To do so, it seems that I have to cross everything out and start again. And again.

> Every attempt
> Is a wholly new start, and a different kind of failure
> Because one has only learnt to get the better of words
> For the thing one no longer has to say, or the way in which
> One is no longer disposed to say it.
> —*East Coker*

Or, as Eliot also put it, "Twenty years largely wasted." But, as one continues the process—the luxury or folly—of educating oneself in public, at what point, if ever, can one make that call?

I am quite serious when I say that one of my main motives for publishing is to be freed from the task of rewriting the same piece over and over again. Even so, after the proofs, there are still demands for an abstract. Worse yet, however obscure the journal in which one publishes, there is still the danger that someone might read it. It is not that I do not want to communicate, although I am happiest doing that where there can be some exchange of ideas. One of the drawbacks of publishing is that people tend to define you by what you have written, sometimes long ago. Your past interests are assumed to be your current ones. That is no more than a nuisance until you start believing it yourself. It is one thing for a scholar to try to make sense of a thinker's corpus by identifying certain strands that tie it together and give it continuity. It is another thing altogether to perform a similar operation on one's own work, as if one were writing one's obituary, which is perhaps what we always do anyway, wherever we sit down to write.

So when James Watson telephoned, I was not eager to cast a retrospective gaze over my writings. I did not want to have to recall them and be reminded of much that I have forgotten, perhaps on purpose. I knew that, although I was under no obligation to constitute my work as a unity, I would begin to see connections I had not seen before. I cannot avoid trying to form patterns. We do it all the time, constructing an order where none was apparent, explaining the inexplicable. But I wanted to say, at least in part, echoing Eliot in *Little Gidding,* "These things have served their purpose: let them be." Or maybe I am just being English about the whole thing.

I like to think that someone who already knows me and some of my early work—perhaps beginning with James Watson when he finds this essay in the mail—will be surprised at how I have chosen to present myself, but the sense of surprise would soon evaporate. Retrospectively, it is easy enough to convince oneself that there are no surprises. In any case, I cannot control these responses and any attempt to do so is likely to lead to disappointment. Nevertheless, it is sometimes important to try to find a way of keeping a sense of the unexpected alive. Sometimes it is important to refuse to accept as normal what others have grown used to.

## Selected Bibliography

1982 "Levinas Face to Face—with Hegel." *Journal of the British Society for Phenomenology* 13 (3): 267–276.

1985 *The Question of Lanquage in Heidegger's History of Being.* Atlantic Highlands, N.J.: Humanities Press.

1986a "Levinas and Derrida: The Question of the Closure of Metaphysics." In *Face to Face with Levinas,* ed. R. Cohen, pp. 181–202. Albany: State University of New York Press.

1986b "Hegel and Levinas: The Possibility of Reconciliation and Forgiveness." *Archivio di Filosofia* 54 (1–3): 325–346.

1987a "Deconstruction and the Possibility of Ethics." In *Deconstruction and Philosophy,* ed. J. Sallis, pp. 122–139. Chicago: University of Chicago Press. Translated into German as "Dekonstruktion and die Möglichkeit von Ethik." *Fragmente* 39/40 (1992): 231–248.

1987b "Technology and the Ethics of Praxis." *Acta Institutionis Philosophiae et Aestheticae* (Tokyo) 5: 93–108.

1987c "Fundamental Ontology, Metontology and the Ethics of Ethics." *Irish Philosophical Journal* 4 (1/2): 76–93.

1988a "The Trace of Levinas in Derrida." In *Derrida and Differance,* ed. with D. Wood, pp. 13–29. Evanston: Northwestern University Press.

1988b "Levinas: Philosophy and Beyond." In *Philosophy and Non-Philosophy since Merleau-Ponty.* Continental Philosophy Series, ed. Hugh J. Silverman, vol. 1, pp. 232–258. New York: Routledge.

1988c "'Failure of Communication' as a Surplus: Dialogue and Lack of Dialogue between Buber and Levinas." In *The Provocation of Levinas: Rethinking the Other,* ed. with D. Wood, pp. 100–135. London: Routledge.

1988d "The Silent Anarchic World of the Evil Genius." In *The Collegium Phaenomenologicum: The First Ten Years,* ed. Giuseppina Moneta, John Sallis, and Jacques Taminiaux, pp. 257–272. Dordrecht: Kluwer.

1988e "The Infinite Task of Confession: A Contribution to the History of Ethics," *Acta Institutionis Philosophiae et Aestheticae* (Tokyo) 6: 75–92.

1989a "Seeing Double: Destruction and Deconstruction." In *Dialogue and Deconstruction: The Gadamer-Derrida Encounter,* ed. R. Palmer and D. Michelfelder, pp. 233–250. Albany: State University of New York Press.

1989b "Rereading *Totality and Infinity.*" In *The Question of the Other: Essays in Contemporary Continental Philosophy,* ed. A. Dallery and C. Scott, pp. 23–40. Albany: State University of New York Press.

1989c "Persons and Masks: The *Phenomenology of Spirit* and Its Laws." *Cardozo Law Review* 10 (5/6): 1695–1711.

1989d "Locke and the Politics of Desire." *Acta Institutionis Philosophiae et Aestheticae* (Tokyo) 7: 97–110.

1990a "One-Way Traffic: The Ontology of Decolonization and Its Ethics." In *Ontology and Alterity in Merleau-Ponty*, ed. Galen A. Johnson and Michael B. Smith, pp. 67–80. Evanston: Northwestern University Press.

1990b "Rousseau and the Supplement to the *Social Contract*: Deconstruction and the Possibility of Democracy." *Cardozo Law Review* 11 (5/6): 1539–1564.

1990c "The Ethics of Suspicion." *Research in Phenomenology* 20: 3–18. Translated into German as "Die Ethik des Verdachts." *Fragmente* 39/40 (1992): 79–96.

1991a "Skepticism in the Face of Philosophy." In *Rereading Levinas*, ed. with Simon Critchley, pp. 149–161. Bloomington: Indiana University Press.

1991b "The Constitution of the People: Frederick Douglass and the Dred Scott Decision." *Cardozo Law Review* 13 (4): 1281–1296.

1991c "The Poor Box and the Changing Face of Charity in Early Modern Europe." *Acta Institutionis Philosophiae et Aestheticae* (Tokyo) 10: 33–54.

1992a "No More Stories, Good or Bad: De Man's Criticism of Derrida on Rousseau." In *Derrida: A Critical Reader*, ed. D. Wood, pp. 137–166. Oxford: Blackwell.

1992b "At War within Oneself: Augustine's Phenomenology of the Will in the *Confessions*." In *Eros and Eris: Contributions to a Hermeneutical Phenomenology*, ed. P. van Tongeren et al., pp. 57–65. Dordrecht: Kluwer.

1992c "Who Is My Neighbor? Who Is the Other? Questioning the Generosity of Western Thought." In *Ethics and Responsibility in the Phenomenological Tradition*, ed. Richard Rojcewicz, pp. 1–31. Pittsburgh: Duquesne University, Simon Silverman Phenomenology Center.

1992d "Locke's Almost Random Talk of Man: The Double Use of Words in the Natural Law Justification of Slavery." In *Metaphysik—Grundlegungsprobleme Heute*, ed. Rudolph Berlinger. *Perspektiven der Philosophie* 18: 293–318.

1992e "The Anglican Bishop and the Pagan Priests: Warburton and the Hermeneutics of Egyptian Hieroglyphs." *Archivio di Filosofia* 60 (1–3): 131–144.

1993a *Heidegger in Question: The Art of Existing*. Atlantic Highlands, N.J.: Humanities Press.

1993b "The Ghetto and Other Gated Communities." *Acta Institutionis Philosophiae et Aestheticae* (Tokyo) 11: 37–54.

1993c "On Deconstructing Nostalgia for Community within the West: The Debate between Nancy and Blanchot." *Research in Phenomenology* 23: 3–23.

1993d "Politics beyond Humanism: Mandela and the Struggle against Apartheid." In *Working through Derrida*, ed. Gary Madison, pp. 94–119. Evanston: Northwestern University Press.

1994a "Repetition and Tradition: Heidegger's Destruction of the Distinction between Essence and Existence in *Basic Problems of Phenomenoloqy*." In *Reading Heidegger from the Start: Essays in His Earliest Thought*, ed. T. Kisiel and J. van Buren, pp. 123–136. Albany: State University of New York Press.

1994b "Cultural Diversity and the Limits of Toleration: Locke's Legacy." *Acta Institutionis Philosophiae et Aestheticae* (Tokyo) 12: 9–23.

1994c "'You Don't Know What I'm Talking About': Alterity and the Hermeneutic Ideal." In *The Specter of Relativism*, ed. Lawrence K. Schmidt, pp. 178–194. Evanston: Northwestern University Press.

1994d "'Only the Persecuted . . .': Language of the Oppressor, Language of the

Persecuted." In *Ethics as First Philosophy*, ed. Adriaan Peperzak, pp. 77–86. New York: Routledge.

1995a "'I Will Tell You Who You Are': Heidegger on Greco-German Destiny and *Amerikanismus.*" In *From Phenomenology to Thought: Errands and Desire*, ed. Babette E. Babich, pp. 301–313. Dordrecht: Kluwer.

1995b "'Ich mag in keinen Himmel, wo Weisse sind.' Herder's Critique of Eurocentrism." *Acta Institutionis Philosophiae et Aestheticae* (Tokyo) 13: 69–81.

1995c "Sartre's Gaze Returned: The Transformation of the Phenomenology of Racism." *Graduate Faculty Philosophy Journal* 18 (2): 201–221.

1995d "Heidegger and the Invention of the Western Philosophical Tradition." *Journal of the British Society for Phenomenology* 26 (3): 240–254.

1995e "Heidegger's Other Sins of Omission." *American Catholic Philosophical Quarterly* 69 (2): 333–350.

1996a "Casting the Slough: Fanon's New Humanism for a New Humanity." In *Frantz Fanon: A Critical Reader*, ed. Lewis R. Gordon, T. Denean Sharpley-Whiting, and Renee T. White, pp. 113–121. Oxford: Blackwell.

1996b "The Double Face of the Political and the Social: Hannah Arendt and America's Racial Divisions." *Research in Phenomenology* 26: 3–24.

1996c "'And Yet I Swear This Oath': Broken Promises, Binding Promises." *Acta Institutionis Philosophiae et Aestheticae* (Tokyo) 14: 17–33.

1996d *Emmanuel Levinas: Basic Philosophical Writings*, ed. with Adriaan Peperzak and Simon Critchley. Bloomington: Indiana University Press.

1997a "African Philosophy's Challenge to Continental Philosophy." In *Postcolonial African Philosophy*, ed. Emmanuel Eze, pp. 183–196. Oxford: Blackwell.

1997b "Opening the Future: The Paradox of Promising in the Hobbesian Social Contract." *Philosophy Today* 41 (1): 77–86.

1997c "What Goes Around Comes Around: Derrida and Levinas on the Economy of the Gift and the Gift of Genealogy." In *The Logic of the Gift*, ed. Alan Schrift, pp. 256–273. New York: Routledge.

1997d "Eckhart's Anachorism." *Graduate Faculty Philosophy Journal* 19 (2)–20 (1): 81–90.

1997e "The Limits of the European Idea of Development." In *Social Development: Between Intervention and Integration*, ed. Jacob Rendtorff, Adam Diderichsen, and Peter Kemp, pp. 185–203. Copenhagen: Rhodos.

1997f "The Violence of the Face: Peace and Language in the Thought of Levinas." *Philosophy and Social Criticism* 23 (6): 81–93.

1997g "Philosophy's Paradoxical Parochialism: The Reinvention of Philosophy as Greek." In *Cultural Readings of Imperialism: Edward Said and the Gravity of History*, ed. Keith Ansell-Pearson, Benita Parry, and Judith Squires, pp. 212–226. London: Lawrence and Wishart.

1997h "Ethische Aporien: Derrida, Levinas und die Genealogie des Griechischen," trans. Peter Gehring and Hans-Dieter Gondek. In *Einsätze des Denkens. Zur Philosophie von Jacques Derrida*, ed. Hans-Dieter Gondek and Bernard Waldenfels, pp. 345–384. Frankfurt: Suhrkamp.

1998a "Hegel at the Court of the Ashanti." In *Hegel after Derrida*, ed. Stuart Barnett, forthcoming. London: Routledge.

1998b "Can Development Theory Break with Its Past? Endogenous Development in Africa and the Old Imperialism." *African Philosophy* 11 (1): 23–34.

1998c "Wer ist der Dritte? Überkreuzung von Ethik und Politik bei Levinas," trans. Antje Kapust. In *Der Anspruch des Anderen,* ed. B. Waldenfels and I. Därmann, pp. 87–110. Munich: Wilhelm Fink.

1998d "'Stuck Inside of Mobile with the Memphis Blues Again.'" In *Theorizing Multiculturalism,* ed. Cynthia Willett, pp. 276–298. London: Blackwell.

1998e "'An Ethics of Violence Justifying Itself': Sartre's Explorations of Violence and Oppression." *Bulletin de la Société Américaine de Philosophie* 10 (2): 102–117.

1998f "Why Is a Suburb? Ghettos of Domesticity." *Acta Institutionis Philosophiae et Aestheticae* (Tokyo) 16: 95–97.

1998g "Different Styles of Eschatology: Derrida's Take on Levinas's Political Messianism." *Research in Phenomenology* 28: 3–19.

# THREE

## Of Mystics, Magi, and Deconstructionists

◨

# JOHN D. CAPUTO

I passed my intellectual youth consorting with saints and mystics and medieval masters who told me spellbinding tales and opened my eyes to an altogether new and astonishing world. I took to works of philosophy not because I needed to study philosophy in order to learn theology, but because I did not perceive a distinction between philosophy and theology. Philosophy and theology seemed to me indistinguishable keys to the magical world that was unlocked for me by the magisterial figures who dominated this world. These figures were like wise men to me, magi who knew things that eye has not seen nor ear heard, who broke the spell of empiricism and the commonplace for me. Their world was enchanted, aglow and radiant, a world of magic, of insight and depth and beauty, inhabited by men who could regularly find God in a sunflower.

There were many masters, many magi, in those days, mostly but not entirely French Catholic intellectuals: Maritain and Gilson, of course, but also Teilhard de Chardin, Josef Pieper, Chenu, Simone Weil, Sertillanges, and a brilliant young French Jesuit killed in World War I, Pierre Rousselot, whose *L'intellectualisme de saint Thomas* inspired my first serious philosophical work. Rousselot advanced a vision of *intellectus* as the faculty of union, as the seat of the soul's union with God in eternity, so that knowledge for Rousselot was union, *idem fieri,* not representational correspondence, *adequatio.* He denounced the notion that dominated neoscholasticism of the intellect as a faculty of concepts and subverted this movement from its mystical-religious moorings by modeling the intellect after modernity's pale conceptual ghosts. A concept, Rousselot said, is the sole recourse of an impoverished intellect, an *intellectus* at the very bottom of the chain of intellects. The weakness of the human intellect takes the form of concept formation, much the way a book of photographs tries to take the place of actually visiting Paris or Rome. Conceptual reasoning is a function of the *debilitas intellectus,* St. Thomas said, of the weakness of our minds.

Organizing his work around the classical medieval distinction between *intellectus* and *ratio*, Rousselot launched what appears to me now, in retrospect, to be my first critique of modernist rationality, of *ratio* as the procrustean bed into which the subject tries to force the things themselves. I was already instinctively trying to become a postmodern, to twist free of the tradition from Descartes to Hegel, before I even knew what modernity was, before I had seriously studied it. My first serious scholarly inquiry was into the "analogicity"—the hierarchical diversity—of *intellectus* in Thomas Aquinas, in which I tried to demonstrate the intrinsic likeness and diversity of the divine, angelic, and human intellects. Part of the magic of that magical world was that it was populated with spirits; I was interrupted from a study of the angelic intellect on the day that President Kennedy was shot in Dallas. When a few years later I read Heidegger's *Der Satz vom Grund,* his brilliant delimitation of modernist rationality, conducted in the name of the rose that lives "without why," every gesture, every move, every strategy in Heidegger's lectures was instantly familiar to me and resonated with instincts in me that were older than I could say, with convictions that I had long held, that had long held me. Here, in Heidegger, I encountered a way of thinking at the end of modernity that had carefully and meditatively worked its way through modernity and that had in the process repeated and recovered the richness of the premodern, which is the sense that I attached to his word *destructio* which never for a moment seemed to me at all destructive.

St. Thomas was, of course, the intellectual sun of this firmament, the solar source, the *agathon* of the other forms, the cause of the growth and knowledge of the other masters, the *fons et origo* to which one returned again and again. His lean, lucid Latin was the first foreign language I mastered, the first experience I had of learning something in a foreign tongue, and in his powerful prose all the magic of this enchanted world was concentrated, intensified, and magnified. Thomas did not know everything, I realized, but he knew the principles of everything; he knew everything *in principio.* That did not have the sense for me of an encyclopedic Hegelian tour de force, of a closed conceptual net, which has always seemed to me a ruse; it suggested, instead, a meditative stillness, an infinitely deep resource, a thinking in touch with the unfathomable heart of things, open-ended and ungrasping. The medieval masters were not modernist systematizers, not conceptual hunters and trappers, but mystics and saints with a transfixing sense of *pietas,* of the most deeply personal piety towards the things themselves, toward God and the world and toward the masters who had preceded them. They were religious, which means transfixed by a sense of *re-ligare* and *ob-ligare* of the bonds that bound them to a being that was deeper and older and more mysterious than they could say (even though they had a lot to say).

It was from out of that enchanted world, from the midst of that magical beginning, that I encountered Heidegger, who was for me at first a modern, or metamodern, or postmodern magus who spoke wondrous words about Being and Being's history and meditative thinking. He invoked one of the oldest and most beautiful words of the Rhineland mystics, *Gelassenheit*, uttered by one of the most magical and magisterial of the medieval magi, Meister Eckhart. My first serious study of Heidegger—my doctoral dissertation—focused on *Der Satz vom Grund*, a book which was for me then and which is still today a brilliant delimitation of the history of "metaphysics" as the history of *ratio*. *Ratio* for Heidegger means the constriction and narrowing of a poetic *nous*, of a poetico-meditative experience of the upsurge of *physis*, of the emergent beauty of *aletheia*. The multiple ringing of *Der Satz vom Grund* as it was orchestrated by the elderly Heidegger (he was 66 years old when he gave these lectures) resonated for me with the medieval distinction between *intellectus* and *ratio*. Heidegger had—quite magnificently—retrieved, repeated, reinvented, and reconfigured this distinction in a searching late modern or postmodern critique of modernity, the high point of which was a powerful meditation on Angelus Silesius's verse, "The Rose is Without Why." The expression *ohne warum* was, I soon discovered, Meister Eckhart's, as was a good deal of the heart and inspiration of Silesius's *Cherubinic Wanderer*.

My first book, *The Mystical Element in Heidegger's Thought* (1978), for which I retain today the greatest affection, began where my dissertation left off. I studied the remarkable structural and historical relationship between "the thought of Being" and the mystical unity of the soul with God in the Meister. As a young man, I learned with fascination, Heidegger had studied Eckhart and had planned a lecture course on medieval mysticism in 1919, though the course was not delivered; I discovered that Heidegger too had had a Catholic beginning. That book was followed by a companion book, *Heidegger and Aquinas: An Essay on Overcoming Metaphysics* (1982), in which I showed that the same sort of mystico-religious way out of modernity and metaphysics that was to be found in Meister Eckhart and that paralleled Heidegger's *Überwindung* was also locatable in Thomas Aquinas, so long as you understood Aquinas mystically, the way he was understood by Rousselot. This, I argued, was a more fruitful way to deal with the Heidegger-Aquinas relationship than the typical Thomistic trope of trying to evade the charge of *Seinsvergessenheit* by beating Heidegger over the head with the Thomistic metaphysics of *esse*.

With the publication of *Heidegger and Aquinas,* I am now inclined to

say, my youth ended and my magical period came to a close. I had completed the circuit set in motion in me by the medieval magi who awakened
my intellectual life and who provided the context for my encounter with
Heidegger. My whole approach to Heidegger up to then had been in terms
of premodern and religious sources. Then I met up with Derrida, neither
religious nor premodern, and still less a magus (his uncomprehending critics to the contrary notwithstanding), but a merciless demystifier, a great
deconstructor. Then things began to change and the forest, *Schwarzwald-
ian* and otherwise, began to get disenchanted. The first shoot in the deconstructed forest was *Radical Hermeneutics: Repetition, Deconstruction and
the Hermeneutic Project* (1987), a book that tried to "articulate" Heidegger, not with Eckhart or Aquinas, but with Derrida. There I tried to forge
a more "demythologized" Heidegger, a Heidegger without the myth of Being's homeland and maternal language, and a more hermeneuticized Derrida, a Derrida tied to the concerns of factical life.

In the final three chapters of this book, I like to think, I found my own
voice. I tried to take a colder, more deconstructed look at things, to face up
to the "difficulty of life," the difficulty of "factical life," i.e., life without the
support of metaphysical foundations, on the one hand, or of the consola-
tions of religion, on the other. Substituting the metaphorics of the flux for
the metaphysics of Being, I began to think of human life as a kind of coping,
a willingness to deal with the endlessly shifting sands of life. I chose not to
describe this hermeneutics in terms of *phronesis*, which has to do with the
skill of applying a schema to variable situations, which governed Gadamer's
more conservative version of hermeneutics and which assumes some kind
of stable horizon or schema of interpretation. I spoke instead of a certain
meta-*phronesis*, cut to fit a more postmodern situation in which the difficulty of life consisted in a conflict among the schemata themselves. For is
not the postmodern situation, as Lyotard called it, a matter of the incom-
mensurability of competing schemata, so that the difficulty is that there are
too many different kinds of prudent men to imitate, not to mention quite a
few prudent women as well? It was from this standpoint that I undertook a
threefold task: (1) to formulate a theory of post-metaphysical rationality,
which tried to imagine what reason would look like at the end of modernity; (2) to unfold an "ethics of dissemination," in which the violence with
which we subscribe to principles would give way to an openness to the little
ones, the bits and fragments who are scattered and ground under by our
love of principles; (3) to sketch the possibility of a postmodern religion. If
things had become more decidedly post-metaphysical for me, they had also
become post-mystical, and the religious had come to mean the mysterious,
the abyss of I know not what that infiltrates and disturbs my sleep, that

lends itself at once and undecidably to an irreligious, Nietzschean interpretation as well as to the religion of Augustine, Eckhart, and Angelus Silesius. When things are "without why" they are as liable to be understood in terms of the groundless play of events as in terms of God's loving but hidden hand.

Having already begun to question, on strictly philosophical grounds, a great deal of Heidegger's romanticizing meta-narrative about the history of Being, the publications of Victor Farías (whatever its limitations) and especially Hugo Ott (whose work was more judicious but for that reason even more damning) convinced me that Heidegger's *Seinsgeschichte* was not only a transparent myth but also a dangerous myth that communicated with a hellish politics. My disenchantment took form in *Demythologizing Heidegger* (1993), a book intended as a judicious but uncompromising account of the limitations of Heidegger's thought. My earlier readings of Heidegger now seem to me to be one-sided, not because they were religious, but because they were too uncritical and apolitical. Today, under the impulse of Derrida, Lyotard, and Levinas, I have come to see the danger of Heidegger's "phainesthetics," a hyper-aesthetics of Being's shining glory, fueled by a monomaniac care for the history of Being's glow that goes hand in hand with a systematic indifference to the concrete sufferings of historical human beings.

*Against Ethics: Contributions to a Poetics of Obligation with Constant Reference to Deconstruction* (1993) is my most impish, impious, impudent, perhaps even imprudent, but certainly most personal statement to date. Here I strike the pose of a modern- or postmodern-day Johannes de Silentio who has no head, not only for the System, but for the History of Being and who has lost contact with the Great Greek Beginning. (If *Radical Hermeneutics* is a kin of Kierkegaard's *Repetition, Against Ethics* is a kind of postmodern *Fear and Trembling*.) For better or worse, *Against Ethics* is where I stand (or fail to stand), what has become of me, today. I have more and more been taken by the thought of the anonymous, of the impersonal horizon by which we are everywhere surrounded, by the ring of impersonality that closes in all around us. I wonder now if what I once called the divine, the dark night and bottomless abyss of the Godhead, is not simply the anonymity of a nameless night, a darkness pure and simple, rather the veil of a deeper, more divine dimension. I wonder if we do not all speak a lost language, a language that will have been lost when once the earth drops back into the sun and turns to ash. It is in this light, or lack of light, that I try to think through the experience of "obligation," as a light that burns gently in this nocturnal abyss, meekly protesting the endless and encompassing void. Calling upon the resources of Lyotard and Levinas, in addition to making "constant reference to deconstruction," I advance a non-foundational account of obligation, where obligation is something that "happens," a fact as it were, as if it were a fact, but without the deep back-up of God or the *agathon* or pure practical reason. I treat obligation as a finite transaction between flesh and flesh, the subject matter of a poetics, not a noetics, which turns not on principles and universals, or freedom and autonomy, but on the claim that descends upon us from the singular ones, the bits and fragments left out of "ethics." Obligation is what is left of the ethical after ethics, the residue left behind by ethics, which is always a certain metaphysics. Obligation is something that happens—in the midst of a cosmic night, in the middle of a disaster. We are all siblings of the same dark night, disturbed by the same demons, haunted by the same specters. That is our discomforting comfort, our disturbing consolation, the faith of an infidel.

The work in which I am currently engaged is to develop a certain more sober, more post-mystical, deconstructionist notion of religion, which is a faith without doctrine, a God without Being, a community that cannot say "we." This is, to be sure, to come back to where I started, to take up the questions of my earlier years, albeit with the full realization that one can never go home again.

## Selected Bibliography

1970 "Being, Ground and Play in Heidegger." *Man and World* 3: 26–48.

1971a "Heidegger's Original Ethics." *New Scholasticism* 45: 127–138.

1971b "The Rose in without Why: The Later Heidegger." *Philosophy Today* 15: 3–15.

1973 "Time and Being in Heidegger." *The Modern Schoolman* 50: 325–59.

1974a "Kant's Refutation of the Ontological Argument." *Journal of the American Academy of Religion* 42: 686–691.

1974b "Meister Eckhart and the Later Heidegger, Part I." *Journal of the History of Philosophy* 12: 479–94.

1974c "Phenomenology, Mysticism and the *Grammatica Speculativa*." *Journal of the British Society for Phenomenology* 5: 101–117.

1975a "The Nothingness of the Intellect in Eckhart's *Parisian Questions*." *The Thomist* 39: 85–115.

1975b "Meister Eckhart and the Later Heidegger, Part II." *Journal of the History of Philosophy* 13: 61–80.

1977 "The Question of Being and Transcendental Phenomenology: Husserl and Heidegger." *Research in Phenomenology* 7: 84–105.

1978 "Fundamental Themes in Eckhart's Mysticism." *The Thomist* 42: 197–225.

1979a "The Presence of Others: A Phenomenology of the Person." *Proceedings of the American Catholic Philosophical Association* 53: 45–58.

1979b "Transcendence and the Transcendental in Husserl's Phenomenology." *Philosophy Today* 23: 205–216.

1982 *Heidegger and Aquinas: An Essay on Overcoming Metaphysics.* New York: Fordham University Press.

1983a "Heidegger's God and the Lord of History." *New Scholasticism* 57: 439–464.

1983b "The Thought of Being and the Conversation of Mankind: The Case of Heidegger and Rorty." *Review of Metaphysics* 36: 661–687. Reprinted in *Hermeneutics and Praxis,* ed. Robert Hollinger, pp. 248–271. Notre Dame: University of Notre Dame Press, 1985.

1984a "Husserl, Heidegger, and the Question of a Hermeneutic Phenomenology." *Husserl Studies* 1: 157–158. Reprinted in *A Companion to Martin Heidegger's "Being and Time,"* ed. Joseph Kockelmans, pp. 104–126. Current Continental Research, no. 550. Washington, D.C.: University Press of America, 1986.

1984b "Kant's Ethics in Phenomenological Perspective." In *Kant and Phenomenology,* ed. T. Seebohm, pp. 129–146. Current Continental Research, no. 004. Washington, D.C.: University Press of America.

1984c "Prudential Insight and Moral Reasoning." *Proceedings of the American Catholic Philosophical Society* 58: 50–55.

1984d "'Supposing Truth to Be a Woman . . .': Heidegger, Nietzsche, Derrida." *Tulane Studies in Philosophy* 32: 15–22.

1985 "Three Transgressions: Nietzsche, Heidegger, Derrida." *Research in Phenomenology* 15: 61–78.

1986a "Cold Hermeneutics: Heidegger and Derrida." *Journal of the British Society for Phenomenology* 17: 252–275.

1986b "Heidegger's Philosophy of Science." *Rationality, Relativism and the Human Sciences,* ed. J. Margolis, pp. 43–60. Dordrecht: Nijhoff.

1986c "Telling Left from Right: Hermeneutics, Deconstruction, and the Work of Art." *Journal of Philosophy* 83: 678–685.

1986d *The Mystical Element in Heidegger's Thought.* Athens: Ohio University Press, 1978. Revised paperback edition, with a new introduction, New York: Fordham University Press.

1987a "Derrida: A Kind of Philosopher." *Research in Phenomenology* 17: 245–259.

1987b *Radical Hermeneutics: Repetition, Deconstruction and the Hermeneutic Project.* Bloomington: Indiana University Press.

1987c "The Economy of Signs in Husserl and Derrida: From Uselessness to Full Employment." In *Deconstruction and Philosophy,* ed. John Sallis, pp. 99–113. Chicago: University of Chicago Press.

1988a "Beyond Aestheticism: Derrida's Responsible Anarchy." *Research in Phenomenology* 18: 59-73.

1988b "Demythologizing Heidegger: *Aletheia* and the History of Being." *The Review of Metaphysics* 41 (March): 519-546. Translated into German as "Heidegger Entmythologigisieren: Aletheia und die Seinsgeschichte." In *Twisting Heidegger: Drehversuche paradistishchen Denkens,* ed. Michael Eldred, pp. 66–91. Cuxhaven: Junghans-Verlag, 1993.

1988c "On Mystical and Other Phenomena." In *Phenomenology in America,* ed. Calvin Schrag, pp. 318–322. Dordrecht: Reidel.

1988d "Presidential Address: Radical Hermeneutics and the Human Condition." *Proceedings of the American Catholic Philosophical Association* 61: 2–15.

1989a "An Ethics of Dissemination." In *The Ethics of the Other,* ed. Charles Scott, pp. 55–62. Albany: State University of New York Press.

1989b "Gadamer's Closet Essentialism: A Derridean Critique." In *Dialogue and Deconstruction: The Gadamer-Derrida Encounter,* ed. Richard Palmer, pp. 258–264. Albany: State University of New York Press.

1989c "Mysticism and Transgression: Derrida and Meister Eckhart." *Continental Philosophy* 2: 24–39.

1990a "Derrida and the Study of Religion." Co-authored with Charles Winquist. *Religious Studies Review* 16 (January): 19–25.

1990b "Radical Hermeneutics and Religious Truth: The Case of Sheehan and Schillebeeckx." In *Phenomenology of the Truth Proper to Religion,* ed. Daniel Guerriere, pp. 146–172. Albany: State University of New York Press.

1991 "Hyperbolic Justice: Deconstruction, Myth and Politics." *Research in Phenomenology* 21: 3–20.

1992a "Heidegger's Scandal: Thinking and the Essence of the Victim." In *The Heidegger Case: On Philosophy and Politics,* ed. Tom Rockmore and Joseph Margolis, pp. 265–281. Philadelphia: Temple University Press.

1992b "How to Avoid Speaking of God: The Violence of Natural Theology." In *The Prospects for Natural Theology,* ed. Eugene Long, pp. 128–150. Washington, D.C.: Catholic University of America Press.

1992c *Modernity and Its Discontents.* Co-authored with James Marsh and Merold Westphal. New York: Fordham University Press.

1993a *Against Ethics: Contributions to a Poetics of Obligation with Constant Reference to Deconstruction.* Bloomington: Indiana University Press.

1993b *Demythologizing Heidegger: Studies in the Philosophy of Religion.* Bloomington: Indiana University Press.

1993c *Foucault and the Critique of Institutions,* ed. with Mark Yount. University Park: Pennsylvania State University Press.

1993d "Heidegger and Theology." In *The Cambridge Companion to Heidegger,* ed. Charles Guignon, pp. 270–288. Cambridge: Cambridge University Press.

1993e "Heidegger, Kierkegaard and the Foundering of Metaphysics." In *"Fear and Trembling" and "Repetition,"* ed. Robert Perkins, pp. 201–224. International Kierkegaard Commentary, vol. 6. Macon, Ga.: Mercer University Press.

1993f "In Search of the Quasi-Transcendental: The Case of Derrida and Rorty." In *Working through Derrida,* ed. Gary Madison, pp. 147–169. Evanston: Northwestern University Press.

1993g "On Not Knowing Who We Are: Foucault and the Night of Truth." In *Foucault and the Critique of Institutions.* University Park: Pennsylvania State University Press.

1994a "Reason, History and a Little Madness: Towards a Hermeneutics of the Kingdom." *Proceedings of the American Catholic Philosophical Association* 68: 27–44.

1994b "*Sorge* and *Kardia:* The Hermeneutics of Factical Life and the Categories of the Heart." In *Reading Heidegger from the Start: Essays in His Earliest Thought,* ed. Theodore Kisiel and John van Buren, pp. 327–343. Albany: State University of New York Press.

1994c "The Age of Repetition." *Southern Journal of Philosophy* 32 (Supplement): 171–177.

1995a "Bedevilling the Tradition: Deconstruction and Catholicism." In *(Dis)continuity and (De)construction: Reflections on the Meaning of the Past in Crisis Situations,* ed. Josef Wissink, pp. 12–35. Kampen, the Netherlands: Pharos.

1995b "Infestations: The Religion of the Death of God and Scott's Ascetic Ideal." *Research in Phenomenology* 25: 261-268.

1995c "Instants, Secrets, Singularities: Dealing Death in Kierkegaard and Derrida." In *Kierkegaard in Post/Modernity,* ed. Martin Matuštík and Merold Westphal, pp. 216–238. Bloomington: Indiana University Press.

1995d "Presenting Heidegger." *American Catholic Philosophical Quarterly* 64 (May): 129–133.

1996a "A Community of the Impossible." *Research in Phenomenology* 26: 25–37.

1996b "Dark Hearts: Heidegger, Richardson, and Evil." In *From Phenomenology to Thought, Errancy, and Desire,* ed. Babette Babich, pp. 267–275. Dordrecht: Kluwer.

1996c "Phenomenology and Beyond." Introduction to *Selected Studies in Phenomenology and Existential Philosophy,* vol. 21. *Philosophy Today* 40. Co-edited with Lenore Langsdorf.

1997a "Dasein." In *Encyclopedia of Phenomenology,* pp. 133–137. Dordrecht: Kluwer.

1997b *Deconstruction in a Nutshell: A Conversation with Jacques Derrida,* ed. with commentary. New York: Fordham University Press.

1997c "Other Openings." Introduction to *Selected Studies in Phenomenology and Existential Philosophy,* vol. 22. *Philosophy Today* 41. Ed. with Debra Bergoffen.

1997d *The Prayers and Tears of Jacques Derrida: Religion without Religion.* Bloomington: Indiana University Press.

# F O U R

## From Imagination to Place
### *Memories of a Wayward Thinker*

E

# EDWARD S. CASEY

Emerging from graduate school in 1967—where I had written a dissertation on "Poetry and Ontology" that took up the question of poetic imagination—I conceived the project of writing a series of books on basic mental acts or psychical phenomena: imagination, memory, feeling, and thinking. Little did I know that it would take the next twenty years just to write the first two volumes in this series! At that time, my inspiration was overtly phenomenological and, more specifically, Husserlian. I hoped to study the four mental acts on the basis of an intentional, diphasic model of mind, in accordance with a distinction between noetic and noematic phases. I had learned this model from my teachers at Northwestern, William Earle and James Edie, and from Paul Ricoeur at the Sorbonne. The applicability of the model seemed unproblematically extensive: Does not every aspect of human mentation lend itself to analysis in such terms? I could not conceive of any effective limit to the model; its scope, indeed its very truth, seemed assured.

My theoretical optimism was bolstered by what I found when I attempted a close description of imagination for my first book, *Imagining* (1976). This mental act lent itself readily to the Husserlian paradigm, even though Husserl himself had never fully attended to it. Building on previous attempts of Fink and Sartre, I discerned an act phase and an object phase, each with its own complexities: three kinds of act (imaging, imagining-that, imagining-how) and several strata of the imaginative presentation (specific content, world-frame, margin). Further reinforcing my conviction as to the feasibility of a phenomenology of mental acts was the way in which imagining, regarded as a total phenomenon, can be described as at once controlled and spontaneous, self-contained and self-evident, indeterminate and purely possible. These neatly paired "essential traits" all emphasized the status of imagination as an act that is strictly discontinuous with perception and memory and thinking. Hence I argued for the "thin autonomy" of this act, its independence of other acts and contents, its apparently self-sufficient freedom of mental maneuver.

In considering memory, however, I began to encounter obstacles to the ambitious methodology of my research. Although I did offer an initial noetico-noematic account in the early chapters of *Remembering* (1987), I soon discovered that many memorial phenomena do not fit into any diphasic, mentalistic approach. I abandoned an exhaustive study of eidetic traits (contained in a second, unpublished volume) to which this approach led. For I found that, to begin with, there are a number of intermediate phenomena—e.g., reminding, recognizing, reminiscing—that could fit into an intentional account only by being forced onto a prescribed Procrustean bed. These "mnemonic modes" may be quite continuous with perception (especially in the case of recognition), or with words (i.e., in reminiscing), or with indicative signs (particularly in reminding). Together, the three modes constitute a complex interim space between mind and world, drawing mind out of its intentionalistic confinement and into the world that surrounds it on all sides.

It was at just this point that I came to criticize the very mentalism that had gone unquestioned in *Imagining*. I did this just as I launched into the topic of body memory, neglected by virtually every major Western thinker, with the notable exceptions of Bergson and Merleau-Ponty. The latter had spoken of a specifically "corporeal intentionality," but such intentionality is precisely such that it cannot be analyzed into an act phase and object phase, which characterize mental acts alone, just as Brentano had foreseen in his inaugural discovery of intentionality in *Psychology from an Empirical Point of View* (1874). Body memory, which I investigated by focusing on bodily trauma, erotic experiences, and habitual bodily actions, entails a massive immersion in the environing life-world—to the point that the respective contributions of body and world are often no longer discernible. I discussed such parameters of body memory as density, depth, and the co-immanence of past and present. These parameters point to the "thick autonomy" of memory, its ability to involve us ineluctably in the life-world. The same non-ethereal autonomous action—amounting to a special form of memorial freedom, distinctively different from the untethered freedom at stake in imagining—is found in acts of commemoration, whose ritual and social aspects I underlined in a chapter that took four years to write. (The reason for the delay, the literal moratorium, in writing about commemoration had to do with unresolved issues of mourning, above all mourning for my parents, both of whom had died when I was in my twenties.)

Both body memory and commemoration require *places* in which to occur: the place of bodily stance or movement, places of commemorative action. The more I pondered the ramifications of both kinds of memory, the more I realized that each entails an enduring embroilment in concrete places —the particular scenes and settings where remembered events have happened. These events do not occur in thin air; they happen *somewhere,* somewhere in particular. Their locus of happening is their place of occurrence, and any adequate account of remembering must take account of the emplacement of *all* memories in what I have come to call the "place-world." Neither mind nor body—singly or together—can bear the burden of memory. Places, however, have the requisite perduring power to situate and subtend our complex and ongoing memorial life. And yet, I asked myself, who has discussed *place memory* in the West? Proust alludes to it and draws upon it yet offers no complete description of it. A paradox quickly arises: on the one hand, the fact of the massive emplacement of memory; on the other hand, the striking fact that place memory *per se* has rarely, if ever, been given its due in Western accounts of remembering. Indeed, I reflected, how often has place itself—even apart from its importance for memory— been treated thoroughly in Western thought, especially in the last three centuries? An entire vista of place-work opened up suddenly, along with a pointed challenge: how to do justice to place, plain old place?

A lecture I delivered in 1983 at Northwestern University—on the occasion of the twentieth anniversary of the Society for Phenomenology and Existential Philosophy (I had been present at the founding meeting in Evanston in 1963)—was entitled "Keeping the Past in Mind." In that pivotal paper I argued that the past cannot be kept exclusively in mind, not by any means. It is also found in the body, in actions taken with others, in language, and in landscape. With this last suggestion—the embeddedness of the past in landscape—I took a further step toward acknowledging the importance of place and, thereby, toward escaping the confinement of mentalism (i.e., the belief that, in order to be experienced, an entity or event has to be represented by an idea or some other cognitive item within the mind). For the next ten years, I considered the role of place in human life and beyond ("beyond" because place is also critical in the life of other species, indeed of the entire animate and inanimate world). In so doing, I realized that the places I have lived in have had a decisive impact on my thinking, feeling, and style of living—in fact on every aspect of my ongoing life. I had composed *Imagining* while at Yale, where munificent private support had underwritten a text that reflected the removed life I led in New Haven. *Remembering* had been begun at Yale, especially its early chapters, but its later, more expansive and speculative chapters were written at Stony Brook, where I had gone in 1978 as an associate professor. The more diverse and less structured experiences I enjoyed on Long Island had much to do with the different way I was beginning to think and write during this mid-life period.

The result of this decade of reflection on the priority of place ("place is the first of all things," said Aristotle in the *Physics*), was *Getting Back into Place: Toward a Renewed Understanding of the Place-World* (1993). This was the third volume of mine published by Indiana University Press, yet it decidedly altered the plan of the originally projected series of books. I was going off course, it seemed. Or was I? My own sense was that I was getting ever more deeply into the direction I had first staked out in *Imagining*—but precisely by going under, or around, the mind that was the *focus imaginarius* of that first work. Place presented itself as the common ground of imagining and remembering and doubtless of feeling and thinking as well. Yet it is not their simple foundation, something simply solid on which one builds as upon a material bedrock or rational principle. It is a decidedly porous ground, a leaking loam, filled with soil of many types and with many underground roots and tubers as well. It is "rhizomatic" in the discourse of Deleuze and Guattari, "an-archic" in Schürmann's language, a "being-in-common" (but not a "common being") in Nancy's terms. Place is the common domain of all that we experience and remember, including experiences and memories themselves. How, then, to render justice to such a massively crucial thing as place?

In my first foray into the topic, I treated place not as a single phenomenon, since no such thing as "place" exists in and of itself. It is not itself simply located, nor does it proffer simple location to other things (where "simple location" is meant in Whitehead's sense of a strict locus point that makes no reference to other loci in the immediate environment). Place is a matter of diverse directions (cardinal and otherwise) and dimensions (e.g., up/down, back/front), which I attempt to describe in this first book on place—directions and dimensions that draw in turn upon our corporeal powers of emplacement. In becoming oriented in place and as a means of consolidating that orientation, built places are crucial. I explore the Hermetic and Hestial aspects of human dwellings before contrasting these aspects with basic features of wild places such as arc, atmosphere, surrounding array, things, sensuous surface, and ground itself. The issue of what constitutes a homeplace as well as what it means to travel *between* secure and settled places preoccupy the last chapter, "Homeward Bound," of *Getting Back into Place*. The question of displacement—of not being steadily located anywhere—is on the agenda throughout the book, and I here consider the special significance of journeys and nomadism.

In the course of writing this book, I became aware of a very special lacuna in philosophical literature: the absence of a concerted treatment of place in the history of philosophy. The role of place in philosophical thinking has ranged from a position of central significance—i.e., in ancient Greek thought, including its Hellenistic and neoplatonic outgrowths—to one of utter neglect, as has occurred increasingly since the Renaissance. I realized to my amazement that the very term "place"—in any of its western European linguistic forms—had dropped out of serious philosophical discourse after the death of Leibniz in 1715. Its return was at best sporadic (e.g., in Kant's early essay on "The Distinction of Material Regions in Space"), and was overshadowed by the dominance of time in philosophical discussions that extend from the publication of the *Critique of Pure Reason* in 1781 to Bergson's *Time and Free Will* (1889), Husserl's lectures on time-consciousness (1904–1905), and the appearance of *Being and Time* (1927). How can one attempt to question, perhaps even begin to reverse, this outright temporocentrism if not by a renewed attention to the peculiarities of place? Not in order to advocate a lococentrism but, instead, to inculcate an increased sensitivity to something that is part and parcel of our very being-in-the-world. How can we be in the world at all without being emplaced there? Do we not have to measure up—all the more so at this postmodern moment—to the indispensable importance of place in our individual and collective lives?

In my own case, the measuring up is carried out in a series of three further projected books on place, two of which have now been completed. One takes up the hidden history of the idea of place in Western philosophy and is entitled *The Fate of Place;* another, *Representing Landscape,* investigates the role of place in landscape painting and maps; the third will explore the position of place in other cultures, such as that of certain Native Americans. My hope is that, having completed this cycle of four studies of place, I can return to the series of books I first envisioned in 1967, writing the final two volumes on feeling and thinking. Before this, however, I will finish a book on which I am now working, to be entitled *The World at a Glance.*

I wish to add a few observations on questions of method, source, and influence, as well as on my sense of responsibility as a philosopher. In my undergraduate years at Yale, the primary influences on my thinking were Kierkegaard, Dewey, and Freud; in graduate work, Heidegger and Bachelard (the two central figures in my dissertation), Ricoeur and Dufrenne (with both of whom I studied in Paris in the mid-1960s); and more recently, Derrida, Lacan, Deleuze and Guattari, and Irigaray. Some thinkers are of enduring importance: Aristotle, Descartes, Kant, Bergson, Husserl. If it was from Husserl that I took inspiration for my methodology in investigating imagination, I have found that I have come gradually but quite decisively to depart from phenomenological method—not in order to indulge a deliberately post-phenomenological or deconstructionist propensity, but rather to become more open to the contribution of other approaches to my own philosophical interests. The impact of psychoanalysis upon my work, for example, has been considerable, and is most evident in *Remembering.* Important to me is not only the psychoanalysis of Freud but also that of Jung and Hillman, as is evident in a collection of essays I have published under the title *Spirit and Soul: Essays in Philosophical Psychology* (1991). I have also undertaken psychoanalytic training at the Western New England Institute for Psychoanalysis and regularly teach courses that examine philosophical aspects of psychoanalysis. I hope soon to publish a collection of essays in Freudian and Lacanian psychoanalytic theory.

More recently and specifically in my work on place, I have been taking anthropology into serious account, not just in an effort to avoid ethnocentrism but more particularly as an attempt to practice what Kant, in the *Critique of Judgment,* calls "a broadened way of thinking," arguing that in overcoming a "narrow mind" a person "overrides the private subjective conditions of his judgment, into which so many others are locked, as it were, and reflects on his own judgment from a universal standpoint (which he can determine only by transferring himself to the standpoint of others)."—Even if it is doubtful that one can attain an *allgemeine Standpunkt,* one can still attempt to put oneself into the position of others in other cultures—to imagine oneself to be in their *place* to the extent that this is possible without superimposing one's own cultural categories on that place. And if it remains true that one begins and ends with one's own concrete emplacement in one's own culture, an imaginative journey through another culture, guided by insightful figures from that culture (as well as by its best-informed observers), can be immensely valuable, indeed indispensable, in coming to understand more deeply what is happening back home in local culture.

In fact, I regard such cultural broadening as a first responsibility of a philosopher who takes up topics of general human interest. A second responsibility is to discuss these topics themselves in a comparatively jargon-free and non-technical way, so that one's writings will appeal to the intelligent lay reader. This latter responsibility is a second kind of broadening, this time an *Erweiterung* of one's audience and not just of one's own thought. In the end, the two broadenings go hand in hand: each extension of responsibility complements and reinforces the other.

My most consistent desire and design in philosophy has been to illuminate, in diverse and novel ways, subjects of continual concern to human beings, and to accomplish this in the most lucid and forthright manner I can effect. That I have been inspired by figures in the Continental tradition, and most particularly by those associated with the phenomenological tradition, does not mean that I am primarily responsible to these figures. Rather (as Husserl himself says) I am mainly responsible to myself for gaining telling insights into any given subject, and to others—students and colleagues and readers—for conveying these insights in the liveliest and most compelling way. Methods and sources, influences and ambitions fade in the face of this double commitment to tell the philosophical truth.

## Selected Bibliography

1969 "Meaning in Art." In *New Essays in Phenomenology*, ed. J. M. Edie. Chicago: Quadrangle.

1970 "Truth in Art." *Man and World* 3 (4): 351–369.

1971a "Expression and Communication in Art." *Journal of Aesthetics and Art Criticism* 30 (2): 197–207.

1971b "Imagination: Imagining and the Image." *Philosophy and Phenomenological Research* 31: 475–490.

1971c "Man, Self, and Truth." *The Monist* 55: 218–254.

1972 "Freud's Theory of Reality: A Critical Account." *Review of Metaphysics* 35 (4): 659–690.

1974a *Explorations in Phenomenology*. Co-edited with D. Carr. The Hague: Nijhoff.

1974b "Toward a Phenomenology of Imagination." *Journal of the British Society for Phenomenology* 5 (1): 3–19.

1974c "Toward an Archetypal Imagination." *Spring: An Annual of Archetypal Psychology and Jungian Thought,* pp. 1–32.

1975 "L'imagination comme intermédiare." In *Vers une esthétique sans entrave,* ed. G. Lascault. Paris: Union Générale d'Editions.

1976a *Imagining: A Phenomenological Study.* Bloomington: Indiana University Press.

1976b "The Image/Sign Relation in Husserl and Freud." *Review of Metaphysics* 30 (2): 207–225.

1977a "Imagination and Phenomenological Method." In *Husserl: Expositions and Appraisals,* ed. F. Elliston and P. McCormick. Notre Dame: University of Notre Dame Press.

1977b "Imagining and Remembering." *Review of Metaphysics* 31 (2): 187–209.

1978 "Perceiving and Remembering." *Review of Metaphysics* 32 (3): 407–436.

1980 "Freud and Piaget on Childhood Memory." In *Piaget, Philosophy, and the Human Sciences,* ed. H. J. Silverman. Atlantic Heights, N.J.: Humanities Press.

1981a "Literary Description and Phenomenological Method." *Yale French Studies* 61: 176–201.

1981b "Sartre on Imagination." In *The Philosophy of Jean-Paul Sartre,* ed. P. A. Schilpp. La Salle, Ill.: Open Court.

1983a "Hegel, Heidegger, Lacan: The Dialectic of Desire." Co-authored with J. M. Woody. In *Interpreting Lacan,* ed. J. H. Smith and W. Kerrigan. New Haven: Yale University Press.

1983b "Keeping the Past in Mind." *Review of Metaphysics* 37 (1): 77–95.

1984a "Commemoration and Perdurance in the *Analects,* Books I and II." *Philosophy East and West* 34 (4): 389–399.

1984b "Habitual Body and Memory in Merleau-Ponty." *Man and World* 17 (3/4): 279–297.

1984c "Origin(s) in(of) Heidegger/Derrida." *Journal of Philosophy* 81 (10): 601–610.

1985a "Findlay's Philosophy of Mind." In *Studies in the Philosophy of J. N. Findlay,* ed. R. S. Cohen et al. Albany: State University of New York Press.

1985b "Memory and Phenomenological Method." In *Phenomenology in Practice and Theory,* ed. W. S. Hamrick. The Hague: Nijhoff.

1986a *The Life of the Transcendental Ego,* ed. with D. Morano. Albany: State University of New York Press.

1986b "The Place of Space in the Birth of the Clinic." *Journal of the Philosophy of Medicine* (special issue on Foucault).

1987a "Derrida's Deconstruction of Heidegger's Views on Temporality: The Language of Space and Time." In *Phenomenology of Temporality: Time and Language.* Pittsburgh: Duquesne University, Simon Silverman Phenomenology Center.

1987b *Remembering: A Phenomenological Study.* Bloomington: Indiana University Press.

1987c "The World of Nostalgia." *Man and World* 20: 361–384.

1988 "Levinas on Memory and the Trace." In *The Collegium Phaenomenologicum: The First Ten Years,* ed. Giuseppina Moneta, John Sallis, and Jacques Taminiaux. Dordrecht: Kluwer.

1990a "Heidegger in and out of Place." In *Heidegger: A Centenary Appraisal.* Pittsburgh: Duquesne University, Simon Silverman Phenomenology Center.

1990b "Place, Form, and Identity in Postmodern Architecture and Philosophy." In *After the Future,* ed. G. Shapiro. Albany: State University of New York Press.

1990c "The Subdominance of the Pleasure Principle." In *Pleasure beyond the Pleasure Principle,* ed. R. A. Glick and S. Bone. New Haven: Yale University Press.

1991a *Spirit and Soul: Essays in Philosophical Psychology.* Dallas: Spring.

1991b "'The Element of Voluminousness': Depth and Place Re-examined." In *Merleau-Ponty Vivant,* ed. M. Dillon. Albany: State University of New York Press.

1992a "Forgetting Remembered." *Man and World* 25 (3/4): 281–311.

1992b "Remembering Resumed: Pursuing Buddhism and Phenomenology." In *In the Mirror of Memory,* ed. J. Gyatso. Albany: State University of New York Press.

1992c "Retrieving the Difference between Place and Space." *Journal of Philosophy and the Visual Arts* (Spring).

1993a "Anima Loci." *Sphinx: A Journal for Archetypal Psychology and the Arts* (special issue).

1993b *Getting Back into Place: Toward a Renewed Understanding of the Place-World.* Bloomington: Indiana University Press.

1993c "On the Phenomenology of Remembering: The Neglected Case of Place Memory." In *Natural and Artificial Minds,* ed. R. Burton. Albany: State University of New York Press.

1996a "Embracing Lococentrism." *Human Studies* 19 (4): 459–465.

1996b "How to Get from Space to Place in a Very Short Stretch of Time: Phenomenological Prolegomena." In *Senses of Place,* ed. Steven Feld and Keith Basso. Santa Fe: School of American Research Press.

1997a "Imagination." Co-authored entry in *The Encyclopedia of Phenomenology,* ed. L. Embree. Dordrecht: Kluwer.

1997b "Memory." In *The Encyclopedia of Phenomenology,* ed. L. Embree. Dordrecht: Kluwer.

1997c "Joseph Margolis on Interpretation." *Man and World* 30 (2): 127–138.

1997d "Smooth Places and Rough-Edged Places: The Hidden History of Place." *Review of Metaphysics* 51 (2): 267–296.

1997e "Sym-phenomenologizing." *Human Studies* 20 (2): 169–180.

1997f *The Fate of Place: A Philosophical History.* Berkeley: University of California Press.

1997g "The World at a Glance." In *Chiasms,* ed. Fred Evans and Len Lawlor. Albany: State University of New York Press, forthcoming.

# FIVE

## From Bad Infinity to Hyper-Reflection

## BERNARD FLYNN

My entry into philosophy was sudden and unpremeditated. In the antediluvian days of required courses, I was happily compelled to take a course in logic at Duquesne University. In retrospect it was, in fact, not a very good course; but again happily, I did not know it then. Rather I was completely taken by it. The very idea of posing the most fundamental questions—about life, the world, the nature and limits of knowledge—filled me with an enthusiasm that has never diminished.

On second thought, perhaps it was not so unpremeditated. As a child I was plagued by a certain phenomenon that continues to play a role in the type of philosophy that was to become my life work, namely, the *mise en abime*. But for me it did not take the form of facing mirrors reflecting each other to infinity. If Lacan is to be believed, my fascination with the mirror took shape at an earlier stage. In any case, for me it was linked to the issue of the infinite divisibility of matter. The "little metaphysician" was struck by the label on a can of kitchen cleanser called Old Dutch Cleanser. On this can was a picture of an old "Dutch" woman. In one hand she held a stick, not to defend herself against Nietzsche but rather to chase away dirt. In her other hand she held a can of Old Dutch Cleanser, on which was a picture of a Dutch woman with a stick and a can of Old Dutch Cleanser, and so on to infinity. I studied this label with a magnifying glass and deviled my mother with the question of how far it could go. Indeed, Hegel's bad infinity was the first philosophical concept that I entertained.

At Duquesne in those days, a student was introduced to philosophy through Thomism in bloodcurdling textbooks in which, at the end of each chapter, came a page or two devoted to the refutation of all philosophers other than Aquinas. There was a brief period during my sophomore year when I thought that Descartes and Kant must have been the stupidest people who ever lived. Later on I was fortunate to have a genuine medievalist, John Rowan, as a professor. Even so, it took me almost a decade to be able to appreciate Aquinas as a great philosopher.

In the same year in which I was introduced to the mysteries of logic, I also read Dostoevsky's *The Brothers Karamazov*. After reading all night, I finished the book at dawn and thought to myself: this is faith, and I no longer have it. Religious faith lingered for a while, but no longer as a vital dimension of my life. Genuine faith had given way to the idea of faith. I could have said what Merleau-Ponty reported to Sartre concerning his religious faith: "One believes. One believes that one believes, but one does not believe." This was a decision, if that is what it was, that I have never been inclined to reconsider. Kierkegaard notwithstanding, believing things for which there is no evidence is not, to my mind, a good idea. Again, it took a while before I stopped viewing the faith of others as anything other than a moral fault.

It was only in the last two years of my undergraduate study at Duquesne, and then in graduate school, that I got to the real thing—the true *wurst,* as Hannah Arendt referred to the subject matter of *The Life of the Mind*. During this time, I seriously read the history of philosophy and, of course, phenomenology with a certain reverence. Perhaps this was a thin sublimation of an erstwhile religious faith, perhaps not. I still wince when I receive a graduate student paper that purports to "refute" Hegel. The philosophers whom I studied at this time have become my lifelong companions.

During the '60s I immersed myself in the texts of Plato, Aristotle, Descartes, Kant, Hegel, and Husserl. In 1963, I and some friends, including Al Lingis, who was to become my dissertation director, along with a few young comrades from the Dubois Club of America, organized the first Pittsburgh demonstration against the war in Vietnam. (The Dubois Club of America was in fact the youth group of the Communist Party; nonetheless, Nixon outdid himself by claiming that its name was a Communist deception because it sounded so much like the Boys Club of America.) At the 1964 Easter demonstration in Washington, D.C. against the war, I joined Students for a Democratic Society. This event marked my entry into political philosophy in general and Marxism in particular. At this time I made an extensive study of the works of Marx and they remain for me classics in the sense in which Merleau-Ponty spoke of a classic in his Preface to *Signs:* a text from which we draw further thought, including the reasons for which we no longer accept them as true. Never did I become a great fan of any of the Marxist regimes except, alas, the Cuban. Many of us thought then that Cuba was different, and as the historian Ron Radosh recently wrote, "We were right, Cuba was different, it was worse."

The year before I wrote my dissertation on Sartre, I presented a paper in Lingis's seminar defending Sartre against Merleau-Ponty's critique in his "Sartre and Ultrabolshevism." A year later I wrote an article claiming that

Merleau-Ponty's critique was on the mark in every respect, a position that I still hold. After having disabused myself of Sartre's "Cartesian Marxism," I began to pursue a study of Heidegger, in particular his writings after the turn; curiously for someone of my background, I was untroubled at the time by his politics. Also in conjunction with my reading of Nietzsche, I concerned myself with the concept of "metaphysics." The thought of Nietzsche, Heidegger, and, from another direction, Saussure and Freud—with and without Lacan—convinced me that the "neo-Cartesian" starting point of phenomenological reflection in the works of Husserl, Sartre, and, as I then believed, Merleau-Ponty was profoundly problematized.

From Heidegger's thought I learned to be sensitive to the extent to which we are not the origin of our thinking, the extent to which Language speaks, and the extent to which our thought is a response to epochal givens. From Nietzsche, and also from Foucault and Marx, I learned to ask of a text not only "What does it mean?" but also "Who is speaking?" What form of life does this text express and promote? From Freud I learned that man is not master in his own house and furthermore, as Mikkel Borsch-Jacobsen adds, that the house is haunted. Freud's doctrine of the multiplicity of psychic "agencies," the plurality in the mind, and the alterity at the heart of ipseity —the it—troubled the unity of the Cartesian Cogito, the Kantian transcendental unity of apperception, and the Husserlian transcendental ego. I tried to learn all these lessons without forgetting the critique of psychologism and historicism that I had learned from Husserl's "Prolegomena to Pure Logic" and "Philosophy as a Strict Science."

All of these lessons were reinforced by my reading of the Structuralists, particularly de Saussure's *Course in General Linguistics*. If meaning is constituted through language by a diacritical process, and if language is a system of differences without positive terms, then any reference to subjective acts of sense-giving seems to be precluded.

Foucault viewed the philosophical concept of Man, the subject, as having been generated through the discursive regularities of the *episteme* of surface and depth which came into being in the nineteenth and twentieth centuries—a figure of recent origin soon to be effaced. Subjectivity is thus a metaphysical conception, and metaphysics in the thought of Nietzsche and Heidegger, in different ways, begins by the bifurcation of the sensible world and the "true world": our history is the process by which "the true world has become a fable." According to Heidegger, the forgetfulness of Being and the forgetfulness of this forgetfulness are functions of Being's self-donation and at the same time its withdrawal—epoch and at the same time *epoche*. Metaphysics historicizes itself as errancy, as the re-elaboration of ontological hierarchies: from Greek thought to the philosophy of the Middle Ages, to the modern metaphysics of subjectivity and finally to the epoch of technology when all ontological hierarchies are flattened in the donation of Being as standing reserve. In our epoch, he claims, metaphysics "has gone through the sphere of prefigured possibilities." It is exhausted.

I became, and still am, both fascinated and troubled by this conception of the notion of metaphysics. Fascinated because it seems to me that it points to a fundamental transformation of the nature of philosophy, beginning with Kant and proceeding, though not in a straight line, to our own situation, in which very few philosophers would claim access to a founding stratum of the supersensible. Even those who do so emphatically deny that they are doing it—Habermas, for example. Troubled in two respects: on the one hand, there are philosophers who have no place in it. Take the case of Vico, a thinker who in 1725 made a profound critique of the Cartesian Cogito. On the other hand, and more importantly, it is over-totalizing. For example, after a discussion of the principle of sufficient reason in the *Principle of Reason,* Heidegger remarks parenthetically that it is no accident that Leibniz invented actuary tables and thus basically invented life insurance. But one must ask: can life insurance really be understood as an instantiation of the principle of sufficient reason? I think not. Life insurance is of use to neither a feudal aristocrat nor a serf. Very complex historical processes have to take place—the rise of alienable property, the formation of an urban middle class, and so forth. Can history really be understood exclusively through the history of philosophy?

Husserl has taught us that we must return to the things themselves; and Aristotle, phenomenologist *avant la lettre,* has told us that we must "save the appearances." If it is the case that subjectivity is a metaphysical concept, it is nonetheless also an experience and as such must have a place in our reflection. At this point in my life, I rediscovered the writings of Merleau-Ponty, texts which I and many others had far too hastily consigned to the realm of metaphysics. His chapter on the Cogito in the *Phenomenology of Perception* includes a profound critique of the Cartesian Cogito, arguing that for the subject of the Cogito, passivity, finitude, and time can have no meaning.

Then, in *The Visible and the Invisible,* Merleau-Ponty develops an auto-critique of his previous works, in which he finds that they retain too much of a philosophy of the Subject. Nevertheless, in *The Visible and the Invisible,* through his conception of the flesh, of reversibility, we find a way to speak about our finite inherence in the world. In his late writings, one discovers not only a critique of the separation of the sensible and the supersensible, of perception and language, but also a way to philosophize without effecting such separations. It was to his conception of the intertwining of the visible and the invisible, an invisible which is not the contrary of the visible but an invisible *of* the visible, that I was drawn. For Merleau-Ponty the intelligible world is not opposed to the sensible world but is encrusted in the joints of the sensible, as "its lining and its depth."

Also I was attracted to his conception of hyperreflection, a type of reflection which does not propose to reach beneath phenomena in order to arrive at the conditions of possibility, but rather to reach the place of its finite insertion into the "there is" of the world, of Being. In the Preface to *The Visible and the Invisible,* Lefort cites a line from Kafka which characterizes the late philosophy of Merleau-Ponty:

> The things presented themselves to me not by their roots, but by some point or other situated toward the middle of them.

Through Merleau-Ponty's works I was able to reconcile the critique of metaphysics with a type of thinking that would still be phenomenology.

Now let us return to the subject of political philosophy. After moving away from Marxism in my search for a political philosophy that would remain critical, I turned for a time to the Frankfurt School. But perhaps my "overexposure" to Heidegger as a youth ill fitted me for Critical Theory, and in particular for its most advanced proponent, Habermas. I could not but see in the Lukacsian inspiration of Critical Theory, as Heidegger says, a resurrection of classical metaphysics in altered form. In my book, *Political Philosophy at the Closure of Metaphysics,* I devoted a chapter to Habermas in which I demonstrated this in some detail.

In the mid-seventies, I had the good fortune to meet, and subsequently to become friends with, the philosopher Claude Lefort. In his work I discovered a type of political philosophy which put into practice what Merleau-Ponty called hyperreflection. At the same time I also began to read the writings of Hannah Arendt. I was particularly taken by her notion of the contempt that philosophers have for *doxa,* and thus for the domain of the political, except insofar as it could be viewed as an *instantiation* of an idea, a theory.

Strongly influenced by these two thinkers, I began to write *Political Philosophy at the Closure of Metaphysics.* This work is divided into two parts. In the first part, I looked at three political philosophers—Marx, Habermas, and Foucault, who in their own self-representation of their works took into account something like the end, or closure, of metaphysics; and they viewed their own thought as a step beyond it. I argued that unproblematized metaphysical concepts were in fact operative in their allegedly "post-metaphysical" thinking.

In a chapter entitled "The Real through Desire and Language," I began with Marx, according to whom the end of philosophy is achieved in Hegel's thought. Marx's advance beyond Hegel consists of the realization that practice must not replace, but rather realize, philosophy. Against the Hegelian philosophy of Spirit, Marx contends that to encounter the Real is to be affected by it, as happens in the case of desire, where the affected is touched by the *immediate* presence of the object. Sexual desire gives rise to the first society, the family. Against this, using the concept of the symbolic order borrowed from Lacan, I argued that in fact desire is never immediate but is always already mediated through a system of signifiers, namely the kinship structure. Then, employing the work of Levi-Strauss, I claimed that the family is not founded on the immediate relationship between a man and a woman but is mediated through a system of exchange necessitated by the interdiction against incest. I attempted to show that in the *German Ideology,* Marx held a motivated theory of language, one, that is, immediately related to sensual activity, which is dissolved by the division of mental and physical labor. Against such a conception, again borrowing from Lacan, I argued that Language is always already mediated, that it is always the discourse of the Other. And I suggested that there is in one strain of Marx's thinking a foreclosure of the symbolic order which is not unrelated to the totalitarian fate of Marxism.

In the chapter on Habermas, I showed that his reading of Freud, a reading in which he claims that the unconscious is derived from consciousness, annuls the most profound dimension of Freud's thought in the service of a philosophy of transparency. I contended that in his later works, Habermas's theory of language as the bearer of validity claims greatly impoverishes language in its capacity to reveal the world. This critique drew heavily on the conceptions of language of both Saussure and Heidegger.

Addressing Foucault, I demonstrated that there is in his work a metaphysics of power, which is to say that "beneath" the phenomena of the political-juridical structure of a modern *nation,* there is to be found the immediate operations of power, and that this leads Foucault to a denegation of the symbolic dimension of the social. In a way, Foucault replicates the Marxist distinction between substructure and superstructure.

The second part of my book dealt with thinkers who, in my opinion, were more successful in elaborating a political philosophy "outside" the bounds of metaphysics. Here I invoked Arendt's conception of the irreducibility of *doxa* to any form of theory and her notion of the autonomy of the political as a domain of speech and action, a position the opposite of Foucault's. Nevertheless, criticizing her reliance on Kant's theory of judgment in her conceptualization of the political, I argued that insofar as Kant's theory of judgment relies on the subjective universality of the faculties, it too is metaphysical.

As might be expected from what I have said so far, my chapter on Merleau-Ponty focused on the extent to which he was able to subvert the opposition of the sensible and the intelligible, of perception and language.

The book ended with a chapter on the thought of Lefort, which drew attention, contrary to Heidegger, to the historical mutations in the symbolic dimension of society effected by political events, particularly the democratic revolutions of the eighteenth century. Lefort depicts these events as generative of a new *dispositif symbolique* that contains in latent form both democracy and totalitarianism, types of regimes which are not explicable as the instantiations of philosophical theories. Lefort's work defends the irreducibility of politics to theory; he is against the view that politics is an instantiation of philosophical ideas. His thought rejoins the classical tradition of political philosophy, in which the question of the nature of the regime is paramount.

In conclusion let me say that the thought of Jacques Derrida has also played an important role in my philosophical development. From him I have taken what I think is a more nuanced conception of metaphysics, since, according to him, the "philosophy of presence" is never in fact realized; rather it is a desire that is subverted in its very execution. Nevertheless, I have lately been entertaining very serious doubts about the ability of the philosophy of difference to think identity, which, like the notion of the subject, is a metaphysical concept but also an experienced phenomenon.

I am currently writing a book-length study on the political philosophy of Lefort, since I believe that he, more than anyone, has given us the concepts to think the world as we find it.

Philosophy conceived of as a process of interrogation, without the prospect of achieving an end, continues to motivate my efforts to think in order to know the world, but also to effect a transformation of myself. Freedom begins at the point of our deliverance from dogmatism, but we underestimate at our own risk the potential for dogmatism to rise again.

And I still wonder about the Dutch Lady with the stick.

## Selected Bibliography

1973a "The Question of Ontology: Sartre and Merleau-Ponty." In *The Horizons of the Flesh: Critical Perspectives on the Thought of Merleau-Ponty,* ed. Garth Gillan. Carbondale: Southern Illinois University Press.

1973b *An Introduction to Husserl's Phenomenology.* Albany: State University of New York Press. (Booklet.)

1973c *The Marxist Dialectic: The Development of the Concept of the Dialectic from the Second International to the Structuralism of Althusser.* Albany: State University of New York Press. (Booklet.)

1978a "Methodology in the Work of Michel Foucault." *Philosophy and Social Criticism*: 147–158.

1978b "Michel Foucault and the Husserlian Problematic of a Transcendental Philosophy of History." *Philosophy Today* 22 (3): 224–239.

1982 "Sexuality, Knowledge and Power in the Thought of Foucault." *Philosophy and Social Criticism*: 329–349.

1983 "Descartes and the Ontology of Subjectivity." *Man and World* 16: 3–23.

1984a "Textuality and the Flesh: Derrida and Merleau-Ponty." *Journal of the British Society for Phenomenology* 15 (2). Translated into French as "Chair et Textualite: Merleau-Ponty et Derrida," in *Actualites de Merleau-Ponty, Les Cahiers de Philosophie* 7 (1989).

1984b "The Question of an Ontology of the Political: Arendt, Merleau-Ponty and Lefort." *International Studies in Philosophy*.

1985a "Kant's Doctrine of Subjectivity: From Finitude to the Absolute." *Philosophy Today* 29 (4): 284–302.

1985b "Reading Habermas Reading Freud." *Human Studies: A Journal for Philosophy and the Social Sciences* 8: 57–76.

1986 "Political Theory and the Metaphysics of Presence." *Philosophy and Social Criticism* 11 (3): 245–259.

1987a "Claude Lefort: The Political Forms of Modern Society." *Philosophy and Social Criticism* 13 (1): 85–103.

1987b "Foucault and the Body Politics." *Man and World* 20: 65–84.

1988 "Arendt's Appropriation of Kant's Theory of Judgment." *Journal of the British Society for Phenomenology* 19 (2): 128–140.

1989 "Derrida and Foucault: Madness and Writing." In *Derrida and Deconstruction*, ed. Hugh J. Silverman. Continental Philsophy, vol. 2. New York: Routledge.

1991 "The Places of the Work of Art in Arendt's Philosophy." *Philosophy and Social Criticism* 17 (3). Translated into French as "Positions de l'oeuvre d'art dans la philosophie de Hannah Arendt," in *Dossier: Art et Phenomenolgie, La Part de l'Oeil, Revue annuelle* 7: 73–81.

1992a *Political Philosophy at the Closure of Metaphysics*. Atlantic Highlands, N.J.: Humanities Press.

1992b "The Concept of the Political and Its Relationship to Plurality in the Thought of Arendt." In *Hannah Arendt et la Modernite*, Annales de l'Institut de la Philosophie de l'Universite de Bruxelles. Paris: Vrin.

1994a "Between Ethics and Politics in the Thought of Lefort." In *Dissensus Communis: Between Ethics and Politics*, ed. Philipe Van Haute. Kampen: Kok/Pharos Press.

1994b "Merleau-Ponty and Derrida: Convergence/Divergence." In *Ecart and Difference: Merleau-Ponty and Derrida on Seeing and Writing*, ed. Martin Dillon. Atlantic Highlands, N.J.: Humanities Press.

1994c "Merleau-Ponty and Nietzsche on the Visible and the Invisible." In *Merleau-Ponty: Difference, Materiality, Painting*, ed. Veronique Foti. Atlantic Highlands, N.J.: Humanities Press.

1997a "The Philosophy of Lefort." In *A Companion to Continental Philosophy*, ed. Simon Critchley. Oxford: Blackwell.

1997b "Phenomenological Ethics." In *How Natural Is the Ethical Law?*, ed. Paul Cobben and Ludwig Heyde. Tilburg: Tilburg University Press.

1997c "Benjamin und Merleau-Ponty: Sprache/Verlust/Restitution." In *Walter Benjamin und Die Französische Moderne*, ed. Asnof Noor. Freiburg: Rombach Verlag.

1998a "Merleau-Ponty et la Position Philosophique du Scepticisme." In *Merleau-Ponty: Notes cours sur L'origine de la géométrie de Husserl suivi de Recherches sur la phénoménologie de Merleau-Ponty*, ed. Renaud Barbaras. Paris: Presses Universitaires de France.

1998b "Truth in Painting/Eye and Mind." In *Painting and Truth: Derrida/Heidegger/Kant*, ed. Hugh J. Silverman and Wilhelm S. Wurzer. Atlantic Highlands, N.J.: Humanities Press.

1998c "Foucault and Marx: The Law as Praxis." In *Foucault: Archaeology/Genealogy*, ed. Hugh J. Silverman. Continental Philosophy, vol. 7. London: Routledge.

1998d "Secularization and Modernity: Vattimo/Blumenberg." In *Reading "The End of Modernity,"* ed. Hugh J. Silverman and Wilhelm S. Wurzer. Atlantic Highlands, N.J.: Humanities Press.

# SIX

# Continental Philosophy on Another Continent

# THOMAS R. FLYNN

It is curious that so-called "Continental" philosophy is not recognized as such by philosophers on the European continent. Another instance of Molière's Monsieur Jourdain's not realizing that he had been speaking prose all his life? Or does it indicate a special feature, perhaps a failing, of philosophical thought and practice in the English-speaking world? Why would a student of philosophy in America turn to Continental thought for intellectual stimulation and guidance? Since I take it that the essays in this volume reflect a kind of intellectual biography of their authors, I shall attempt to answer these questions in the narrative mode, exploiting the concreteness while acknowledging the limitations of a personal perspective.

My philosophical education was broadly "humanistic." It began with a thorough grounding in what has been called the "Thomistic synthesis" of Aristotle, neo-Platonism, and Biblical thought, with particular emphasis on the act of existing and the (much maligned but ineluctable) question, "Why is there anything at all rather than nothing?" From the outset, I sensed that philosophy should be addressing personally urgent, nontrivial questions, ones that "made a difference" in a person's life. To me, the seemingly abstract questions, "Is the real completely intelligible? Does it all make sense?" were and continue to be pressing ones. Aquinas's distinction between *studiositas* and mere *curiositas* seemed to articulate the difference that drew me; the former was related to wisdom, the latter the child of sloth. Accordingly, I was convinced that philosophy must be experiential, not just conceptual, in its origin and method; language, yes, but the *experience* of language and the language of experience broadly conceived, had to be the touchstones of philosophical activity. No doubt, this is why I would later find phenomenology so attractive.

Circumstance more than logical necessity brought me into contact with attempts to confer an epistemological legitimacy on this metaphysics, first through a Cartesian foundationalism (the Louvain school of Léon Noël), and then via the influence of German idealism, especially the later Fichte (Maréchal and the so-called "transcendental" Thomists). It was the latter who captured my loyalty through their emphasis on being as the object of the unrestricted desire to know. The personal influence of Bernard Lonergan at the Gregorian University in Rome, where I studied systematic theology for four years, was decisive in that respect. His *Insight: A Study of Human Understanding* remains one of the most important books I have ever read. Ironically, perhaps, this introduced me to nineteenth-century German thought. Lonergan seemed to be doing a kind of hermeneutical phenomenology *malgré-lui*.

But there was another tributary to this formation, namely, the "existentialist," and it pursued its course in relative innocence of the other stream of thought. My undergraduate honors thesis dealt with the concept of choice in Kierkegaard, a topic which was just emerging in importance in the English-speaking world. What I found attractive about such thinking was its "personalism" more than its so-called nihilism or its theses of meaninglessness and revolt. But the latter could not be ignored; they constituted the shadow, if not the substance, of authenticity, in my view, and had to be addressed with fairness and even a certain intellectual sympathy. In retrospect, I must admit that Sartre's penchant for "thinking against himself" and Foucault's "ethic of an intellectual" as "thinking otherwise than before" (*se déprendre de soi-même*) were already operative at this early stage of my development. Had *skepsis* enfeebled the will to *sophia*? The link, if I were to forge one, between my metaphysics and this newly fashionable style of thinking would have to be a theism at once experiential and theoretical (experience and reason "breaking and foaming on the rocks of faith," as Josef Pieper once wrote). If a "philosophy of the concrete" is what moved people from German idealism toward existential phenomenology in the '30s (e.g., Sartre's famous encounter with Husserl's thought via Raymond Aron's proposed description of the cocktail before them), I believe that it was a kind of *orthopraxis* (*une foi vivante*) within a practical community that provided the *cantus firmus* for the intellectual polyphony (if not cacophony) in which I would henceforth be engaged.

It was perhaps inevitable that these streams of thought would find their confluence in Heidegger and the more ontological "existentialists" rather than in Nietzsche, at least as he was read in the early '60s. Phenomenology respected the experiential measure of philosophical reflection, and existential, hermeneutical phenomenology with its "preontological understanding" of Being seemed the most satisfactory way to explore the inexhaustible richness of that horizon. I read widely in existentialist literature during my years in Italy and deepened this reading with growing exposure to the Augustinian and Franciscan traditions in metaphysics and theology. The matter of *voluntarism,* whose attraction I felt both in these medieval authors and in their existentialist heirs, still fascinates and repels me. In many ways it appears the easiest solution. But I cannot bring myself simply to cut the Gordian knot (the voices of Aristotle and Thomas still ring true). Yet it seems impossible to untie it while you are hanging from the cord; your weight removes all slack!

After several years teaching at the college where I had first studied philosophy (Carroll in Helena, Montana), I entered the doctoral program at Columbia in 1966. The department was in transition from a historical orientation (with a lingering hint of naturalist metaphysics) to an analytic one. This afforded me the opportunity to study analytic philosophy as I had thus far failed to do. But the program was sufficiently tolerant to enable me to pursue my interests in "existentialist" thought as well. Then there was the enormous intellectual stimulation of New York City itself. On reflection, I believe that I learned more from the city than from the University. It was from the city, with its relentless motion both physical and intellectual, that I felt the questions arising in concrete fashion, questions that analytic philosophy failed to address and that existential thought parried with ambiguity. My theological background would not let me look away, but a certain excess of speculation (elitism?) prevented me from facing them squarely: Vietnam, social and economic exploitation, the nascent feminist movement: 1968. These hit Columbia harder than any other American university except perhaps Berkeley. This too was due in part to the city. The university closed early that term, and I went off to Paris to begin research on my dissertation and to experience what were to be the "events of May."

"You can always make something out of what you've been made into." This is the motto of Sartrean humanism which I discovered during those years and which continues to sustain me. "You can always make something out of" is the message of hope that his vintage existentialism set forth, despite a tendency to overshadow it with phrases like "futile passion" and "hell is others." This is the side of Sartre that I and others discovered early on. The other side, the "what you've been made into," emerged only in the late '50s and '60s. It contributed to the spirit of '68 and impressed on me a deeper sense of the fact, the nature, and the conditions of *collective responsibility.* This became the subject of my dissertation and was rewritten and published as a book—*Sartre and Marxist Existentialism: The Test Case of Collective Responsibility* (1984). I have retained this interest in the theory of responsibility to this day and find it one of the theoretical links between my existentialist and my postmodern interests. An ethic of responsibility is central to both styles of thought, even if the latter has only recently come to appreciate that need. (When I asked Foucault about it, for example, he responded that he had heard enough of "responsibility" under the Vichy regime!)

Most of my research and publication for the next two decades focused on Sartre or on topics to which he had introduced me. Like a brilliant friend, though we never met, he expanded my horizons to include literature and politics, painting and social theory, psychology and history. But these were always broached in a manner that did not stray far from questions of ontological possibility and moral responsibility with which I continued to feel at home. Fortunately, Sartre did not want disciples. So I have never felt unfaithful for following him in my own fashion. His writings placed me in dialogue with some of the seminal minds of the age. It was Sartre's critique that introduced me to Foucault.

By then I had what Isaac Deutcher calls an "ideological interest" in contemporary French thought. Foucault was Sartre's successor, if not heir, in this conversation. He addressed issues in the '70s and the '80s that often complemented Sartrean stands in the previous decades, even as he sought to free himself from Sartre's intellectual hegemony. I found in Foucault a congenial respect for freedom and ethical, if not moral, concerns, as well as a brilliant propensity to "think otherwise." But now the specter of voluntarism with its ambivalent allure reappeared with a vengeance: reason itself was at stake. True, Sartre had previously distinguished dialectical from analytic reason, which he characterized as proletarian and bourgeois respectively, but he remained tied to certain "absolutes," viz., the absolute of consciousness-freedom and the absolute of being-in-itself (the cabinet where historical facts are preserved). With Foucault I found myself in a state of Nietzschean free fall: the earth cut loose from its sun. With him and other "postmoderns," one seemed to be undergoing a crisis of criteria, a judgment reiterated by Lyotard and others. With a grant from the A.C.L.S. (American Council of Learned Societies), I attended the last lectures Foucault delivered before his untimely death in 1984. These dealt with plain-speaking (*parrhesia*) and the "good" Cynics who practiced it in opposition to the essentialist tradition. I remain convinced that "parrhesiast" best captures Foucault's philosophical character and style and that it tempers the apparent inconsistency between his "theory" and his social activism so criticized by Habermas and others. I also suspect that "parrhesiasm," to coin a term, is the best we can hope for in our "postmodern" condition.

A book from my graduate studies that left a lasting impression was Dewey's *The Quest for Certainty*. This because it so questioned my prior foundationalist tendencies without requiring that I slip into nihilistic despair. Although I do not consider myself a "pragmatist," I find this position especially relevant to the current philosophical scene and to my place in it. On the one hand, it reminds me that many of the criticisms directed against recent French philosophy (charges of relativism, nihilism, and the like) were aimed at the American pragmatists of an earlier generation. But civilization did not collapse and the philosophical world was in fact enriched by the pragmatists' reflections. To be sure, there is the contrary belief that pluralism is intrinsically execrable, that "error" has no rights, and that philosophy is the guardian and dispenser of truth to the other disciplines. But I find such a position incredible. Which is not to say that I do not remain convinced that philosophy must face the question of the meaning of being in one way or another or that, as Gilson used to say, "metaphysics always buries its undertakers." That too we have learned from the history of philosophy. For the "postmodern" is more a style than an epoch. As a style, it has always been with us (it is as old as Diogenes and the "good" Cynics). As an epoch, it is already showing signs of absorption in the counterpoint of ongoing philosophical discussion. Such is the lesson of history for this, our "time of need."

If the matter of responsibility transported me from existentialist to postmodern writers, it was a renewed interest in the meaning-direction (*sens*) of history that enabled me to bring Sartre and Foucault into direct comparison and contrast. The major project in which I am currently engaged is a two-volume study entitled "Sartre, Foucault and Historical Reason." I have reconstructed an existentialist theory of history on the basis of the entire Sartrean corpus, but especially his posthumously published works in volume 1 (1997b), in order to contrast it with a Foucauldian "mapping" of history in poststructuralist terms in the second volume. The possibilities and limits of each approach should come into view and with them, the characteristic features of existentialist and poststructuralist thought in general will emerge for critical assessment. Of course, one cannot compare the incomparable (as Lyotard has argued strikingly with the concept of "differend") and so one must look for a *tertium comparationis,* as the logicians say. Such a mediating term I find in the "moral" realm broadly conceived to include both the ethical and the aesthetic. And to the extent that "history" is a prescriptive, not a descriptive term, the concept of "responsibility" is relevant to both sides of the equation. Perhaps the intersection of the historical and the moral will yield the "concrete" philosophy that has attracted me so consistently.

I have never surrendered my interest in theological questions, which I believe continue to press themselves on thinkers even in a "disenchanted" world. My next major project will be a book-length study, tentatively entitled "(Postmodern) Faith and (Enlightenment) Reason." It is my intent to bring to bear what several decades of study of existentialist and post-existentialist Continental philosophy have to say about the perennial question concerning the relation between religious faith and reason. Critics have already begun to note the "theological" turn taken by French phenomenologists in recent years. Ironically, the very atmosphere of pluralism and tolerance generated by postmodern thought opens space to think in a variety of ways, including the theological. But could it be that, as a condition for such freedom of movement, the traditional bond between metaphysics, reason, and theology must be loosened, if not severed entirely? That would require a kind of investigation more sympathetic to Augustine, Bonaventure, and Meister Eckhart than I had intended to pursue. The experiential would supplant the conceptual, and critical distance might well be sacrificed for "committed" thinking and "witnessing" to what Lyotard calls "singularities." Another whack at the Gordian knot? But this would revive interests that I once had nourished in a premodern context. Perhaps these authors will assume a new fascination when viewed from the hither side of the modern/postmodern divide.

Aristotle describes the "wise person" on several occasions. At one point he speaks of the wise one as "knowing how to put things in order." In another, he reminds us that the wise person does not seek a greater degree of precision than the subject-matter allows. To the extent that philosophy is still the love of wisdom and not a mere pastime (*curiositas* again), it may be seen as tempering this rage for order. Modern thought tended to connect individuals algorithmically or through constituting subjects. What we term "postmodern" thought favors the more subtle order of randomness, the unity of multiplicity, and the "othering" functions of diacritics, agonistics, and *differance*. Yet it seems that we are inescapably tied to sameness of some kind, even if it be merely the Wittgensteinian crisscrossing and overlapping of family resemblances. One need not slip back into Platonic or even Aristotelian modes of discourse in order to find a measure of order in the multiplicities that surround us. Indeed, the *moral* "order" may well be the place from which to redefine (if not rebuild) these parameters.

## Selected Bibliography

1973 "The Alienating and the Mediating Third in the Social Philosophy of Jean-Paul Sartre." In *Studies in Philosophy and in the History of Philosophy*, vol. 6, ed. John K. Ryan. Washington, D.C.: Catholic University of America Press.

1975 "The Role of the Image in Sartre's Aesthetic." *Journal of Aesthetics and Art Criticism* 33: 431–442.

1976a "The Use and Abuse of Utopias." *The Modern Schoolman* 43: 235–264.

1976b "Praxis and Vision: Elements of a Sartrean Epistemology." *Philosophical Forum* 8: 21–43.

1977 "An End to Authority: Epistemology and Politics in the Later Sartre." *Man and World* 10 (4): 448–465.

1979 "L'Imagination au Pouvoir: The Evolution of Sartre's Political and Social Thought." *Political Theory* 7: 157–180.

1980a "Vision, Responsibility, and Factual Belief." *Journal of Chinese Philosophy* 7: 27–36.

1980b "Sartre-Flaubert and the Real/Unreal." In *Existence and Dialectic: Contemporary Approaches to Jean-Paul Sartre,* ed. Hugh Silverman and Frederick Elliston. Pittsburgh: Duquesne University Press.

1980c "Angst and Care in the Early Heidegger: The Ontic/Ontologic Aporia." *International Studies in Philosophy* 12: 61–76.

1980d "Another Sartrean Torso: Critique of Dialectical Reason." *Social Theory and Practice* 6: 91–107.

1981a "Mediated Reciprocity and the Genius of the Third." In *The Philosophy of Jean-Paul Sartre,* ed. Paul Arthur Schilpp. La Salle, Ill.: Open Court.

1981b "Existential Hermeneutics: The Progressive-Regressive Method." *Eros* 8: 3–24.

1982 "Beginnings without End." Review essay of R. D. Cummings's *Starting Point: An Introduction to the Dialectic of Existence. Man and World* 15: 197–205.

1983a "From 'Socialisme et Liberté' to 'Pouvoir et Liberté': Sartre and Political Existentialism." In *Phenomenology in a Pluralistic Context,* ed. William McBride and Calvin Schrag. Albany: State University of New York Press.

1983b "Jean-Paul Sartre." In *Thinkers of the Twentieth Century: A Biographical, Bibliographical and Critical Dictionary,* ed. Elizabeth Devine et al. Detroit: Gale Research.

1984a *Sartre and Marxist Existentialism: The Test Case of Collective Responsibility.* Chicago: University of Chicago Press.

1984b "Collective Responsibility and Obedience to the Law." *Georgia Law Review* 18: 845–861.

1984c "Truth and Subjectivation in the Later Foucault." *Journal of Philosophy* 82: 531–540.

1985 "Merleau-Ponty and the Critique of Dialectical Reason." In *Hypatia,* ed. William Calder, Ulrich Goldsmith, and Phyllis Kenevan. Boulder: Colorado Associated University Press.

1987a "Foucault and the Career of the Historical Event." In *At the Nexus of Philosophy and History,* ed. Bernard P. Dauenhauer. Athens: University of Georgia Press.

1987b "Dying as Doing: Philosophical Thoughts on Death and Authenticity." In *Death: Completion and Discovery,* ed. Charles A. Corr and Richard A. Pacholski. Lakewood, Ohio: Association for Death Education and Counseling.

1988a "Foucault as Parrhesiast: His Last Course at the College de France." *Philosophy and Social Criticism* 12 (2–3). Reprinted in *The Final Foucault,* ed. James Bernauer. Cambridge: MIT Press. Japanese translation, 1991.

1988b "Foucault and Historical Nominalism." In *Phenomenology and Beyond: The Self and Its Language,* ed. Harold A. Durfee and David F. T. Rodier. Dordrecht: Kluwer.

1988c "Time Redeemed: Maritain's Christian Philosophy of History." In *Understanding Maritain*, ed. Diel Hudson and Matthew Mancini. Macon, Ga.: Mercer University Press.

1988d "Skizze für eine Theorie der Geschichte in der Philosophie Sartres: Die *Carnets* und die *Cahiers.*" In *Sartre—ein Kongress*, ed. Traugott Knig. Reinbeck: Rowohlt Verlag.

1988e "History as Fact and as Value: The Posthumous Sartre." In *Inquiries into Values*, ed. Sander H. Lee. Lewiston, N.Y.: Edwin Mellen Press.

1989 "Foucault and the Politics of Postmodernity." *Nous* 23: 187–198.

1990a "Phenomenology and Faith: From Description to Explanation and Back." *American Catholic Philosophical Quarterly* 64 (supplement): 40–50.

1990b "Sartre and Technological Being-in-the-World." In *Lifeworld and Technology*, ed. Lester Embree and Tim Casey. Lanham, Md.: University Press of America.

1991a "Sartre and the Poietics of History." In *Proceedings of the Sartre Society of Canada* 1 (1), ed. A. van den Hoven and W. Skakoon. Windsor, Ontario: University of Windsor.

1991b "Foucault and the Spaces of History." *The Monist* 74 (2): 165–186.

1992a "Authenticity," "Simone de Beauvoir," and "Jean-Paul Sartre." In *Encyclopedia of Ethics*, 2 vols., ed. Lawrence Becker, vol. 1, pp. 67–69, 241–242; vol. 2, pp. 1121–1124. New York: Garland.

1992b "Sartre and the Poetics of History." In *The Cambridge Companion to Sartre*, ed. Christina Howells. Cambridge: Cambridge University Press.

1992c "The Possibility/Impossibility of a Foucauldian Ethic." In *Joyful Wisdom: Sorrow and an Ethic of Joy*, ed. David Goicoechea and Marko Zlomislic. St. Catharines, Ontario: Thought House.

1992d "Sartre, The Last Ten Years." Review essay of works on Sartre's philosophy by Thomas Busch and by William McBride. *Research in Phenomenology* 22.

1993a *Dialectic and Narrative*, ed. with Dalia Judowitz. Albany: State University of New York Press.

1993b "Foucault and the Eclipse of Vision." In *Modernity and the Hegemony of Vision*, ed. David Michael Levin. Berkeley: University of California Press.

1993c "Truth Is a Thing of This World." Review essay of James W. Bernauer, *Foucault's Force of Flight*. *Research in Phenomenology* 23: 193–201.

1993d "Partially Desacralized Spaces: The Religious Availability of Foucault's Thought." *Faith and Philosophy* 10 (4): 471–485.

1993e "Sartre and the Paradox of Committed History." In *Modern Concepts of Existentialism*, ed. Peter L. Eisenhardt et al. Jyräskylä, Finland: University of Jyräskylä Press.

1994a "Philosophy of Existence 2: Sartre." In *Continental Philosophy in the Twentieth Century*, ed. Richard Kearney. London: Routledge.

1994b "Existentialism," "Foucault," and "Sartre." In *The Encyclopedia of Time*, ed. Sam Macey. New York: Garland.

1994c "Foucault and the Mapping of History." In *The Cambridge Companion to Foucault*, ed. Gary Gutting. Cambridge: Cambridge University Press.

1995a "Inauthentic and Authentic Love in Sartrean Existentialism." In *The Nature and Pursuit of Love*, ed. David Goicoechea. Amherst, N.Y.: Prometheus Books.

1995b "History and Histories: Weiss and the Problematization of the Historical." In *The Philosophy of Paul Weiss*, ed. Louis Hahn. La Salle, Ill.: Open Court.

1995c "Phenomenology of Ethics, Sartrean." In *The Encyclopedia of Phenomenology*, ed. Lester Embree. Dordrecht: Kluwer.

1995d "The Future Perfect and the Perfect Future: History Has Its Reasons. . . ." Presidential Address, A.C.P.A., 1994. *American Catholic Philosophical Quarterly* 68 (supplement). (Proceedings, 1994): 1–15.

1996a "The Essence of Man." *The World & I* 11 (2): 253–259.

1996b "Reconstituting Praxis: Toward a Sartrean Theory of History." *American Catholic Philosophical Quarterly* 70 (4): 597–618.

1996c "Authenticity," "Bad Faith," "Existentialism," "Existential Psychoanalysis," and "Sartre, Jean-Paul." In *The Encyclopedia of Philosophy*, Supplement, ed. Donald M. Borchert. New York: Macmillan.

1997a "Ethics in Sartre." In *The Encyclopedia of Phenomenology*, ed. Lester Embree. Dordrecht: Kluwer.

1997b *Sartre, Foucault and Historical Reason*. Vol. 1 of *Toward an Existentialist Theory of History*. Chicago: University of Chicago Press.

1998a "Sartre, Jean-Paul," "Authenticity," and six brief contributions: "Dialectical Reason," "Facticity," "The Look," "Bad Faith," "Nothingness," and "Negation." In *Dictionary of Existentialism*, ed. Haim Gordon. Westport, Conn.: Greenwood Press, forthcoming.

1998b "Truth(s) in Painting: Sartre, Foucault, and Derrida." In *Reading Truth in Painting*, ed. Hugh J. Silverman and Wilhelm S. Wurzer. Albany: State University of New York Press, forthcoming.

1999a "The Philosopher-Historian as Cartographer: Mapping History with Michel Foucault." *Research in Phenomenology*, forthcoming.

1999b "Sartre on Violence, Foucault on Power: A Diagnostic." *Bulletin de la Société des Philosophes de la langue française*, forthcoming.

1999c "Times Squared: The Historical Times of Sartre and Foucault." In *Recent Phenomenologies of Time*, ed. John Brough. Dordrecht: Kluwer Academic Publishers, forthcoming.

# SEVEN

# Hermeneutics and Natural Science

## Patrick A. Heelan

When the trajectories of philosophy and natural science, as different as they are, crossed in the past, they influenced one another in fateful ways. Analytical philosophy of science is the residue of such a crossing that reflects both the enormous prestige of theoretical physics and a strong cultural preference for the *Naturwissenschaften* over the *Geisteswissenschaften*. The privilege given to theory and to modern physics was carried over into the philosophy of science, and even to philosophy itself. Until recently, Continental Philosophy tended to dwell almost exclusively on the deformations associated with theoretical thinking. Recalling, however, that theory enters essentially into all inquiry, its positive role needs also to be researched within the traditions of Continental Philosophy. A hermeneutical philosophy then should ask: how should theory function within philosophy so as to fulfill the philosophical grounding of its own as well as of natural scientific claims? The goal of my research has been to answer this question and to redirect the philosophy of science accordingly.

As for myself, before taking up philosophy as a career, I studied theoretical physics and did research in theoretical geophysics (some of which is still regularly cited even after forty years), I studied relativistic cosmological models under Erwin Schrödinger and John Singe at the Institute for Advanced Studies in Dublin and taught the subject to graduate students, and I worked as a post-doc at Princeton under Eugene Wigner on the localization of elementary particles, using quantum field theory. I found that this scientific material contained enough philosophical "mysteries" to last many lifetimes. I also found, however, that most of them were related to one another and were generated by the assumption that science and its philosophy constitute merely theoretical knowledge of different orders. While addressing specific questions, I found myself grappling with deep systemic weaknesses in both analytic and Continental Philosophy focused on the mediations that transform lifeworld experience into theory and theory into knowledge about the lifeworld. Among the chief philosophical "mysteries" (read "challenging topics") I addressed once I had exchanged the practice of physics for the profession of philosophy, were these:

1) The intentionality of quantum theoretic research, quantum logic as a logic of embodied contexts, and the problem of causality and localization in quantum mechanics;

2) The epistemological (social, hermeneutical, historical, technological) status of measurement and laboratory data as praxis-laden rather than as theory-laden;

3) Perception and the embodied knower, including the hermeneutics and the group transformation structure of perception and the phenomenology of theoretically designated laboratory entities;

4) The geometry of visual space, and the assessment of machine perception;

5) Problems for personalistic theistic religion created by a too theoretical interpretation of science and all knowledge.

My introduction to philosophical research was influenced in equal parts by the writings of Edmund Husserl, Martin Heidegger, Maurice Merleau-Ponty, Hans-Georg Gadamer, and Paul Ricoeur, and the lectures of Jean La-drière at the University of Louvain, which is the location of the Husserl Archives. I also owe much to the influence of Bernard J.F. Lonergan, especially his *Insight*. My phenomenological research was tempered from the start, then, by recourse to Aristotle, Aquinas, and Kant. Later I was to find among my American colleagues some who moved me further in the direction of existential hermeneutics, such as William Richardson, Joseph J. Kockelmans, Theodore Kisiel, Hugh Silverman, and Babette Babich. I discovered many of the more technical details of philosophy and the history of science in discussion with the analytic philosophers at the Pittsburgh Center for the History and Philosophy of Science, where I was in 1983 as a senior fellow.

What I learned from Lonergan is the importance of the starting point in any inquiry. Insight into insight or the "phenomenology" of insight became for me the starting point for a philosophy of science. A similar but richer message came from the phenomenological tradition with its emphasis on "*die Sache selbst,*" the object constituted as known by language, community, history, technology, and the human body and revealed through the intentionality of inquiry. One begins, not as Plato, Descartes, and Hume did, with the question: What can we know? (for we don't know whether we are competent to answer it) but as Aristotle, Aquinas, Husserl, Heidegger, and Lonergan did, with the question: what is knowing? Which leads to the further question, what is inquiry? For the answers to these *must be* in some sense self-evident; the Being of Knowing *must be* in some sense the Knowing of Being.

My first book, *Quantum Mechanics and Objectivity* (1965), studied the intentionality-structure of quantum mechanics under the original Bohr-Heisenberg account, and criticized the later, more frequently held, objectivist account of John von Neumann and Eugene Wigner that construed the quantum theory as a new universal physics. In the Bohr-Heisenberg account, the quantum theory spoke about the (observed) microsystem as it was revealed to a macroscopic observer through the process of measurement. Measurement for Bohr and Heisenberg was central; it was quantitative, technological, social, historical, linguistic and teleological. It was the action of one part of the humanly inhabited cosmos on another that strangely (one of the mysteries of quantum mechanics!) had the capacity to change both knower and known. I defended the view that this mysterious capacity did not lie in the non-physical or spiritual agency of the human Mind, as proposed by von Neumann and Wigner, but in the intentional character of the measurement process and its ability to shape the way an object—here a quantum mechanical object—is "dressed" to make its appearance as a cultural object within the context of a particular culture, in this case a historical scientific community.

I was to do much further study on these and other topics, among them quantum logic, measurement, locality, and causality which are names for the set of particularly recalcitrant problems associated with the quantum theory.

Quantum logic studies the deviance in truth-functionality that seems to characterize experimental sentences in quantum mechanics. For many logicians, quantum mechanics seems to involve either a third truth-value intermediate between T(ruth) and F(alsity), say, I(ndeterminacy) or a range of truth-values between 0 and 1. In either case, there is deep uneasiness about the objective goals of both science and logic. I found the basic paper of Birkhoff and von Neumann incoherent and claimed that in keeping with Bohr-Heisenberg's original interpretation of quantum mechanics it was sufficient to hold that any experimental sentence formulated in quantum mechanics becomes truth-functional (T or F) only conditional to the fulfillment of a local embodied context—in this case, the prior implementation of a specific measurement situation. In my view, since truth-functionality in quantum mechanics is context-dependent, quantum logic should be addressed as a specific case of contextuality in sentential logic. This solution, though often anthologized in quantum logic collections, offended against several dominant perspectives: the nominalism of the logical empiricists and the objectivism inherent in the new universalist interpretation of quantum mechanics. It also offended on one side the secularist historico-political leanings of the founders of logical empiricist school, and on the other the New Age religious longings of those who looked to science for spiritual inspiration. The articulation of the notion of contextuality requires sophisticated tools and techniques that stem naturally from continental approaches to knowledge, using, for example, such notions as intentionality, phenomenology, constitution, history, embodiment, and hermeneutics. Such philosophic tools are simply not available to objectivist social science or analytic (ratonalist or empiricist) philosophy. The use of continental tools unlocked for me some of the "mysteries" of the quantum theory and opened up for me a large field of inquiry that I hope others will be able to enter and appropriate in due time.

Among the topics of outstanding importance for the understanding not just of quantum mechanics but of all empirical science is measurement, for the measurement process is that which brings model-defined "theoretical entities" into the domain of human culture and perception, revealing them as cultural entities of scientific laboratory culture. Among these cultural entities, some are perceptual entities under the philosophical criteria implicit in Husserl's (Hilbert-inspired) analysis of the noetic-noematic group theoretic invariances of a perceptual object under the variation of its characteristic profiles. By measurement, theoretical and quantitative language gets translated into a cultural and perceptual language: Look! we say, that trace is (one of the characteristic group theoretic profiles of) a proton with 10 Mev energy in the local setup. Measurement then is where theoretical language gets "dressed" within a social, historical, and technological context with local perceptual "clothes." Measurement is a hermeneutic performance, a playing and replaying of a game, or like a musical or theatrical performance. Bob Crease has developed this notion in a book called *The Play of Nature.*

My approach to the problems of localization and causality in quantum mechanics was influenced by a study I began in the late sixties (and recently revisited) of the pictorial space of Vincent Van Gogh's painting *The Bedroom at Arles,* which led to a comparison between visual/pictorial spaces on the one hand and scientific spaces on the other. The Van Gogh study was sparked by discussions at a seminar (on differential geometry) led by Erwin Schrödinger and by a lecture I gave at Fordham University on pictorial spaces at the invitation of my friend, the distinguished art historian Irma B. Jaffe. The metric structures of visual and pictorial spaces fascinated me because they turned out, on analysis, to be different from the Euclidean metric structure of physics, which both culture and philosophy assume to be the one and only, "true," "real" and "actual" space of experience. This problem led to my second book.

*Space-Perception and the Philosophy of Science* (1983/1988) is a book about the philosophy of science, but it is often read as a book about vision. It uses vision as a starting point and a helpful illustration of how to address the analysis of science from the standpoint of an embodied, hermeneutical and phenomenological philosophy. I claim that the shapes and dimensions we actually see in life and in pictures do not fit a Euclidean space but belong rather to members of the two-parameter family of finite hyperbolic Riemannian spaces. (The two Riemannian parameters are correlated with the size of the space and the "center" of the local zone of quasi-Euclidean vision.) The finitude of space was accepted by Plato, Aristotle, and nearly all of the ancient philosophers, and by most people till the middle of the fourteenth century, when the cultural elite began to entertain belief in a single infinite—terrestrial and heavenly—Euclidean space following the discovery of mathematical perspective and the ability to figure the heavens as measurable, like the earth. This inclination to favor the authority of Euclidean theory over practical perception was full-blown by the times of Descartes and Newton, and has persisted right up to the present day. The conclusion of part I of my book is that visual perception, clued hermeneutically to the (unreflective) appreciation of the environmental context, has at its disposal and uses a diverse family of Riemannian metric spaces within which to deploy the presentation of self to the world and vice versa.

In *Space-Perception,* I address the following questions: What philosophical weight should be given to the cultural revolution that narrowed the options of theory to just the Euclidean? What "reality" weights should be assigned respectively to the diversity of modes of spatial perception compared with the uniqueness of Euclidean space? Do answers to these questions throw any light on the "mysteries" of quantum mechanics?

I take the lifeworld to be the primary cognitive activity within which reality is given to humans. This is always in a local (social, cultural, and historical) situation, and its furniture is "dressed" characteristically (for that local situation) according to the Husserlian-Hilbertian theoretical criteria referred to above. Measured reality must be legitimated by these criteria. This principle, however, takes issue both with rationalist criteria (the privilege of theory over practice) and with the empiricist criteria (the privilege of measured data over cultural perception). One of the paradoxes of scientific modernity is a tension in common usage between theory and practice, perception and measurement. This paradox is resolved only when it is understood that reality (in a philosophical analysis) is never given in a unique way, since experience always takes place in a local space for a local community and, therefore, in spaces with possibly different metrical structure. If reality is the phenomenological *'die Sache selbst,'* then this is given only within the local 'being-in-the-world' of a laboratory culture.

One of the "mysteries" of quantum mechanics is that particles are not localized spatial entities before they are measured. I propose that this is because there is no constituted, local lifeworld space prior to the implemented measurement process in which they can make their appearance. Setting up a measurement process constitutes the local lifeworld space (here, of the local laboratory culture) in which the particle can display itself as a localized entity. The "localization" problem in quantum mechanics disappears, with this analysis; a problem of understanding, however, remains. Quantum mechanics appears to be saying that in a world where all real entities are necessarily localized, quantum particles appear not to be localized. What it is really saying is that in a world where real spatiality is always of a local lifeworld kind, the relevant lifeworld space has first to be constituted before objects can be taken to be localizable entities and ready to be "dressed," through the implemented measurement process, to display themselves to the local lifeworld community that is the inquiring community.

Following the same analysis, the "causality" problem in quantum mechanics also disappears. Causality (in the Humean sense) is defined as the lawful ordering of localized events in before/after sequences. Clearly, if in quantum mechanics things are not localized prior to measurement, they cannot be said to participate in orderly before/after sequences of interactions before a space-constituting measurement process has been chosen.

So much for quantum mechanics. A final word on machine perception: if visual and other perceptual spaces are hermeneutically engendered and Riemannian, then the machine processing of Euclidean optical signals can go only so far before it encounters the need to be guided by top-down Riemannian concepts that have their legitimation only in the narratives of human culture. Machine processing beyond this point is possible only if the machine is already a servant of the culture and not its master. Human perception, unlike machine perception, can endorse or withdraw from cultural changes stimulated, say, by "seeing machines," designed to automate some cultural process. Cultural processes, then, are and must always be more than machine processes in which they are embodied.

I will end with some brief and speculative reflections on science and religion contained in a paper entitled "Bernard J. F. Lonergan as a Contemporary Christian Philosopher: Lonergan and the Measures of God" that was read at a symposium of scientists, philosophers, and theologians at Notre Dame University in 1993. It asks whether people's religious and spiritual lives are based on purely rational, say, philosophical arguments, or on embodied lifeworld experiences. These are, as it were, the "measures of God" in contrast with arguments for God. Modern physics with its theological background took human reason to be pure and disembodied. General relativity and the quantum theory in their abstract forms as universal theories of nature are often presented to modern readers as revealing the divine reason, Hawking's "Mind of God," permeating all things. Quantum mechanics, because of the "mysteries" associated with it, is particularly prone to a religious interpretation that often takes the form of a New Age pantheism. Redirecting science and its philosophy away from abstract theory toward the body (biological and technological) that human reason uses brings in historical, social, technological, hermeneutical, and esthetic elements into the analysis of the practice of human reason. Reason takes on more the character of chiaroscuro, of light and shadow. Light as the unconcealed meaning and shadow as its concealed infrastructure, namely, the body, that structures the basic metaphors we use. If the reason we bring to modern science is chiaroscurist reason, human reason in all its manifestations may also be chiaroscurist, including the reason we bring to religion. With this turn a new emphasis can be brought to the rational study of religion, one that is based on the physical culture and experience of religious communities, its sacramentality.

## Selected Bibliography

1965 *Quantum Mechanics and Objectivity.* The Hague: Nijhoff.

1967 "Horizon, Objectivity and Reality in the Physical Sciences." *International Philosophical Quarterly* 7: 375–412.

1970a "Quantum Logic and Classical Logic: Their Respective Roles." *Synthese* 22: 3–33.

1970b "Complementarity, Context-Dependence and Quantum Logic." *Foundations of Physics* 1: 95–110.

1972a "Nature and Its Transformations." *Theological Studies* 33: 486–502.

1972b "Towards a New Analysis of the Pictorial Space of Vincent van Gogh." *Art Bulletin* 54: 478–492.

1972c "Hermeneutics of Experimental Science in the Context of the Life-World." *Philosophia Mathematica* 9: 101–144; also in *Interdisciplinary Phenomenology,* ed. D. I. Ihde and R. Zaner, pp. 7–50. The Hague: Nijhoff.

1974 "Discussion: 'Hermeneutics of Experimental Science in the Context of the Life-World,' commentary on Professor Theodore Kisiel's commentary on my paper." *Zeitschrift fur allgemeine Wissenschaftstheorie* 5: 124, 135–137.

1975 "Heisenberg and Radical Theoretic Change." *Zeitschrift fur allgemeine Wissenschaftstheorie* 6: 113–138.

1983a *Space-Perception and the Philosophy of Science.* Berkeley and Los Angeles: University of California Press. Paperback 1988. See "HEELAN, Patrick," by Jean Ladrière, in *Encyclopédie Philosophique Universelle,* vol. 3: *Les Oeuvres Philosophiques,* Tome 2 dirigé par Jean-François Mattei, 1993, pp. 3322–3324.

1983b "Natural Science as a Hermeneutic of Instrumentation." *Philosophy of Science* 50: 181–204.

1983c "Perception as a Hermeneutical Act." *Review of Metaphysics* 37: 61–76.

1983d "Natural Science and Being-in-the-World." *Man and World* 16: 207–216.

1983e "Space as God's Presence." *Journal of Dharma* 8: 63–86.

1985 "Machine Perception." In *Philosophy and Technology II: Information Technology and Computers in Theory and Practice,* ed. Carl Mitchum, pp. 131–156. Boston: Reidel.

1986a "Interpretation and the Structure of Space in Scientific Theory and in Perception." *Research in Phenomenology* 16: 187–199.

1986b "Perceived Worlds Are Interpreted Worlds." In *New Essays in Metaphysics,* ed. Robert Neville, pp. 61–76. Albany: SUNY Press.

1987 "Husserl's Later Philosophy of Science." *Philosophy of Science* 54: 368–390.

1988a "Husserl, Hilbert and the Critique of Galilean Science." In *Edmund Husserl and the Phenomenological Tradition,* ed. Robert Sokolowski, pp. 157–173. Washington, D.C.: Catholic University of America Press.

1988b "The Primacy of Perception and the Cognitive Paradigm: Reply to De Mey." *Social Epistemology* 1: 321–326.

1988c "A Heideggerian Meditation on Science and Art." In *Hermeneutic Phenomenology,* ed. J. J. Kockelmans, pp. 257–275. Washington, D.C., and Pittsburgh: University Press of America and CARP.

1988d "Experiment and Theory: Constitution and Reality." *Journal of Philosophy* 85 (10): 515–524.

1989a "Husserl's Philosophy of Science." In *Husserl's Phenomenology: A Textbook,* ed. J. Mohanty and W. McKenna, pp. 387–428. Pittsburgh and Washington, D.C.: CARP and University Press of America.

1989b "After Experiment: Research and Reality." *American Philosophical Quarterly,* 26 (4): 297–308.

1989c "Yes! There Is a Hermeneutic Philosophy of Natural Science: Rejoinder to Markus." *Science in Context* 3: 469–480.

1991a "Hermeneutic Phenomenology and the Philosophy of Science." In *Gadamer and Hermeneutics: Science, Culture, and Literature,* ed. Hugh Silverman, pp. 213–228. Continental Philosophy IV. New York: Routledge.

1991b "Hermeneutical Phenomenology and the History of Science." In *Nature and Scientific Method: William A. Wallace Festschrift,* ed. Daniel Dahlstrom, pp. 23–36. Washington, D.C.: Catholic University of America Press.

1992a "Experiment as Fulfillment of Theory." In *Phenomenology and Indian Philosophy,* ed. D. P. Chattopadhyaya, L. Embree, and J. N. Mohanty, pp. 169–184. New Delhi: Council for Philosophical Research.

1992b "Remarks on the Rivalry between Science and Perception." *On Making: Pratt Journal of Architecture* 4: 163–171. New York: Rizzoli.

1992c "Ignation Discernment, Aesthetic Play, and Scientific Inquiry." In *Minding the Time,* ed. William O'Brien, pp. 3–17. Washington, D.C.: Georgetown University Press.

1993 Article on HEELAN, Patrick, by Jean Ladrière, in *Encyclopédie Philosophique Universelle,* vol. 3: *Les Oeuvres Philosophiques,* Tome 2 dirigé par Jean-François Mattei, "HEELAN, Patrick," pp. 3322–3324.

1994 "Galileo, Luther, and the Hermeneutics of Natural Science." In *The Question of Hermeneutics: Festschrift for Joseph Kockelmans,* ed. Timothy Stapleton, pp. 363–374. Dordrecht: Kluwer.

1995a "An Anti-epistemological or Ontological Interpretation of the Quantum Theory and Theories Like It." In *Continental and Postmodern Perspectives in the Philosophy of Science,* ed. B. Babich, D. Bergoffen, and S. Glynn, pp. 55–68. Aldershot: Avebury Press.

1995b "Quantum Mechanics and the Social Sciences: After Hermeneutics." *Science and Education* 4: 127–136.

1995c "Heidegger's Longest Day: Twenty-five Years Later." In *From Phenomenology to Thought, Errancy, and Desire: Essays in Honor of William J. Richardson, S.J.*, ed. Babette Babich, pp. 579–587.

1997a "Herméneutique de la Science Expérimentale: La Mécanique Quantique et les Sciences Sociales." In *Herméneutique: sciences et textes,* ed. Francois Rastier, Jean-Michel Salanskis, and Ruth Scheps, pp. 277–292. Collection, Philosophie d'Aujourd'hui. Paris: PUF.

1997b "Why a Hermeneutical Philosophy of Natural Science?" *Man and World* 30: 271–298.

1997c "Context, Hermeneutics, and Ontology in the Experimental Sciences." In *Issues and Images in the Philosophy of Science,* ed. Dimitri Ginev and Robert S. Cohen, pp. 107–126. Boston Studies in the Philosophy of Science, vol. 192. Boston and Dordrecht: Kluwer.

1998a "Scope of Hermeneutics in the Philosophy of Natural Science." *Studies in the History and Philosophy of Science* 29: 273–298.

1998b "Hermeneutical Philosophy and Pragmatism: A Philosophy of Science." *Synthese* 115: 269–302.

1998c "The Authority of Science: A Postmodern Crisis." *Studia Culturologica: Divinatio* 6: 3–17.

1999a "Nietzsche's Perspectivalism and the Philosophy of Science." In *Nietzsche's Epistemological Writings and the Philosophy of Science,* ed. Babette Babich and Robert S. Cohen. Boston Studies in the Philosophy of Science. Boston and Dordrecht: Kluwer, forthcoming.

1999b "Bernard J. F. Lonergan as a Contemporary Christian Philosopher: Lonergan and the Measures of God." In *The Questions of Christian Philosophy Today,* ed. Francis Ambrosio. New York: Fordham University Press, forthcoming.

# EIGHT
## Adventures in Continental Philosophy

▣

## Douglas Kellner

In 1968, I was studying Continental Philosophy at Columbia University when the student uprising erupted. My primary philosophical allegiances at the time were to phenomenology and Existentialism and I was frankly unprepared for the explosive impact of the student rebellion. Students all over the United States and Europe were demonstrating against the Vietnam War, taking over university buildings and even entire campuses, and in Paris in May '68, it appeared that a new French revolution was in the making. To help understand these events, I went back and read the works of Herbert Marcuse, and by the time his *Essay on Liberation* appeared in 1969, I better understood both Marcuse's writings and the philosophical underpinnings of the student movement to which I was increasingly attracted.

In 1969, I left Columbia to write my dissertation on "Heidegger's Concept of Authenticity" with the support of a German government fellowship (DAAD). I chose to pursue this project at the University of Tübingen, in the small southwestern German town where Hegel, Hölderlin, Schelling, and other luminaries had studied and which was reputed to be an excellent place to study a broad range of German philosophical traditions.

Tübingen also was permeated with the spirit of '60s radicalism and I bought pirate editions (*Raubdruck*) at the University Mensa of Karl Korsch's writings on Marxism, Lukacs's *History and Class Consciousness*, Horkheimer and Adorno's *Dialectic of Enlightenment,* and other texts of the Frankfurt School. I also became involved in a Critical Theory study group and sat in on Ernst Bloch's seminars on the great philosophers and on imperialism, fascism, and other political topics. From Bloch, I learned among other things that philosophy was highly political and that politics required philosophical analysis and critique.

Near the end of my research on Heidegger, I picked up Adorno's *Jargon der Eigentlichkeit* and discovered some early essays by Marcuse on his teacher Heidegger, which contained a sharp critique of Heidegger's thought and proposed a synthesis of phenomenological Existentialism and Marxism, of Heidegger and Marx, that would overcome the limitations of these traditions. I found Marcuse's critique of Heidegger convincing and his proposed synthesis of Heidegger and Marx fascinating. I also thoroughly investigated Heidegger's relation to National Socialism and thus was not surprised by the later revelations in the Farias and Ott volumes.

I was rapidly moving toward the Critical Theory of the Frankfurt School, a move intensified by a year in Paris. After two years in Germany, I had more or less completed my dissertation on Heidegger and received a good grounding in German philosophy. I was eager to improve my knowledge of French and to immerse myself in French philosophy and culture. During a thirteen-month sojourn in Paris in 1971–1972, I accordingly devoted myself to French language and philosophy and also drafted the first version of a book on Herbert Marcuse, whose work continued to fascinate me.

While in Paris, I was fortunate to hear the lectures of Levi-Strauss, Foucault, Deleuze, and Lyotard and to read their latest works, as well as the texts of Baudrillard, Derrida, and others. I initially read Derrida as a curious version of Heideggerian philosophy and read Foucault, Baudrillard, and Lyotard as supplementing the Frankfurt School. I saw parallel attempts to develop syntheses of Marx, Freud, and critical philosophy in both contemporary German and French thought and did not see the differences as so fundamental as they appear to many today. Thus, for me, it was not a choice between the Germans or the French, but a matter of drawing on both traditions to develop new philosophical syntheses.

Upon returning to the States in 1972, I offered myself for sale for a position in Continental Philosophy at the APA slave market and sold myself to the University of Texas at Austin, where I have labored ever since. I was offered a job teaching Marxist philosophy and my years in Europe gave me a good grounding in the Marxian tradition and made the Texas offer attractive. It was a fortunate choice, as Texas has a strong tradition in Continental Philosophy and a pluralistic department that has allowed a broad range of philosophical inquiry (although Texas has its anti-continental philosophy police squads, and there have been struggles between different factions).

Though it was not obvious to me at the time, I had accumulated an enormous amount of cultural capital during my three years in Germany and France that enabled me to write a series of books on both the Frankfurt School and contemporary French thought over the next two decades. My books on Critical Theory include *Herbert Marcuse and the Crisis of Marxism* (1984), *Critical Theory, Marxism, and Modernity* (1989), and (with Stephen Bronner) *Critical Theory and Society: A Reader* (1989). My books *Karl Korsch: Revolutionary Theory* (1977), *Passion and Rebellion: The*

*Expressionist Heritage* (1983), co-edited with Stephen Bronner, *Postmodernism/Jameson/Critique* (1989), and the many articles I have written on Marx and Marxism were nourished during my two years in Germany and subsequent research trips. My books *Jean Baudrillard: From Marxism to Postmodernism and Beyond* (1989), *Postmodern Theory: Critical Interrogations* (with Steven Best, 1991), *Baudrillard: A Critical Reader* (1994), and *The Postmodern Turn* (also with Steven Best, 1997) were made possible by the work that I did on French theory during a year in France and subsequent visits to France.

As noted, I have tried to synthesize German and French traditions rather than to oppose them, and this project animated a book co-authored with Michael Ryan, *Camera Politica: The Politics and Ideology of Contemporary Hollywood Film.* The idea was to combine Critical Theory and poststructuralist methods to interrogate the politics and ideology of Hollywood film. My two books on television also drew on both German and French traditions but attempted to rethink the problematics of the Frankfurt school critique of the culture industries through a concrete study of American television. This project informed my *Television and the Crisis of Democracy* (1990) and *The Persian Gulf TV War* (1992). In all of these works, I see Continental Philosophy as providing weapons of critique and tools of analysis that can be applied to concrete issues and problems.

I have also applied the insights of Continental Philosophy to a vast array of cultural phenomena, and my *Media Culture: Cultural Studies, Identity and Politics Between the Modern and the Postmodern* (1995) attempts to reconceptualize the project of cultural studies by using the tools of Continental Philosophy.

I thus do not use Continental Philosophy as abstract dogma to be worshipped religiously, but as a body of living thought for application to contemporary problems and issues. The best of Continental Philosophy is critical and dialogical, and its major thinkers have often drawn on the most productive elements of their predecessors, while overcoming those aspects that are no longer useful or relevant.

I have always found a broad range of Continental Philosophy attractive. And yet I am not happy with the current division of Anglo-American philosophy into continental vs. analytical perspectives. While much that passes for analytical philosophy today is useless, much that parades as Continental Philosophy is dogmatic and scholastic. But both the tools of conceptual analysis and the perspectives of Continental Philosophy can be applied together in specific tasks and projects. Philosophy, in my optic, is both analysis and synthesis, deconstruction and reconstruction. Consequently, I would defend pluralistic perspectives that draw on the best work of all traditions.

Indeed, it is somewhat ridiculous for philosophers in the United States to worship and fetishize European philosophers whose works developed in a very specific socio-historical environment and whose ideas may or may not be relevant to American conditions. Instead, we should see Continental Philosophy as an important tradition whose ideas can be rethought, reconstructed, and developed in new ways in our own unique historical situation. Our own tradition of American philosophy also has some important resources, though I find the continental thinkers to be of more use for my own projects. Yet we need to take seriously American traditions of philosophy as well, and to see what insights and contributions are found in our native traditions.

On the whole, contemporary American philosophy, like other areas of philosophy, seems frozen, in a state of paralysis. While the dominant analytical philosophy suffers from sclerosis, a hardening of the categories, a premature senility, suffering a long, slow, public death, the situation of Continental Philosophy is also dispiriting. In the 1980s, it looked as though contemporary philosophy was entering a fruitful state of pluralism with a blossoming of Continental Philosophy, mutating into "Theory," crossing over into every discipline. On the philosophical front, there was also a reappropriation of Dewey and pragmatism, of other strands of American philosophy, as well as the move into new fields such as philosophy of technology, environmental philosophy, feminism, African American philosophy, Latino philosophy, media philosophy, and the philosophy of electronic culture and communication.

These trends continue within the broader philosophical-intellectual world, but often not in philosophy departments, and they have been pushed to the margins of the academic discipline of philosophy. Most distressing, not only has reaction and retrenchment set in with analytic philosophy, but Continental Philosophy is becoming increasingly narrow and biased. Individual continental philosophers are taken as the voice of Truth, of the revealed Word, and coteries of Kantians, Hegelians, Marxists, Husserlians, Heideggerians, and others seek refuge in the ideas and systems of *their* philosophers, contemptuously believing that they are in the truth, that everyone else is superficial and caught up in minor philosophies, in philosophical untruth. Thus, Continental Philosophy is falling into a narrow scholasticism, a dogmatism, a web of commentaries or readings that stay within the bounds of the traditional systems, that marginalize those who do not stay within the bounds, that are eclectic or original in their thought.

Thus the ontotheological dimension of philosophy that Derrida decried has its Renaissance in contemporary Continental Philosophy. Living philosophy, however, is always synthesis, always in motion, always taking in the new, absorbing new ideas, trends, theories, and content, constantly developing and reshaping philosophy, building on the best that went before but going in new directions. The master thinkers, of course, create original syntheses, putting their own stamp, their own vision, on their syntheses, thus creating something new in the process.

Ultimately, Continental Philosophy provides me with the possibility of seeing philosophy as an adventure containing all the traditional domains of philosophy, as well as social theory, cultural criticism, and social and political critique. While some analytic philosophers develop their arguments in journal articles or books that often focus on very narrow topics, the great continental thinkers provide vast philosophical vistas that include philosophy of history, metaphysics, social theory, aesthetics, ethics, politics, and other normative concerns. The great continental thinkers were concerned with the key issues of their day and drew on the relevant sciences, ideas, and discourses of their time.

I share this focus on today and its problems—a focus also found in Dewey and American pragmatism. In this sense, I suppose, my work is very much in the tradition of the Frankfurt School, which also transcended narrow disciplinary boundaries and undertook studies of a vast array of contemporary phenomena from supradisciplinary perspectives. This project continues to appeal to me, as does its attempt to relate theory to practice, to politicize theory, and to make theory an instrument of social action. The weekly TV show, *Alternative Views,* that I did for eighteen years with Frank Morrow also fits into this project and realizes as well the Deweyan concept of the public intellectual, the application of philosophical notions and abilities to issues of public concern in a public forum. Thus, rather than seeing the end of philosophy in a postmodern turn, I see philosophy as confronting new challenges in an era of new media, technologies, cultural forms, and political configurations and believe that the adventure of Continental Philosophy can best carry on by engaging these phenomena.

## Selected Bibliography

1973 "The Frankfurt School Revisited: A Critique of Martin Jay's *The Dialectical Imagination.*" *New German Critique* 4: 131–152.

1974 "The Latest Sartre: Reflections on *On a raison de se revolter.*" *Telos* 22: 188–201.

1975 "Korsch's Revolutionary Historicism." *Telos* 26: 70–93.

1976 "Utopia and Marxism in Ernst Bloch." Co-authored with Harry O'Hara. *New German Critique* 9: 11–34.

1977a "Capitalism and Human Nature in Adam Smith and Karl Marx." In *The Subtle Anatomy of Capitalism,* ed. Jesse Schwartz, pp. 66–86. Santa Monica: Goodyear Publishing Company.

1977b *Karl Korsch: Revolutionary Theory.* Austin: University of Texas Press. British edition, New York: Pluto Press. Translated into Spanish as *El Marxismo Revolucionario de Karl Korsch* (Mexico City: Premice).

1977c "Television Socialization." *Mass Media/Adult Education* 46: 3–20.

1978 "Ideology, Marxism, and Advanced Capitalism." *Socialist Review* 42: 37–65.

1979 "TV, Ideology and Emancipatory Popular Culture." *Socialist Review* 45: 13–53. Reprinted in *Technology and Human Affairs* (St. Louis: Mosby, 1981) and in *Television: The Critical View* (New York: Oxford University Press, 1979, 1982, 1987). German translation in *Dollar und Traume* 3 (1981): 93–112.

1980a "Television Images, Codes, and Messages." *Televisions* 7 (4): 2–19.

1980b "Television Research and the Fair Use of Media Images." In *Fair Use and Free Inquiry: Copyright Law and the New Media,* ed. John Shelton Lawrence and Bernard Timberg, 2nd ed., pp. 92–108. Norwood, N.J.: Ablex Communications and Information Sciences Press.

1981a "Brecht's Marxist Aesthetic: The Korsch Connection." In *Bertolt Brecht: Political Theory and Literary Practice,* ed. Betty Weber and Herbert Heinin, pp. 29–42. Athens: University of Georgia Press.

1981b "Marxism, Morality, and Ideology." *Canadian Journal of Philosophy* 7 (supplementary volume): 93–120.

1981c "Network Television and American Society." *Theory and Society* 10 (1): 31–62. Reprinted in *Mass Communication Review Yearbook*, vol. 2. New York: Sage Publications, 1982.

1982a "Karl Korsch and Marxism." In *Continuity and Change in Marxism,* ed. N. Georgopoulos, pp. 232–247. Atlantic Highlands, N.J.: Humanities Press.

1982b "Kulturindustrie und Massenkommunikation: Die Kritische Theorie und ihre Folgen." In *Sozialforschung als Kritik,* ed. Wolfgang Bonss and Axel Honneth, pp. 482–514. Frankfurt am Main: Suhrkamp.

1982c "Television Myth and Ritual." *Praxis* 6: 133–155.

1983a "Critical Theory, Commodities and the Consumer Society." *Theory, Culture, and Society* 1 (3): 66–84.

1983b "Science and Method in Marx's *Capital.*" *Radical Science Journal* 13: 39–54.

1984a "Authenticity and Heidegger's Challenge to Ethical Theory." In *Thinking about Being: Aspects of Heidegger's Thought,* ed. Robert W. Shahan and J. N. Mohanty, pp. 159–176. Norman: University of Oklahoma Press.

1984b "Critical Theory, Max Weber, and the Dialectics of Domination." In *The Weber–Marx Dialogue,* ed. Robert J. Antonio and Ronald Glassman, pp. 89–116. Lawrence: University of Kansas Press.

1984c *Herbert Marcuse and the Crisis of Marxism.* Berkeley: University of California Press.

1985 "Public Access Television: *Alternative Views.*" *Radical Science Journal* 16: 79–82. Other versions of this article were published in *Humanity and Society* 9 (February 1985), and in *American Media and Mass Culture,* ed. Donald Lazere. Berkeley: University of California Press, 1987.

1987a "Baudrillard, Semiurgy, and Death." *Theory, Culture and Society* 1 (4): 125–146.

1987b *Kwame Nkrumah.* New York: Chelsea House.

1987c "The Great American Dream Machine: The Ideological Functions of Popular Culture in the United States." In *Democracy Upside-Down,* ed. Fred Exoo, pp. 107–140. New York: Praeger.

1988a *Camera Politica: The Politics and Ideology of Contemporary Hollywood Film.* Co-authored with Michael Ryan. Bloomington: Indiana University Press.

1988b *Ernesto "Che" Guevara.* New York: Chelsea House.

1988c *Passion and Rebellion: The Expressionist Heritage,* ed. with Stephen Eric Bronner. 2nd ed. New York: Columbia University Press.

1988d "Postmodernism as Social Theory: Some Problems and Challenges." *Theory, Culture and Society* 5 (2-3): 240–269.

1988e "(Re)Watching Television: Notes toward a Political Criticism." Co-authored with Steven Best. *Diacritics* (Summer): 97–113

1989a "Boundaries and Borderlines: Reflections on Jean Baudrillard and Critical Theory." *Current Perspectives in Social Theory* 9: 5–22.

1989b *Critical Theory and Society: A Reader,* ed. with Stephen Eric Bronner. New York: Routledge.

1989c *Critical Theory, Marxism and Modernity.* Baltimore: Johns Hopkins University Press.

1989d *Jean Baudrillard: From Marxism to Postmodernism and Beyond.* Stanford: Polity Press and Stanford University Press.

1989e "Kulturindustrie und Ideologiekritik." *Tute,* special issue on *Ästhetik und Politik am Ende des Industrieszeitalters. Herbert Marcuse,* pp. 56–63.

1989f *Postmodernism/Jameson/Critique,* ed. Washington, D.C.: Maisonneuve Press.

1989g "Reading Images Critically: Toward a Postmodern Pedagogy." *Boston Journal of Education* 170 (3): 31–52. Reprinted in *Postmodernism, Feminism and Cultural Politics,* ed. Henry Giroux. Albany: State University of New York Press.

1990a "From *1984* to *One-Dimensional Man:* Reflections on Orwell and Marcuse." *Current Perspectives in Social Theory* 10: 223–252.

1990b "Sexual Politics in the 1980s." In *Terms of Endearment vs. Independence Day: Representations of Gender in Popular Culture,* ed. Diane Raymond, pp. 231–246. Bowling Green, Ohio: Bowling Green Popular Press.

1990c *Television and the Crisis of Democracy.* New York: Westview Press.

1990d "The Postmodern Turn in Social Theory: Positions, Problems, and Prospects." In *Frontiers of Social Theory: The New Syntheses,* ed. George Ritzer, pp. 255–286. New York: Columbia University Press.

1991a "Film, Politics and Ideology: Reflections on Hollywood Film in the Age of Reagan." *Velvet Light Trap* 27 (Spring). Chinese translation in *Continuum* 5 (1): 9–24.

1991b *Postmodern Theory: Critical Interrogations.* Co-authored with Steven Best. New York: Guilford Press.

1991c "Postmodernismus als Kritische Gesellschafts theorie? Herausforderungen und Probleme." In *Abschied von der Aufklarung,* ed. Heinz-Hermann Kruger. Oplande: Leske and Budrich.

1992a "Postmodernism, Identity, and the Politics of Popular Culture." In *Postmodernism and Identity,* ed. Scott Lash and Jonathan Friedman, pp. 141–172. London: Hutchinson.

1992b "Televisión y Postmodernidad." *Archipielago* 8: 89–100.

1992c *The Persian Gulf TV War.* New York: Westview Press.

1993a "Critical Theory and Social Theory: Current Debates and Challenges." *Theory, Culture, and Society* 10 (2): 43–61.

1993b "Film, Politics, and Ideology: Toward a Multi-perspectival Film Theory." In

*Movies and Politics: The Dynamic Relationship*, ed. James Combs, pp. 55–92. New York: Garland.

1993c "Marcuse in the 1940s: Some New Textual Discoveries." In *Kritik und Utopie im Werk von Herbert Marcuse*, ed. Institut für Sozialforschung, pp. 301–311. Frankfurt am Main: Suhrkamp.

1993d "Minima Moralia: The Gulf War in Fragments." *Journal of Social Philosophy* 24 (2): 68–88.

1994a "A Marcuse Renaissance?" In *Marcuse: From the New Left to the Next Left*, ed. John Bokina and Timothy J. Lukes, pp. 245–267. Lawrence: University of Kansas Press.

1994b *Baudrillard. A Critical Reader*, ed. with introduction. New York: Blackwell.

1994c "Postmodern Social Theory: Contributions and Limitations." Co-authored with Robert J. Antonio. In *Postmodernism and Social Inquiry*, ed. David Dickens and Andrea Fontana. New York: Guilford Press.

1995a "Intellectuals and New Technologies." *Media, Culture, and Society* 17: 427–448.

1995b *Media Culture: Cultural Studies, Identity and Politics between the Modern and the Postmodern*. New York: Routledge.

1995c "The End of Orthodox Marxism." In *Marxism in the Postmodern Age*, ed. Jack Amarglio et al., pp. 33–41. New York: Guilford Press.

1995d "The Obsolescence of Marxism?" In *Whither Marxism?*, ed. Bernd Magnus and Stephen Cullenberg, pp. 3–30. New York: Routledge.

1996 *Articulating the Global and the Local: Globalization and Cultural Studies*, ed. with Ann Cvetkovich. New York: Westview Press.

1997a "Brecht's Marxist Aesthetic." In *A Bertolt Brecht Reference Companion*, ed. Siegfried Mews, pp. 281–291. Westport, Conn.: Greenwood.

1997b *The Postmodern Turn*. Co-authored with Steven Best. New York: Guilford Press.

1997c "Intellectuals, the New Public Spheres and Techno-Politics." *New Political Science* 41–42: 169–188.

1998a. "Introduction." In *Technology, War, and Fascism*, ed. Collected Papers of Herbert Marcuse, vol. 1 New York: Routledge.

1998b "Multiple Literacies and Critical Pedagogy in a Multicultural Society." *Educational Theory* 48 (1): 103–122.

1998c "Globalization and the Postmodern Turn." In *Globalization and Europe*, ed. Roland Axtmann, pp. 23–42. London: Cassells.

# NINE

## Science, Ontology, Pluralities

🖳

# JOSEPH J. KOCKELMANS

I was born in 1923 in a small town called Meerssen in the southernmost part of the Netherlands, very close to the city of Maastricht. The entire area dates back to Roman days; my town, Meerssen, was founded by the Romans circa 50 B.C. and was originally called Marsana. Later my family moved to Geleen, known for its coal mining industry. There I spent my elementary school years, followed by studies at the Gymnasium in Sittard, another small old town just next to Geleen. I took my qualifying exam in 1942, an affair supervised by the Dutch government.

When I think or speak about my education I feel a certain affinity with Descartes in a number of things he wrote in his *Discourse,* which are quite possibly true for many people who are philosophers by profession. Although it is a fact that I was always one of the best students in my class, I nevertheless "have never ventured to presume that my mind was in any way more perfect than that of the ordinary man." I, too, "have sometimes longed to possess thought as quick, or an imagination as accurate and distinct or a memory as comprehensive or ready, as some others." I, too, have been "nourished on letters since my childhood" and, like Descartes, have had "an extreme desire to acquire instruction." I, too, studied at some of "the finest schools in Europe" where there were many men of learning, and I, too, "learned there all that others learned; and not being satisfied with the sciences that were taught, I even read through all the books that fell into my hands."

In my gymnasium years I was introduced to the literatures of seven languages and cultures, in addition to mathematics, physics, chemistry, biology, and history. We all know that "the languages which one learns . . . are essential for the understanding" of all literature, and that "fables with their charm stimulate the mind and histories of memorable deeds exalt it; and that, when read with discretion, these books assist in forming a sound judgment." I, too, "was aware that the reading of good books is indeed like a conversation with the noblest men of past centuries who were the authors of them, nay a carefully studied conversation, in which they reveal to us none but the best of their thoughts." I had my personal preferences, as indeed Descartes must have had his.

Like Descartes, I, too, was most of all "delighted with mathematics because of the certainty of its demonstrations and the evidence of its reasoning." I liked physics and astronomy even more. Later I was introduced to the great ideas of the leading philosophers of our Western tradition after the pre-Socratics. It is here that I must part from Descartes. For contrary to his view that all that these great thinkers have claimed is dubious, I have always found their great works to be inexhaustible sources of inspiration. I believe that I have learned more from Plato and Aristotle, Augustine and Aquinas, Descartes himself and Hume, Kant and Hegel, and from all who came later, than from any other sources.

In my philosophic studies, I focused initially on the history and philosophy of mathematics. I wrote my dissertation on the science "mathematics" in the Middle Ages and was graduated from the Angelico in Rome in May of 1951. After completing my dissertation I turned immediately to post-doctoral studies in mathematics, physics, and phenomenology. At that time I realized that I did not truly have a philosophical position of my own. I had been educated mainly in the history of philosophy, and had taken some courses in metaphysics and philosophy of science. All of this had led to what might be described as a scholastic position in which there were influences from Plato and Aristotle, Aquinas, and Wolff. I began to make an effort to go beyond this framework, and in so doing turned first to Nicolai Hartmann, whose work I studied carefully and admired more for its rigorous methodology than for its idealist content.

The year 1954 was an important one in my development. I had the good fortune to meet Professor Herman Van Breda, director of the Husserl Archives at Louvain. He helped me to structure my post-doctoral research, which was to involve mathematics, physics, and phenomenology. He put me in touch with Professor Hans Freudenthal, who commissioned one of his assistants, Dr. H. Busard, to introduce me to the various forms of "higher" mathematics that I would need for my further study of physics. Van Breda then guided me to Professor Fokker in Leyden who taught theoretical physics, theory of relativity, and quantum mechanics. Fokker introduced me to the classical "textbooks" (Sommerfeld, Eddington, Weyl, and Kramers), and later to the papers and treatises by Einstein and Heisenberg.

During that period and for many years thereafter I went to Louvain for regular participation in the Tuesday evening seminars conducted by Van Breda. The group involved most of the Higher Institute of Philosophy's faculty members as well as a few post-doctoral students. For several years I listened to discussions of texts by Husserl and later also of works by Merleau-Ponty and Heidegger. Under the influence of the ideas with which I was confronted in these seminars, I gradually moved away from the philosophy of Hartmann and toward the philosophies of Merleau-Ponty and subsequently Heidegger. Once I had discovered a position which seemed livable to me, I first called it "existential phenomenology," but later I came to prefer the expression "hermeneutic phenomenology." The first systematic presentation of my philosophical ideas was given in my inaugural address at the Agricultural University of Wageningen, "Over de Zin der Wijsbegeerte" (On the Meaning of Philosophy). Later I returned to the views expressed in this address in my book *The World in Science and Philosophy*, as well as in several other publications such as "Gedanken zur Frage: Wozu Philosophie?" and *Ideas for a Hermeneutic of the Natural Sciences*.

As I see it, philosophy is neither a religion nor a science in the modern sense of those terms. Nor can philosophy be identified with a system. Yet neither is it a game that tries to solve linguistic puzzles, or deals dialectically with paradoxes and antinomies. Rather, philosophy is science in the sense of *episteme*. It consists in a critical reflection on our important human experiences, and this reflection is to be enacted from the perspective of the totality of all possible meaning or "Being." Philosophy, therefore, is not the privileged domain of research for certain academicians, but is rather a necessary endeavor on the part of every human being who wishes to understand the true meaning of the experiences already lived through.

Everyone who philosophizes finds himself originally in a world which he shares with other human beings. He has a great number of insights in common with his contemporaries; in the everyday attitude, these insights are simply taken for granted. The world is already there before anyone can make a contribution to it. This world appears no longer to constitute a harmonious unity, but consists of a limited number of relatively independent domains of human experiences such as myth, religion, art, socio-political practice, science, technology, and the moral domain. It is from the perspective of Being as this historically comes to pass that the reflecting person tries to mediate critically the experiences which he has had in regard to these large domains of experience.

It should be made clear here that by the term "experience" I do not mean what Locke or Kant understood by the term, but rather what Hegel meant by it. Experience is that which makes someone an experienced person. Experiences can take place in every domain of meaning in a person's life. They are never definitive and they are always open to new experiences; yet an experience can never be just repeated. An experience is an event over which one has no control. It is inherently affected by negativity insofar as it shows to the person who has it that until now he or she has basically misunderstood something. The experience lets something be in a manner in which it has never before been. Experience is thus inherently dialectical. In hermeneutic phenomenology the so-called hermeneutic experiences, i.e., those which are concerned with what has been transmitted in our tradition, occupy a privileged position, because it is *from* these experiences that we live and *through* these experiences that we have been made free. In other words, the term is reserved here for those important moments and events in life when one's entire conception of the world and of oneself changes because of the experiences one has had.

In my own life I have tried to reflect critically on a great number of experiences in the domains of religion and myth, ethics and the arts. Yet most of my work as a philosopher has been in the realm of the sciences. As a matter of fact, as I said, I have had a keen interest in the philosophy of science almost from the very beginning of my career as a philosopher. At first this interest led to reflections on the mathematical sciences—*Philosophy of Mathematics in the Middle Ages* (1953), "On the Mode of Being of Mathematical Entities" (1954), "On the Nature and the Mode of Being of Ideal Space According to Nicolai Hartmann" (1958). Later this interest shifted to the natural sciences—*On Time and Space: The Meaning of Einstein's Relativity Theory for a Phenomenological Philosophy of Nature (1958),* and *Phenomenology and Physics* (1962). All of these publications were written in Dutch. I have maintained this interest for more than thirty years. Recently I have presented my conceptions in a somewhat more systematic fashion in *Ideas for a Hermeneutic Ontology of the Natural Sciences* (1993). On a number of occasions I have concerned myself, also, with philosophical issues that pertain to the behavioral, social, and historical sciences. Most of these ideas were presented in journal articles and book essays.

In my critical philosophical reflections on the sciences, my main interest never was in logical or methodological issues, although obviously I studied and taught the most important insights from this area of research. My own concern has been with ontological issues, with issues of meaning and truth. I am particularly interested in what really happens in the processes of thematization, objectivation, formalization, abstraction, and reduction. Consequently I am also interested in the question of what scientific statements and claims precisely mean, and in what sense they can be called true.

My first teaching appointment at a university came in 1963 at the Agricultural University of Wageningen, the Netherlands, where I taught modern philosophy and philosophical anthropology. A year later I came to the United States for a position at the New School for Social Research in New York that involved teaching a graduate seminar on formal logic and a graduate course on Hume. In 1965 I went to the University of Pittsburgh, where I taught undergraduate courses on a variety of subjects but mainly in the history of modern and twentieth-century philosophy. At the graduate level I taught courses on Hegel, Husserl, Merleau-Ponty, and Heidegger, as well as on the philosophy of science (e.g., philosophical problems of quantum mechanics).

In 1968 I was invited to join the faculty of the Pennsylvania State University. Over these years at Penn State I have regularly taught undergraduate courses in the history of philosophy, philosophy of science, philosophy of religion, and Continental Philosophy. At the graduate level, I first regularly taught a course on the philosophy of the social sciences. Later I joined the Science, Technology, and Society program at Penn State and replaced the course in the philosophy of science with one on science, philosophy, and religion. Beyond this, I have taught Aristotle (metaphysics, physics, ethics), Kant (the first two Critiques), Hegel, Marx, Nietzsche, and very regularly Husserl and Heidegger. For many years I offered an unscheduled seminar on the philosophy of the late Heidegger.

Shortly after my arrival at Penn State I became involved in an interdisciplinary program that was meant to promote interdisciplinary research and teaching. This program was initially funded by a grant from the National Endowment for the Humanities and later by the College of the Liberal Arts. It has been most effective from the very beginning in promoting new types of courses, often team-taught, and in organizing a number of interdisciplinary conferences. In the early years there were bi-weekly or monthly faculty seminars in which some fifteen faculty members of different disciplines gathered to discuss important new publications or issues. Although the program had no faculty members or graduate students of its own, it nonetheless became more and more involved with special, individualized, interdisciplinary graduate majors. Over the years the number of students seeking a Ph.D. degree in an area not covered by a major program at Penn State has grown consistently. Between 1972 and 1999, the program has had some thirty students enrolled annually between the M.A. or M.S. and the Ph.D. degrees. On the average, seven to eight students graduated with a Ph.D. each year. The students who choose an interdisciplinary option come from all colleges of the University, including the engineering programs. Students from the College of the Liberal Arts usually seek to combine philosophy with another discipline— for example, literature, literary criticism, and philosophy; social theory and social and political philosophy; psychology (theory of) and phenomenology. Students who seek this individualized interdisciplinary option are usually the very gifted ones who have very specific career goals; students from third world countries whose governments often want a much broader scholarly education for their subjects than one program ordinarily provides; older students who find it difficult to fit into a group of much younger students; and, finally, disabled students who cannot easily avail themselves of a regular program because of their disability (blindness, partial paralysis, etc.). I function as the director of this interdisciplinary option and am often a member of an interdisciplinary student's committee.

Since coming to the United States and becoming deeply involved in the teaching of undergraduate courses, I have many times reflected on higher education and the place philosophy should have in it. It seems to me that we have gradually come to a point in our colleges and universities where we must ask ourselves whether or not we are still educating our undergraduate students. As I see it, specialization and the departmentalization of the universities which has resulted from it have had a negative impact on the quality of the education we offer to our undergraduates. I mean by this that undergraduates are forced too soon into some form of specialization. True, each university has its countermeasures, but in my experience they are too few and often of little or no consequence. Some years ago a group of faculty members at Penn State proposed a mandatory curriculum for all incoming students in which virtually all of the courses were prescribed and were to be taken by all undergraduates, particularly the courses in mathematics, physics, chemistry, and biology on the one hand, and the social sciences and the humanities on the other. Under this proposal, students would be allowed to prepare themselves for a career or for graduate school only during the final two years of their undergraduate education. Interestingly, only the College of the Liberal Arts was willing to endorse the plan, and it went no further. Our proposed curriculum may not have been the best solution to the problem of premature specialization and the narrowing effect it has on students' minds and lives. But I share the view of many of my colleagues that this issue must be raised. We must engage in ongoing dialogue over this question of how to adapt our institutions of higher learning to our rapidly changing world while at the same time preserving a meaningful liberal arts curriculum.

As an educator I have devoted a substantial amount of my time and energy to the preparation of courses for undergraduates. To ensure that course texts would be available to students at a reasonable price, I have written introductory texts on the philosophy of Husserl and Heidegger, and I have edited several anthologies designed to help undergraduate students find their way into phenomenology, Husserl and Heidegger, philosophy of science, and ethics. In cooperation with Professors Thomas Seebohm, Arion Kelkel, Adrian Peperzak, and Calvin Schrag, I have worked to develop a series of texts in the history of philosophy to be written by the most competent scholars we can find. Each of these books is devoted to one great philosopher of our tradition and contains, in addition to a general introduction, a basic text of the relevant philosopher with a systematic commentary. Twelve volumes have appeared to date and several others are forthcoming.

Over the years I also have published many scholarly books, most of them on issues in the philosophy of science but others that deal with the ideas of leading philosophers such as Husserl and Heidegger. In addition I have published many articles in refereed journals and contributed chapters to anthologies and other books.

I have been an editor, with John Anderson and Calvin Schrag, of *Man and World* and a member of the editorial board of a number of journals (e.g., *Philosophical Quarterly, New Ideas in Psychology, Journal of the Philosophy of Religion*). I have been active in the Society for Phenomenology and Existential Philosophy and served on its executive committee, and I have sat on several committees of the American Philosophical Association (APA) and have served as president of its eastern division.

In my roles at the APA I have always been a staunch defender of pluralism, maintaining that in a pluralistic society, pluralism in philosophy should be promoted and defended so as to make certain that every voice receives a proper hearing. Yet I have also defended the view that all members of the community of scholars should be willing and able to engage in meaningful discourse. Difference of opinion in important matters is a condition of the possibility of meaningful philosophical discourse, as I argue in "Gedanken zur Frage: 'Wozu Philosophie?'" I am fully aware, however, of the difficulties in reaching consensus in pluralist societies. I worry that in societies where people no longer share the same world, the same values, and some significant level of experience in common, it will be virtually impossible to reach consensus on important matters. I have focused in various writings on the implications of these ideas with regard to discourse on moral issues.

Over the years I have been honored in a number of ways, beginning with a gold medal award which I received in the Netherlands from Teyler's Tweede Genootschap for a book on the philosophical implications of the conceptions of time and space underlying the special theory of relativity. I also received a medal from Pennsylvania State University for "Outstanding Achievement in the Arts and the Humanities." I was invited to become a fellow of the Institute for the Arts and Humanistic Studies and later was appointed "Distinguished Professor of Philosophy." Finally, I also hold a doctorate honoris causa in Humane Letters.

As for the other side of things, I like to take long walks "in nature" and to be at a lake in Maine where one can sit in a boat and speculate about the meaning of life and other important issues. Yes, and on unimportant questions as well. I like music very much. I have played the cello, the concert flute, and several recorders. In my frivolous days I also played the saxophone. Currently it is my great pleasure to listen to the incomparable music of Bach, Beethoven, Mozart, Handel, and Haydn at every possible opportunity.

## Selected Bibliography

1958 *Tijd en ruimte de opvattingen van Albert Einstein over de absolute Betrekkingen volgens tijd en ruimte tussen voorvallen in de werkelijkheid en haar betekenis voor de wijsbegeerte der anorganische natuur.* Haarlem: Bohn.
1961 *Phaenomenologie en natuurwetenschap. Een inleiding in de wijsbegeerte der natuurwetenschappen.* Haarlem: Bohn.
1962 *Martin Heidegger. Een inleiding tot zijn denken.* Tielt: Lannoo.
1963a *Edmund Husserl: Een Inleiding tot zijn fenomenologie.* Tielt: Lannoo.
1963b *Over de zin der wijsbegeerte.* Tielt: Lannoo.
1965 *Martin Heidegger: A First Introduction to His Philosophy.* Pittsburgh: Duquesne University Press.
1966 *Phenomenology and Physical Science: An Introduction to the Philosophy of Physical Science.* Pittsburgh: Duquesne University Press.
1967a *A First Introduction to Husserl's Phenomenology.* Pittsburgh: Duquesne University Press.
1967b *Edmund Husserl's Phenomenological Psychology: A Historico-Critical Study.* Pittsburgh: Duquesne University Press.
1967c *Phenomenology: The Philosophy of Edmund Husserl and Its Interpretation,* ed. New York: Doubleday.
1968a *Philosophy of Science: The Historical Background,* ed. New York: Macmillan.
1968b *The World in Science and Philosophy.* Milwaukee: Bruce.
1970a *Inleiding tot en Commentaar van Martin Heideggers: Wat is dat—Filosofie?* Tielt: Lannoo.
1970b *Phenomenology and the Natural Sciences: Essays and Translations,* ed. with T. J. Kisiel. Evanston: Northwestern University Press.
1972a *On Heidegger and Language,* ed. Evanston: Northwestern University Press.
1972b "Stegmüller on the Relationship between Theory and Experience." *Philosophy of Science* 39: 397–420.
1973 *Inleiding tot en Commentaar van Heideggers Brief Over het Humanisme.* Tielt: Lannoo.
1975 "Toward an Interpretative or Hermeneutic Social Science." *Graduate Faculty Philosophy Journal* 5: 73–96.
1976a "Empirische, phanomenologische und hermeneutische Psychologie: Gedanken zu einer mehrdimensionalen Bestimmung des Problems der Psychologie." In *Versuche über Erfahrung,* ed. A. Metraux, pp. 35–49. Bern: Hans Huber.
1976b "On the Meaning and Function of Experience in Husserl's Phenomenology."

In *Der Idealismus und seine Gegenwart*, Festschrift für Werner Marx, pp. 297–317. Hamburg: Felix Meiner.

1977 "Language, Experience, and Communication." *Phänomenologische Forschungen* 5: 90–127.

1978a "Alcune Riflessioni Sulla Concezione della Terra in Heidegger." *Humanitas* 4: 445–468.

1978b "Gedanken zur Frage: 'Wozu Philosophie?'" In *Wozu Philosophie? Stellungnahmen eines Arbeitskreises,* ed. Hermann Lubbe, pp. 213–237. Berlin: Walter de Gruyter.

1978c "Reflections on Social Theory." *Human Studies: A Journal for Philosophy and the Social Sciences* 1: 1–15.

1979a "Dasein's Analysis and Freud's Unconscious." *Review of Existential Psychology and Psychiatry* 16 (1-3): 21–42.

1979b *Interdisciplinarity and Higher Education,* ed. University Park: Pennsylvania State University Press.

1979c "Sociology and the Problem of Rationality." Proceedings of the International Symposium on Rationality Today (Ottawa, October 27–30, 1977). In *Rationality Today,* ed. Theodore F. Geraets, pp. 85–106. Ottawa: University of Ottawa Press.

1980 "Some Reflections on the Meaning and Function of Interpretative Sociology." *Tijdschrift voor Filosofie* 42 (2): 294–324.

1981 "Überlegungen zur Lakatosschen Methodologie der wissenschaftlichen Forschungsprogramme." In *Voraussetzungen und Grenzen der Wissenschaft,* ed. Gerard Radnitzky and Gunnar Andersson, pp. 319–338. Tübingen: Mohr.

1982a "On Art and Language." In *Philosophie et Langage,* ed. J. Sojcher and G. Hottois, pp. 125–146. Brussells: Editions de l'Université de Bruxelles.

1982b *The Challenge of Religion,* ed. with F. Ferré and J. Smith. New York: Seabury Press.

1982c "Hermeneutik und Ethik." In *Kommunikation und Reflexion,* ed. W. Kuhlmann and D. Bohler, pp. 649–684. Frankfurt am Main: Suhrkamp.

1983a "The Foundations of Morality and the Human Sciences." *Analecta Husserliana* 15: 369–386.

1983b "On the Impact of the Human Sciences on Our Conception of Man and Society." *Analecta Husserliana* 14: 51–76.

1984a *Kant and Phenomenology,* ed. with Thomas M. Seebohm. Washington, D.C.: University Press of America.

1984b *On the Truth of Being: Reflections on Heidegger's Later Philosophy.* Bloomington: Indiana University Press.

1985a *Heidegger on Art and Art Works.* Dordrecht: Nijhoff.

1985b "Heidegger on Metaphor and Metaphysics." *Tijdschrift voor Filosofie* 47 (3): 415–450.

1985c *Heidegger and Science.* Washington, D.C.: University Press of America.

1986a *A Companion to Martin Heidegger's "Being and Time."* Washington, D.C.: University Press of America.

1986b "On the Hermeneutic Dimension of the Natural Sciences." *Études Phénoménologiques* 2: 33–81.

1986c "Über Mythos und Wissenschaft: Einige hermeneutische Reflexionen." In *Zur Kritik der wissenschaftlichen Rationalität,* ed. Hans Lenk, pp. 71–101. Freiburg: Alber.

1987a "Einheit und Vielheit in Sittlichkeit und Sittenlehre." In *Einheit und Vielheit,* vol. 14, ed. Odo Marquard, Peter Probst, and Franz Josef Wetz, pp. 36–53. Hamburg: Meiner, 1990.

1987b *Hermeneutic Phenomenology: Lectures and Essays,* ed. Washington, D.C.: University Press of America.

1987c *Phenomenological Psychology: The Dutch School,* ed. Dordrecht: Nijhoff.

1987d "On the Problem of Truth in the Sciences." *Proceedings and Addresses of the American Philosophical Association* 61: 5–26.

1988a "Der Brauch als der alteste Name für das Sein des Seienden: Heidegger über den Spruch des Anaximander." In *Philosophie und Poesie,* ed. Annemarie Gethmann-Siefert, pp. 77–103. Stuttgart: Frommann-Holzboog.

1988b "Zeit und Sprache im Ereignis." In *Sprache, Wirklichkeit, Bewusstsein,* ed. E. W. Orth, pp. 51–81. Freiburg: K. Alber.

1989a *Heidegger's "Being and Time": The Analytic of Dasein as Fundamental Ontology.* Washington, D.C.: University Press of America.

1989b "On the Meaning of Music and Its Place in Our World." In *Kunst und Technik: Gedächtnisschrift zum 100. Geburtstag von Martin Heidegger,* ed. Walter Biemel and Friedrich-Wilhelm von Herrmann, pp. 351–376. Frankfurt: Klostermann.

1989c "Sprache—Hegel und Heidegger." In *Grosse Themen Martin Heideggers: Eine Einführung in sein Denken,* ed. Edelgard Spaude, pp. 60–83. Freiburg: Rombach.

1992 "Twentieth-Century Continental Ethics." In *A History of Western Ethics,* ed. Laurence C. Becker and Charlotte B. Becker, pp. 118–128. New York: Garland.

1993 *Ideas for a Hermeneutic Phenomenology of the Natural Sciences: Contributions to Phenomenology.* Dordrecht: Kluwer.

1994 *Edmund Husserl's Phenomenology.* Lafayette: Purdue University Press.

1997a *Inleiding tot en Commentaar van Martin Heideggers De Spreuk van Anaximander.* Leuven and Assen: Universitaire Press and Van Gorcum.

1997b "On the Hermeneutic Nature of Modern Natural Science." *Man and World,* special issue: "Hermeneutics and the Natural Sciences" 30 (3).

# TEN

# From the School of Suspicion to the Willing Suspension of Disbelief

▣

## DAVID FARRELL KRELL

I shall divide these brief remarks into three sections: (1) education and institutional affiliations; (2) areas of intellectual interest and research; and (3) my hopes for a perfect future. I beg the reader's indulgence for the parade of "I's" that follows. The only possible excuse for such egotism is that the careers of other continental philosophers in America may have followed a similar trajectory, so that out of all this fourth-of-July narcissism will emerge something like a pattern or composite portrait of a Yankee *Geschick des Seins*.

### Education and Institutional Affiliations

My first university degree was in European cultural and intellectual history. Philosophy was always for me merely one part of a larger history that included everything from politics to painting. To the extent that philosophy pretended to be at center stage—to dwell at the origin of all culture or to reflect on the foundations of all learning—it was simply an embarrassment to me, the expression of a lingering bad habit. In a journal I kept during my university days, I recorded my impatience with the philosophers who taught me: an "incredible mix of innocence and arrogance" seemed to mark almost all of them. The first exception was Alphonso Lingis. Later teachers of philosophy in graduate school at Duquesne University in Pittsburgh, principally André Schuwer and John Sallis, caused me to change my mind about the possibilities of philosophy. I was particularly captivated by courses on Plato, Kant, Schelling, Merleau-Ponty, Nietzsche, and Heidegger. In 1969–70, in München, I wrote my doctoral dissertation on Heidegger's two-volume *Nietzsche*, receiving the doctorate from Duquesne in 1971.

At that time I did not know that I was a "continental philosopher." It seemed to me that I was doing the only philosophy there was. It was clear to me, at all events, that what my own language group was doing—in Anglo-American philosophy—was stale, flat, and unprofitable: its linguistic analysis steadfastly refused to engage in any *questioning* that might make a difference, either in metaphysics or in politics; its linguistic expertise seemed to me to be rooted in the colossal Anglo-American ignorance of languages and cultures.

From 1972 to 1983 I taught in Germany, first in Freiburg-im-Breisgau, then later in Mannheim. I became involved in the editing and translating of Heidegger's works, under the genial tutelage of Joan Stambaugh and J. Glenn Gray. It was my good fortune to have the opportunity to work with Heidegger himself, along with Hannah Arendt, during the early years of my sojourn in Germany. It was also my good fortune to have the opportunity to teach at the Anglistisches Seminar in Freiburg and Mannheim with Ulrich Halfmann (still at Mannheim) and Helmbrecht Breinig (now at Erlangen). Heidegger and Arendt—and, later, Derrida—taught me a great deal about the *generosity* of thinking. My friends Halfmann and Breinig, along with other colleagues such as Jupp Schöpp (now at Hamburg) and Jochen Barkhausen, and students such as Michael Walter, Ursula Willaredt, and Ashraf Noor, taught me the meaning of American democracy. For on a German Lehrstuhl (not always considered the seat of democracy) we practiced a genuine democracy of mutual support, constructive criticism, and equal dedication to ideas and to students. Breinig taught me Melville and Twain; Halfmann taught me Faulkner and Morrison; together we pursued this beautiful and demanding love called *literature*. Willingly, we suspended disbelief. My German friends gave me, or at least returned to me, whatever of the U.S.-American tradition I possess, along with the incomparable gifts of Novalis, Hölderlin, and Goethe, Musil, Mann, Trakl, Kafka, and Celan. Probably they also gave me the desire to pursue what below I shall call "my perfect future."

In 1983 Robert Bernasconi invited me to move to Essex University in England. There we helped to develop what I think can be called one of the most vital programs in European thought in the British Isles. In 1988–89, I was on leave from Essex in Cuernavaca, where I worked on my first published piece of fiction. In 1989, I moved to DePaul University in Chicago, where, with the help of energetic colleagues and a supportive administration, it became possible to assemble in one faculty some of the most talented young philosophers working in the continental tradition. Although I became the founding director of the DePaul Humanities Center in 1998, my loyalty to the philosophy department—and to Peg Birmingham, Niklaus

Largier, Mary Jeanne Larrabee, Bill Martin, Will McNeill, Darrell Moore, Michael Naas, and Angelica Nuzzo, among others, friends more than colleagues—is unswerving.

## Areas of Intellectual Interest and Research

While I was studying the history of ideas at the University of Virginia in 1966–67, the "school of suspicion" (which was what Paul Ricoeur called Marx, Nietzsche, and Freud), began to divert me from history of ideas toward philosophy. From the outset, my interest in philosophy was both shaped and disrupted by suspicions concerning philosophy. I took Nietzsche at his word when in an unpublished note from the year 1884 he wrote that he had no desire to convert anyone to philosophy:

> I do not wish to persuade anyone to philosophy: it is inevitable and perhaps also desirable that the philosopher should be a *rare* plant. I find nothing more repugnant than didactic praise of philosophy, as one finds it in Seneca, or worse, Cicero. Philosophy has little to do with virtue. Permit me to say also that the man of knowledge is fundamentally different from the philosopher. —What I desire is that the genuine concept of the philosopher not perish utterly in Germany. (*Kritische Studienausgabe*, 1980, 11: 271)

However severe the problems with philosophers in Germany might have been—and Heidegger in his own sardonic style corroborated Nietzsche's complaint when he opened his first lecture course on Nietzsche in 1936 with the above quotation—the problems with U.S.-American philosophers seemed worse: dogmatic Thomists squabbled with dogmatic positivists, blue-eyed pragmatists pleaded with squint-eyed logicians, and all these debates aroused in me nothing so much as suspicion and the need for enormous distance. (It is therefore a wretched tragicomedy that I see playing itself out in Germany these days, as German-speaking philosophers try to ape The American Way, fawning over Davidson and Putnam as though they were Schleiermacher and Schelling, which they are not. This most vulgar form of Vergangenheitsbewältigung is nearly enough to make one wish one were not a "continental philosopher.")

Nietzsche brought me into philosophy—kicking and screaming, it is true, and through the back door—and for many years it was the major commentaries on Nietzsche that were my principal occupation, from Heidegger's *Nietzsche* and Bataille's *Sur Nietzsche* to Derrida's *Éperons*. Had I been forced to confess my faith, I would have called myself a genealogist, though

I felt more sympathy for Pierre Klossowski than for Gilles Deleuze and Michel Foucault. In spite of my undiminished admiration for Marx, the *Frankfurter Schule* meant nothing to me. It was perhaps as a genealogist that I first read Heidegger's *Being and Time* and became fascinated by the (admittedly doomed) project of a fundamental ontology. It was Heidegger's hermeneutics of facticity, his intimations of mortality, that arrested me. After translating and editing a number of Heidegger's works on the Presocratics and on Nietzsche, and after editing a collection of Heidegger's writings, I published a book entitled *Intimations of Mortality: Time, Truth, and Finitude in Heidegger's Thinking of Being* (1986). I took my title from the darker side of William Wordsworth's famous ode, selecting these lines as an epigraph to the book:

> The clouds that gather round the setting sun
> Do take a sober colouring from an eye
> That hath kept watch o'er man's mortality.

A later book on Heidegger, *Daimon Life: Heidegger and Life-Philosophy* (1992), did not entirely surrender the project of fundamental ontology, but it did manifest a greater distance from Heidegger than the earlier *Intimations* did.

In the same year in which *Intimations* was published, I wrote *Postponements: Woman, Sensuality, and Death in Nietzsche* (1986). This strange little book marked a return to my first love, Nietzsche, viewed from the equally troubling perspectives of sexual difference and theory of tragedy. The lineage of tragedy—its gestation during what Nietzsche called "the tragic age of the Greeks" and its birth in the most perverse and infamous Houses of ancient Greece—seemed to me to be bound up with Hölderlin's and Nietzsche's *Empedocles* dramas, on the one hand, and with Nietzsche's *Zarathustra,* on the other. A later book, *Lunar Voices* (1995), expanded on the Empedoclean and Hölderlinian understanding of tragedy as bound up with sensuality and sexuality as well as with mortality.

*Postponements* was followed by a book on memory (1990), a book most difficult in the writing—and probably in the reading, too. *Of Memory, Reminiscence, and Writing: On the Verge* broke new ground for me. It demanded of me my most sustained readings of Plato, Aristotle, Augustine, Descartes, Hobbes, Locke, Hegel, and Freud, and also my most sustained reading of *reading*—in the style inspired by Jacques Derrida. My *Verge* is doubtless a shapeless, undisciplined book, even though it went through many reshapings and revisings. Its object, the forgotten faculty of memory, has always been my favorite faculty, far more precious to me than the scintillating imagination, the steadfast *sensus communis,* our magisterial power of reason, or even our acute sense perception. And the more *involuntary* memory is, the more I willingly admire it and volunteer to pursue it.

My most recent publications have been on German Idealism and Romanticism, although a small book on architecture has found its way onto the list. The works that most excite me, however, are not philosophical at all—at least, they are not *treatises* of philosophy. If I am granted a future, a perfect future, it will be to do work in the realms of fiction and film-writing.

## The Perfect Future

It is difficult today to be content with U.S.-American academic philosophy, even of the hermeneutical or "continental" persuasion. So much of it is complacently self-righteous, whether it calls itself *ethics* or *politics*. What Lacan in a different yet related context called "the salvationist choirs" [*orphéons salutistes*] are still singing their fervent hymns of militant American Puritanism. And it is difficult to be content with the seedy professionalism of the contemporary U.S.-American philosophical "scene" or "circuit," the German counterpart of which Heidegger lampooned so mercilessly in 1925:

> Today we decide about metaphysics and about even more elevated things at philosophy conferences. For everything that is to be done these days we must first have a meeting, and here is how it works: people come together, constantly come together, and they all wait for one another to turn up so that the others will tell them how it is, and if it doesn't get said, never mind, everyone has had their say. It may very well be that all the talkers who are having their say have understood little of the matter in question, but still we believe that if we accumulate all that misunderstanding something like understanding will leap forth at the end of the day. Thus there are people today who travel from one meeting to the next and who are sustained by the confidence that something is really happening, that they've actually done something; whereas, at bottom, they've merely ducked out of work, seeking in chatter a place to build a nest for their helplessness—a helplessness, it is true, that they will never understand. (Martin Heidegger, *Gesamtausgabe*, 20: 376)

To be sure, there is something puritanical and tyrannical about the lampoon as well. And the gesture of turning one's back on philosophy would smack of the same salvationism it decries. I am therefore not turning my back: a recent book (1998) examines theories of sexuality, disease, and death in Novalis, Schelling, and Hegel. I continue to be drawn to issues in the philosophy of nature and the aesthetic theory of German Idealism and Romanticism. I am also trying at the moment to think about the theory and practice of mourning (*le deuil*) in that most maddening of contemporary European thinkers, that purest of bastards, Jacques Derrida. However, to repeat, the work that most excites me is the fiction—where disbelief can and must be suspended—represented in my *Nietzsche: A Novel* (1996), *Son of Spirit: A Novel* (1997), and, most recently, *The Recalcitrant Art*.

How can I justify the move to fiction—my capitulation to biography and gossip, whether the theme be Nietzsche's madness or Hegel's illegitimate son or Hölderlin's love life? How can I justify the vulgar desire to write screenplays? Justification remains an obsession of philosophy, of course, whereas I am obsessed with something else, something that neither allows nor needs justification. I am obsessed by that neutral voice, the voice of narrative, and the play of visions and images, *eidola*, that Maurice Blanchot tells us haunt the *other* night. My perfect future would consist of a series of such nights, interrupted occasionally by the uncertain daylight of philosophy.

## Selected Bibliography

1972a "Toward an Ontology of Play: Eugen Fink's Notion of *Spiel.*" *Research in Phenomenology* 2: 63–93.

1972b "Socrates' Body." *Southern Journal of Philosophy* 10 (4): 443–451.

1974 "Merleau-Ponty on Eros and Logos." *Man and World* 7 (1): 37–51.

1975a Introduction to *Early Greek Thinking,* by Martin Heidegger. Ed. and trans. with Frank A. Capuzzi. New York: Harper and Row.

1975b "Nietzsche in Heidegger's *Kehre.*" *Southern Journal of Philosophy* 13 (2): 197–204.

1975c "Female Parts in *Timaeus.*" *Arion: A Journal of Humanities and the Classics,* n.s. 2 (3): 400–421.

1976a "Heidegger, Nietzsche, Hegel: An Essay in Descensional Reflection." *Nietzsche-Studien* 5: 255–262.

1976b "Being and Truth, Being and Time." *Research in Phenomenology* 4: 151–166.

1977 Introduction to *Martin Heidegger's Basic Writings,* ed. New York: Harper and Row. 2nd ed., revised and expanded, 1993.

1978a "Phenomenology of Memory: Some Implications for Education." In *Phenomenology and Education,* ed. Bernard Curtis and Wolfe Mays, pp. 131–144. London: Methuen.

1978b "Death and Interpretation." In *Heidegger's Existential Analytic,* ed. Frederick Elliston, pp. 247–255. The Hague: Mouton.

1978c "Schlag der Liebe, Schlag des Todes: On Heidegger and Trakl." In *Radical Phenomenology: Essays in Honor of Martin Heidegger,* ed. John Sallis, pp. 238–258. Atlantic Highlands, N.J.: Humanities Press.

1978d "The Heidegger–Jaspers Relationship." *Journal of the British Society for Phenomenology* 11 (2): 126–129.

1979a–87 Martin Heidegger's *Nietzsche*. 4 vols. Ed. and co-trans., with notes and commentary. New York: Harper and Row. Paperback eds., 1991.

1979b "Art and Truth in Raging Discord: Heidegger and Nietzsche on Will to Power as Art." In *Martin Heidegger and the Question of Literature*, ed. William V. Spanos, pp. 39–52. Bloomington: Indiana University Press.

1980 "Hegel, Heidegger, Heraclitus." In *Heraclitean Fragments*, ed. John Sallis and Kenneth Maly, pp. 22–42. University: University of Alabama Press.

1981a "Memory as Malady and Therapy in Freud and Hegel." *Journal of Phenomenological Psychology* 12 (1): 35–50.

1981b "Results." *The Monist* 64 (4): 467–480.

1981c "A Smile and a Sense of Tragedy: Letters from J. Glenn Gray." *Philosophy Today* 25 (2): 95–113.

1982a "Phenomenology of Memory from Husserl to Merleau-Ponty." *Philosophy and Phenomenological Research* 42 (4): 492–505.

1982b "Work Sessions with Martin Heidegger." *Philosophy Today* 26 (2): 126–138.

1983a "Heidegger/Nietzsche." In *Heidegger*, ed. Michel Haar, pp. 200–210. Paris: Cahiers de l'Herne. Paperback edition, Livre de Poche: 1986, pp. 161–180.

1983b "The Ends of Metaphysics: Hegel and Nietzsche on Holiday." *Research in Phenomenology* 13: 175–182.

1984 "Pitch: Genitality/Excrementality from Hegel to Crazy Jane." *boundary 2: A Journal of Postmodern Literature and Culture* 12 (2): 113–141.

1985a "The Oldest Program toward a System in German Idealism." *The Owl of Minerva* 17 (1): 5–19.

1985b "A Hermeneutics of Discretion." *Research in Phenomenology* 15: 1–27.

1986a *Intimations of Mortality: Time, Truth, and Finitude in Heidegger's "Thinking of Being."* University Park: Pennsylvania State University Press.

1986b *Postponements: Woman, Sensuality, and Death in Nietzsche*. Bloomington: Indiana University Press.

1986c "Hölderlin's 'Hymn to Serenity': A Newly Discovered Poem." Translated, with introduction and commentary. *Graduate Faculty Philosophy Journal* (New School for Social Research) 11 (1): 3–15.

1987a *Exceedingly Nietzsche: Aspects of Contemporary Nietzsche-Interpretation*, ed. with David Wood. New York: Routledge.

1987b "The Perfect Future: A Note on Heidegger and Derrida." In *Philosophy and Deconstruction: The Texts of Jacques Derrida*, ed. John Sallis, pp. 114–121. Chicago: University of Chicago Press.

1988a "Engorged Philosophy: A Note on Freud, Derrida, and Différance." In *Derrida and Différance*, ed. David Wood and Robert Bernasconi, pp. 6–11. Evanston: Northwestern University Press.

1988b "Engorged Philosophy II." In *Postmodernism and Continental Philosophy*, ed. Hugh J. Silverman and Donn Welton, pp. 49–66. Albany: State University of New York Press.

1988c "Knowledge Is Remembrance: Diotima's Instruction at *Symposium* 207c–208b." In *Poststructuralist Classics*, ed. Andrew Benjamin, pp. 160–172. New York: Routledge.

1988d "Paradoxes of the Pineal: From Descartes to Georges Bataille." In *Contemporary French Philosophy: Proceedings of the Royal Institute of Philosophy*, ed. A. Phillips Griffiths, pp. 215–228. Cambridge: Cambridge University Press.

1989 "The Crisis of Reason in the Nineteenth Century: Schelling's *Treatise on Human Freedom* (1809)." In *The Collegium Phaenomenologicum: The First Ten Years*, ed. John Sallis, Giuseppina Moneta, and Jacques Taminiaux, pp. 13–32. Dordrecht: Kluwer.

1990a *Of Memory, Reminiscence, and Writing: On the Verge*. Bloomington: Indiana University Press.

1990b "Beneath the Time of the Line: The Future of Memory." In *Writing the Future*, ed. David Wood, pp. 106–111. New York: Routledge.

1990c "Le plus pur des bâtards." *Revue philosophique de la France et de l'étranger*, special issue "Derrida," ed. Catharine Malabou and Yvon Brès (Presses Universitaires de France) 2: 229–238.

1990d "'I made it on the verge'. . . : A Letter to Daniél Libeskind on the Jewish Museum in Berlin." *Assemblage: A Critical Journal of Architecture and Design Culture* 12: 52–57.

1991a "Madness and Philosophy: Jaspers and Klossowski on Nietzsche's Insanity." *International Studies in Philosophy* 23 (2): 55–63.

1991b "Shattering: Toward a Politics of Daimonic Life." *Graduate Faculty Philosophy Journal* (New School for Social Research), 14 (2) and 15 (1): 153–182.

1991d "Everything Great Stands in the Storm That Blows from Paradise." *Cardozo Law Review* 13 (4): 301–307.

1991e "Lucinde's Shame: Hegel, Sensuous Woman, and the Law." In *Hegel and Legal Theory*, ed. Drucilla Cornell, Michel Rosenfeld, and David Gray Carlson, pp. 287–300. New York: Routledge. Revised and reprinted in *Feminist Readings of Hegel*, ed. Patricia Jagentowicz Mills. pp. 89–107. University Park: Pennsylvania State University Press, 1995.

1992a *Daimon Life: Heidegger and Life-Philosophy*. Bloomington: Indiana University Press.

1992b "Of Spirit and the Daimon: Jacques Derrida's *De l'esprit*." In *Ethics and Danger: Currents in Continental Thought*, ed. Charles E. Scott and Arleen B. Dallery, pp. 59–70. Albany: State University of New York Press.

1992c "National Erotism (Derdiedas Responsibilities)." In *Ethics and Responsibility in the Phenomenological Tradition*, ed. Richard Rojcewicz, pp. 33–56. Pittsburgh: Duquesne University Press.

1993a "Spiriting Heidegger." In *Of Derrida, Heidegger, and Spirit*, ed. David Wood, pp. 11–40. Evanston: Northwestern University Press.

1993b "Immanent Death, Imminent Death: Reading Freud's *Beyond the Pleasure Principle* (1920) with Heidegger's *Being and Time* (1927) and *Metaphysical Foundations of Logic* (1928), though there's something in it for Aristophanes, too. . . ." In *Speculations after Freud*, ed. Sonu Shamdasani and Michael Münchow, pp. 151–166. New York: Routledge.

1994 "To the Orangegrove at the Edge of the Sea: Remarks on Luce Irigaray's *Amante marine*." In *Nietzsche and the Feminine*, ed. Peter Burgard, pp. 185–209. Charlottesville: University Press of Virginia.

1995 *Lunar Voices: Of Tragedy, Poetry, Fiction, and Thought*. Chicago: University of Chicago Press.

1996a *Infectious Nietzsche*. Bloomington: Indiana University Press.

1996b *Nietzsche: A Novel*. Albany: State University of New York Press.

1996c "Thinking Ben Nicholson's Collage Thinking: From the Laurentian Library to the Appliance House, Loaf House, and B-52 Pickup." Published in the *Loaf*

*House Web Site* by the Renaissance Society on the occasion of the Nicholson retrospective in October 1996.

1997a *Son of Spirit: A Novel.* Albany: State University of New York Press.

1997b *The Good European: Nietzsche's Work Sites in Word and Image.* With Donald L. Bates. Chicago: University of Chicago Press.

1997c *Archeticture: Ecstasies of Space, Time, and the Human Body.* Albany: State University of New York Press.

1998a *Contagion: Dire Forces of Nature in German Idealism and Romanticism.* Bloomington: Indiana University Press.

1998b *The Purest of Bastards: Works of Mourning, Art, and Affirmation in the Thought of Jacques Derrida.* University Park, Pa.: Penn State Press, forthcoming.

1999 *The Recalcitrant Art: Diotima's Letters to Hölderlin and Related Missives.* Albany: State University of New York Press, forthcoming.

# ELEVEN

# Understanding
*Learning to Stand on the Earth and Stand under the Sky*

▐▌

# David Michael Levin

Most of my work in the last twenty-five years has been in a field I would like to define as the phenomenology of moral experience. But this description does not yet indicate the singularity of my work. For many years, I have been engaged in questioning the capacities of our embodiment from the standpoint of moral enlightenment: questioning the character of our gestures, for example, and how we "make use" of the gifts of nature we call seeing and hearing. My thinking in this regard has been guided primarily by the hermeneutical method of phenomenology that Heidegger worked out in *Being and Time,* already announcing his decisive break with Husserl in the potentially very radical, very subversive formulation of his Introduction; but the phenomenological studies of Merleau-Ponty have also served as a principal point of reference for my work. From the very beginning of my philosophical life, I found myself drawn to phenomenology, because it seemed to me that this method alone *respects* the reality of our experience as lived and that it alone, therefore, legitimates and empowers subjectivity in its struggle to twist free of the oppressive cultural interpretations that have been imposed on it.

I want to think of embodiment as a complex system of capacities. These capacities are gifts of nature, each one with a potential that can either be appropriately realized, developed, and fulfilled or else neglected, repressed, violated, and denied appropriate cultivation and fulfillment. Since their realization, development and fulfillment are not predetermined by the conditions of nature, this task becomes the joint responsibility of the individual and society. Beyond the biological development of these capacities, there is also their ethical, moral, political, and spiritual development—a *telos* which has been inscribed from time immemorial in the secrets of the flesh, and for which we as individuals must certainly assume some responsibility but toward which we cannot hope to progress without altering the enabling conditions of our society and culture. Thus, if we ask, with Foucault, what kind of body—or what kind of gaze, what kind of listening, what kind of gestural comportment, gestural praxis—our society and culture require of us, we must also ask what kind of society and culture the fulfillment of our potential for seeing and hearing—and our potential as gesturing beings— might need. With this question, we can subject the conditions of our society and culture to a radical critique, deploying as our touchstone the needs and dreams latent in our seeing and hearing, and latent also in the felt sense which is borne—if we will only attend to its silently inscribed claim on our comportment—right in our hands.

Seeing and hearing are, above all, capacities for responsiveness. This responsiveness, taking place, as Levinas would put it, "prior to all freedom," prior to all acts of volition, is the beginning of all ethical responsibility. But we are responsible, both as individuals and as members of a society and culture, for the ongoing development of the responsibility implicit, or latent, in this responsiveness. Developing, cultivating our responsiveness, while at the same time sharpening the critical powers in our perception with regard to the visibility and audibility of oppressive and repressive conditions in our society and culture, could become what I would like to call, borrowing from Foucault, a "practice of the self": a practice of caring for the self that, *a fortiori*, would also be a practice sharpening the self's awareness of others and its ability to care about, and for, the welfare of others.

Since ancient times, philosophers have not only made use of what they saw and heard to construct their philosophical systems; they have also *discursively constructed* (often without acknowledgment) numerous models of seeing and hearing, models of perception, models of sense and sensibility, as required by and for their systems of epistemology and metaphysics. As a philosopher, therefore, I am especially concerned about the *character* of the philosopher's seeing and hearing—and the philosopher's understanding of seeing and hearing. What kind of seeing and hearing do philosophers practice? What kind of perceptiveness is called for? What does the philosopher notice, what see, what observe? To what is the philosopher blind? To what do we shut our eyes? And what does the philosopher hear? To what do we listen? To what are we deaf?

I am interested not only in the self-development and self-fulfillment of the *individual* as a being capable of a uniquely human development of seeing and hearing, i.e., in the relationship between our self-development and self-fulfillment as individuals and the realization, development, and fulfillment of our potential as beings capable of a uniquely human development of seeing and hearing. I am equally interested in the implications of such development for the critique and betterment of society and culture. The great historical project of Enlightenment can, I think, be continued in this way. I accordingly conceive my work as a contribution to critical social theory, connecting in intricate and until now unexplored ways with Benjamin's and Adorno's dialectics of seeing and listening, Marcuse's attempt to articulate and bring about a radical transformation of sensibility, and Habermas's adumbration of an *embodied* rationality. What would it be (like) for this communicative rationality to be embodied in our perception, our seeing and hearing, our gestures, our stride and bearing?

For me, as for many philosophers before me, sight and its principal virtues—clarity, for example, and insight, foresight, and the power to gather beings into a state of simultaneous co-presence—are in large measure responsible for the construction of the ontology dominant in our time. What, then, is the connection between this vision-generated ontology and the ethics, morality, and politics by which we have lived? What is the connection between the will to power driving our technology and the predominant *character* of our vision? To what extent is the character-tendency which has prevailed in the vision of modern times complicit in, and responsible for, the cruelty and violence, the suffering and misery, that some of us can see in the world? To what extent do the terrible things we see in the world around us manifest and reflect the character of our culturally favored way of looking and seeing? To what extent does this way of looking and seeing *reproduce* itself and, correspondingly, the evils that some of us can see? To what extent does the gaze of the philosopher not only *reflect upon* the human condition, but also immediately *reflect,* and thereby itself *reproduce,* its prevailing historical form?

The gift of vision is a challenge; it is also an opportunity. But only, I believe, if we are prepared to root our looking and seeing in the body of feeling. For, as I argued in *The Opening of Vision,* the root of vision is weeping, our vulnerability, our openness to being touched and moved by what we see. Openness to radical alterity, conceived as an anarchic normativity, must be the measure of our engagement with the world. This is the thought that has been guiding my philosophical work with seeing, hearing, gesture, and sensibility.

In the past, hermeneutics has been understood exclusively in relation to the interpretation of texts, or, say, cultural discourses. In my work, however, hermeneutics constitutes the essential phenomenological structure of perception, since perception is always a process of explication, bringing-forth, bringing-out, and is always situated in the interplay of presence and absence, concealment and unconcealment. Phenomenology cannot be faithful to the "truth" of the phenomenon unless it is, in this sense, hermeneutical. Thus we would be thinking about our gestures, and our seeing and hearing, as organs of being with a capacity for engaging hermeneutically—disclosingly, revealingly—with the being of whatever we may be given to behold or hear or in any way handle. The problematic at stake in the hermeneutics of texts and cultural discourses, namely the avoidance of an imperialism of the same in our relation to what is other, is no less at stake, I believe, when it is a question of our gesturing, our seeing and hearing. Here, too, the violence inherent in the logic of identity all too easily dictates the conditions of our perceptivity and gestural praxis.

## Hermeneutical Phenomenology

Many philosophers have claimed empirical, experiential grounding for their thought. However, in spite of good intentions, their thinking has often not only failed to correspond to experience, but to a surprising extent has even subverted and betrayed it. What brought Husserl to the threshold of phenomenology was the problem of meaning: clarifying the meanings of our words by tracing them back to their origin in the acts of transcendental consciousness through which these meanings were first constituted, and re-iterating the meaning-forming process, this time with an explicitly reflexive awareness of the way transcendental subjectivity functions in the process. "Back to the things themselves!" he proclaimed, boldly asserting that the phenomenological method, which he formulated in terms of a sequence of "reductions," is the only authentic positivism, the only true empiricism, and the only way to a realm of knowledge worthy of being called the "science" of all sciences.

Husserl's battle cry summons us to return to the experience of subjectivity and to insist on its claim to a certain validity and legitimacy. In a time when objectivity has become the dominant paradigm of knowledge, truth, and reality, excluding or even denying all reference to experience, this battle cry has played a crucial historical role, a progressive historical role, challenging the hegemony of this paradigm, reaffirming the critical function of subjectivity, and renewing the promise of a rational redemption of lived experience.

But Husserl's phenomenology is ultimately more concerned with the task of rational reconstruction, securing for our knowledge an absolute grounding in the meaning-constitutive activity of transcendental consciousness, than it is with the task of showing us how to reflect on our own experience just as it is lived. In fact, the latter task is not merely rendered subordinate to the task of laying an absolute foundation; it is ultimately annulled.

Thus, what might have served as a method for a creative engagement with our experience as we actually live it became, instead, a method in the service of a metaphysical program.

We need to retrieve the progressive, critical spirit behind Husserl's affirmation of subjectivity and his formulation of the phenomenological method. But this requires that we unhitch the method from his metaphysical agenda.

Every one of the liberation movements that have swept across the Western world in this century is indebted to a *praxis* that can only be called, in effect, the living incorporation of hermeneutical phenomenology. What I mean is that every one of these movements essentially involves the empowerment that comes from *rejecting* the socially imposed constructions that have been interpreting or determining the meaning of one's experience, one's individual and group identity, and *learning* how to think, feel, and act from out of one's own lived experience. For centuries, most people have been *told* what it is that they are or should be experiencing; told, also, *how* they should experience the socially constructed—hence ideologically hegemonic —interpretation of what they are experiencing. Liberation from the sociocultural imposition of meaning therefore essentially involves the subject (whether individual or collective) in a phenomenological gesture, whereby experience just as it is actually lived is finally recognized and its existential meaningfulness is respected as such. For me, then, the significance of phenomenology for life, life in all its dimensions—ethical, social, moral, political, juridical, cultural, and spiritual—is that it insists on recognition and respect for our ownmost experience as it is lived, and that it offers a disciplined method for working hermeneutically with lived experience in order to draw out its implicit or latent potential and carry this potential forward in ways that are felt to be life-affirming and to contribute to the flourishing of meaningful life. This is why I believe that, at the heart of phenomenology, what we find is indeed the dream that the word itself announces: the dream, namely, of the embodiment of reason—an emerging body of understanding, able to stand "poetically" on the earth and stand "poetically" under the sky, drawing elemental support from earth and sky for more appropriate interactions with other human beings, beings of other kinds, and the presencing of the very being of beings as such.

This dream can be realized, however, only if, following Heidegger's formulation in the Introduction to *Being and Time,* we give Husserl's "principle of all principles," and his battle cry, "zu den Sachen selbst!," a much more radical interpretation. Because Husserl's approach is captive to a metaphysical program, it cannot entirely avoid imposing meaning on experience, forcing it into a narrative that in many ways can be distorting. Phenomenology, therefore, must be, as Heidegger says, drawing on the word's

Greek etymology, an approach to experience, an approach to the phenomenon, that *lets* it show itself from out of itself. As Heidegger formulates the phenomenological method in *Being and Time,* it becomes, finally and for the first time, truly empirical, in the radical sense of truly *respecting* the phenomenon as it gives itself. And this means respecting not only its essential becoming, the openness of its nature as the ever-emerging, but also respecting its self-concealment, its withdrawal from the realm of its appearing.

The radicality of the phenomenological method formulated in *Being and Time* consists in the fact that it *detaches* the method from Husserl's metaphysical program, so that it can be entirely given over to hermeneutic articulation, the caring and thoughtful unconcealment of the phenomenon. But Heidegger's fidelity to the hermeneutics of being also depends on a far-reaching critique of the philosophical tradition: on a critique of the domination of the assertion, the constative mode of discourse; a critique of the metaphysically enshrined structure of subject and object; and a critique of the correspondence theory of truth. For phenomenology cannot be entirely devoted to serving the hermeneutic presencing of the phenomenon unless it recognizes the aletheic dimension of truth, the prior event of opening that lays out a field of conditions for the perception and assertion of truth, and recognizes a mode of discourse that is appropriate to the hermeneutics of that which presents itself and that which, as origin, as the event that gives and inaugurates the field for this presence, itself withdraws from truth, a self-concealing background that cannot be retrieved as origin or reduced to the structure of the objective.

Although Heidegger could see in the history of philosophy the repetition of a certain foreclosure, a move that again and again betrayed the wonderful opening laid out, as the task that calls for thinking, with the very broaching of the question of being (Why is there being, anything at all, rather than nothing?), he did not at first realize that his own treatment of this question in *Being and Time* repeated this history of betrayal, articulating the ontological question only to impose a framework of conditions for response that immediately denies the very opening which the question set in motion. It is as if I wanted to get to know you and therefore invited you to tell me about yourself—not by letting you talk freely and by listening in a respectful, open silence, but instead submitted you to an intense interrogation structured entirely according to my own terms, obliging you, for example, to restrict your answers to the set of questions I had already formulated in advance of our encounter and to use only the vocabulary that I wanted you to use.

After the publication of the incomplete manuscript he entitled *Being and Time,* Heidegger soon came to realize that the "analytic of Dasein" which followed his formulation, in the Introduction, of a very radical phenomenological methodology, constituted precisely the same betrayal of the *Seinsfrage* that he lamented in his narrative of the history of philosophy. In other words, he soon recognized in his own work a repetition of the very same foreclosure that he reproached in his precursors. For instead of waiting to receive in an open way what comes from the asking of the question, instead of letting what comes with (from) the question of being simply show itself from out of itself, he had forced the phenomenon, the presencing of being, to show itself in terms of the existential structures he laid down in his *Auslegung* of the being that is constitutive of *Dasein*. This betrays the very hermeneutical openness to the moment of truth that his critique of the correspondence theory of truth and his introduction of the prior event of *aletheia* was intended to secure. Heidegger's so-called "turning" (*Kehre*) therefore involved an attempt to twist free of the framing of the question of being in terms of the existential structures arbitrarily posited in the analytic representation of *Dasein* and an attempt to return to the question of being, working with it, this time, in the radically phenomenological way he had formulated in his Introduction, henceforth maintaining the most rigorous responsibility for responding appropriately to the claim of the question of being as an opening question that calls for a response from our perceptual faculties and our gestural bearing, our *Gebärde*, that would be correspondingly open. The question of being demands an open hermeneutic receptivity to whatever might come, whatever might emerge, from the self-concealing origin of openness into which the question throws us.

## Zugehörigkeit, Gelassenheit, Horchen

In *The Listening Self,* the third volume of my trilogy, I explicate the four moments of hearing. The first two moments are moments not only of development but also moments that are recapitulated in every event of hearing. The third and fourth, however, are "elective" possibilities, realizing to some extent the full dimensionality of our potentiality-for-hearing. (1) *Zugehörigkeit,* our natal bonding, our primordial attunement, the prepersonal, anonymous hearing of infancy, when we are ecstatically open to the "music," the *Grundbestimmung,* of the auditory field of being. (2) Ego-logical listening and hearing, the egocentric hearing of the child and the typical adult, the hearing of *das Man,* anyone-and-everyone, that is attained simply through the normal course of biological and cultural development. Judged in terms of the fourth moment, however, this hearing is a not-hearing: *verhören, überhören.* (3) Skillfully developed listening, trained and disciplined to surpass in some way the normal ability. And finally, (4) hearkening (*Hor-*

*chen*), a radically hermeneutical mode of hearing in which the normal structural relationship between figures of sound and their background (laying out an auditory field for our hearing) is radically altered by virtue of a listening openness—call it *Gelassenheit*—that does not suppress, reify or shut out the *Grundton*, the audibly inaudible tonality of the ground, while *at the same time* attending with interest to the sounds of the figural beings present in the auditory field. Hearkening is thus a double hermeneutical movement, revealing the gift of the auditory field as the gift of that dimensionality by grace of which alone we are first enabled to hear and speak. If, in the draft of the *Geviert,* such double hearing, in resonant correspondence with the doubling of truth in the difference between "truth" and "aletheia," and registering simultaneously both figure and ground—but each in its absolutely distinctive way of phasing—seems to demand of us the nearly impossible, we need perhaps to be reminded that *Dichten,* poetizing, could require nothing less of our historical dwelling. It is perhaps no exaggeration to say that the fate of the earth—and our dwelling—might depend on our admission to this fourth moment. For it is the only moment when our hearing belongs absolutely to alterity.


## Selected Bibliography

1970 *Reason and Evidence in Husserl's Phenomenology.* Evanston: Northwestern University Press.

1977a "Freud's Divided Heart and Saraha's Cure." *Inquiry* 20 (2–3): 165–188.

1977b "Self-Knowledge and the Talking Cure." *Review of Existential Psychology and Psychiatry* 15 (2–3): 95–111.

1978a "The Bodhisattva's Power to Fly." *Gesar* 5 (3): 12–18. Berkeley: The Tibetan Nyingma Institute.

1978b "The Embodiment of Compassion: How We Are Visibly Moved." *Soundings* 61 (4): 515–522.

1978c "Painful Time, Ecstatic Time." *The Eastern Buddhist* 11 (2): 74–112. Kyoto: Otani University.

1979 "Mantra: Sacred Words of Openness and Compassion." *Gesar* 6 (1): 16–22. Berkeley: The Tibetan Nyingma Institute.

1980 "Approaches to Psychotherapy: Freud, Jung and Buddhism." In *Metaphors of Consciousness,* ed. Ronald Valle and Rolf von Eckartsberg, pp. 243–274. New York: Plenum.

1981 "Recollection as Therapeia: Heidegger's Philosophy of History." In *Reflections: Essays in Phenomenology* 2 (1): 5–26. Toronto: Ontario Institute for Studies in Education.

1982 "The Embodiment of Thinking: Heidegger's Approach to Language." In *Phenomenology: Dialogues and Bridges,* ed. Ronald Bruzina and Bruce Wilshire, pp. 61–77. Albany: State University of New York Press.

1982–1983a "Eros and Psyche: A Reading of Merleau-Ponty." In *Merleau-Ponty and Psychology,* ed. Keith Hoeller, *Review of Existential Psychology and Psy-*

*chiatry* 18 (1-3): 219–239. Reprint edition, Atlantic Highlands, N.J.: Humanities Press, 1993.

1982–1983b "Sanity and Myth in Affective Space: A Discussion of Merleau-Ponty." *The Philosophical Forum* 14 (2): 157–189.

1983 "The Poetic Function in Phenomenological Discourse." In *Phenomenology in a Pluralistic Context: Selected Studies in Phenomenology and Existential Philosophy,* vol. 9, ed. William McBride and Calvin Schrag, pp. 216–234. Albany: State University of New York Press.

1984a "Hermeneutics as Gesture: A Reflection on Heidegger's 'Logos (Heraclitus B50)' Study." In *The Thought of Martin Heidegger,* ed. Michael Zimmerman, pp. 69–77. Tulane Studies in Philosophy, vol. 32. New Orleans: Tulane University.

1984b "Logos and Psyche: A Hermeneutics of Breathing." *Research in Phenomenology* 14: 121–147.

1985a "The Body Politic: Political Economy and the Human Body." *Human Studies* 8 (3): 235–278.

1985b *The Body's Recollection of Being: Phenomenological Psychology and the Deconstruction of Nihilism.* Boston: Kegan Paul.

1987a "Clinical Stories: A Modern Self in the Fury of Being." In *Pathologies of the Modern Self: Postmodern Studies on Narcissism, Schizophrenia, and Depression,* ed., pp. 479–537. New York: New York University Press.

1987b "Mudra as Thinking: Developing Our Wisdom-of-Being in Gesture and Movement." In *Heidegger and Asian Thought,* ed. Graham Parkes, pp. 245–269. Honolulu: University of Hawaii Press.

1987c "Psychopathology in the Epoch of Nihilism." In *Pathologies of the Modern Self: Postmodern Studies on Narcissism, Schizophrenia, and Depression,* ed., pp. 21–83. New York: New York University Press.

1988a *The Opening of Vision: Nihilism and the Postmodern Situation.* New York: Routledge.

1988b "Transpersonal Phenomenology: The Corporeal Schema." *The Humanistic Psychologist* 16 (2): 282–313.

1989a "The Body Politic: The Embodiment of Praxis in Foucault and Habermas." *Praxis International* 9 (1–2): 112–132.

1989b *The Listening Self: Personal Growth, Social Change, and the Closure of Metaphysics.* New York: Routledge.

1990a "Existentialism at the End of Modernity: Questioning the I's Eyes." *Philosophy Today* 34 (1): 80–95.

1990b "Justice in the Flesh." In *Ontology and Alterity in Merleau-Ponty,* ed. Galen Johnson and Michael Smith, pp. 35–44. Evanston: Northwestern University Press.

1990c "Postmodernism in Dance: Dance, Discourse, Democracy." In *Postmodernism in Philosophy and the Arts,* ed. Hugh J. Silverman, pp. 207–233. New York: Routledge.

1990d "The Discursive Formation of the Human Body in the History of Medicine." *Journal of Medicine and Philosophy* 15 (5): 515–537.

1991a "Phenomenology in America." *Philosophy and Social Criticism* 17 (2): 103–119.

1991b "Psychology as a Discursive Formation: The Postmodern Crisis." *The Humanistic Psychologist* 19 (3): 1–27.

1991c "Visions of Narcissism: Intersubjectivity and the Reversals of Reflection." In

*Merleau-Ponty Vivant,* ed. Martin Dillon, pp. 47–90. Albany: State University of New York Press.

1993a "Decline and Fall: Ocularcentrism in Heidegger's Reading of the History of Metaphysics." In *Modernity and the Hegemony of Vision,* ed., pp. 297–339. Berkeley: University of California Press.

1996 "What—Is? On Mimesis and the Logic of Identity and Difference in Heidegger and the Frankfurt School." *International Studies in Philosophy* 28 (4): 39–58.

1997a "Keeping Foucault and Derrida in Sight: Panopticism and the Politics of Subversion." In *Sites of Vision: The Discursive Construction of Sight in the History of Philosophy,* ed., pp. 397–465. Cambridge: MIT Press.

1997b *Language beyond Postmodernism: Saying and Thinking in Gendlin's Philosophy,* ed. Evanston: Northwestern University Press.

1997c "Liberating Experience from the Vice of Structuralism: The Methods of Merleau-Ponty and Nagarjuna." *Journal of the British Society for Phenomenology* 28 (2): 116–141.

1998a "Cinders, Traces, Shadows on the Page: The Holocaust in Derrida's Writing." In *Postmodernism and the Holocaust,* ed. Alan Milchman and Alan Rosenberg, pp. 265–286. Amsterdam: Rodopi.

1998b "The Empty Jug." In *Interpreting Visual Culture: Explorations in the Hermeneutics of the Visual,* ed. Barry Sandywell and Ian Heywood, pp. 185–197. New York: Routledge.

1999a "The Embodiment of the Categorical Imperative: Kafka, Foucault, Benjamin, Adorno, Levinas." *Theory, Culture and Society,* forthcoming.

1998d "The Field of Vision: Intersections of the Visible and the Invisible in Heidegger's *Feldweggespräch über das Denken* and Merleau-Ponty's *Working Notes.*" In *Visibility and Expressivity,* ed. Hugh J. Silverman and Wilhelm Wurzer. Evanston: Northwestern University Press, forthcoming.

# TWELVE

# The Unlived Life Is Not Worth Examining

## ALPHONSO LINGIS

How strange that a human, a living organism, is conceived as a material system in which needs and wants agitate it to open its eyes to the outside and seize the contents that satisfy its appetites and leave it to close back upon itself in contentment. How strange that life is conceived negatively, that the spirit is conceived as negativity.

A guppy, a cockatoo, a monkey, a human are organisms that continually generate excess energies that are discharged without thought or need of recompense. These superabundant energies are not simply dissipated; emotions that isolate, frame, crop, color, and shade events of the environment give them direction. Emotions, which dramatize, are the strength of vital movements; the primary emotions are active and thrust an organism into the thick of things.

How strange that emotions are conceived as reactions to things perceived, identified, and evaluated. Emotions break through the packaging and labeling of things that make our environment something only scanned and skimmed over. They are the forces that seek out and engage reality. Emotions are the forces with which we discover nature that summons in what we perused as the text of the universe.

Only those subjugated to the implacable discipline of common sense conceive of laughter and tears reactively—laughter as a relieved, tears as a panicky, reaction to a failure, a local breakdown, in the network of reason and order. An effervescent vitality generates the hilarity that seeks out what is incomprehensible, dysfunctional, preposterous, or absurd in any system where everything works. A brave vitality steadied by pain extends the gaze and the hand in compassion to all that suffers. When hilarity and compassion no longer drive a man or woman, he or she is moribund.

Blessing is the force poured upon the fragments, riddles, and dreadful accidents by a laughter that knows its own power to make them flourish and shine. A father is a blessing for his son not in the providential care that has set aside savings for education, life insurance, and a trust fund, but in the hearty laughter that sends the youth off on his motorcycle to roar the western highways all summer, a laughter that will invigorate the youth's own when he laughs at all the thunderstorms, tight-assed waitresses, and nights in jail in the months to come.

There is no strong grief that does not act by casting curses. Curses are not impotent reactions to the mindless blows of adversity; they are outbursts of torment that know their power to pursue the malevolent into its own lairs. Face to face, you see the force of your curses shatter the composure of the one you curse. Our curses drive the juggernauts of determinism that crush the innocent back into the no-man's-land of the unacceptable. Life knows that, like stars generating energies that produce effects across millions of light-years of empty space, it is a power to produce its effects across distance and time.

How strange is that kind of comprehension that aims to encompass the whole. How strange that kind of understanding that aims to identify everything. Mental life producing only grids and the et cetera. Resentful of disturbances, resentment of the passage of time that washes every content assimilated, it ends in contentment, the torpid satisfaction over content assimilated. Vitality drives another kind of understanding—one that opens up more, goes further. Such understanding is hilarious and grieving, blessing and cursing.

There is an inner momentum in the appetite for reality; emotions are not dissipated when released, but escalate. When one goes off to live in the mountains, one will long to hike all their trails, sleep in their rainy spring nights and winter snow, and climb all their cliffs. Once one gets a feeling for the sea, one longs to sail and dive the oceans. Lust is not content with respectful and considerate caresses and tension release; it wants another, yet wilder, orgasm, it wants orgasms on jet airplanes and in tropical swamps, it wants bondage and whips. One gets sick of the glut of cities, cultures, and nature converted into edited and framed and narrated images on the cathode ray tube; one wants to climb Macchu Pichu, get lost in the favelas of Rio and the slums of Calcutta, get dysentery in Kabul and body lice in the bordellos of Marrakesh, sleep weeks in the Amazonian rain forest and ski Antarctica.

Over the forests and skies, continents and oceans satellite-mapped and computer-programmed for the satisfaction of human wants and needs, laughter and tears, blessing and cursing have gone out of a world become silent and desolate. But blessing is the beginning and end of all environmental or ecological ethics. A curse put on the suffering of all things is the source of all religion.

Perhaps there is nothing more other, remote, foreign to us than someone of our own kind. How strange that philosophy today mainly concerns itself with the relationship between objectivity and intersubjectivity and philosophy yesterday concerned itself with the citizen in the republic of ends or the polis. As though the other concerned us as the agency that promotes our beliefs into truths—another mind, an alter ego—and as our collaborator in the collective work that is called civilization. The strong, active emotions force through to the reality of the other, the reality of otherness. They drive on to someone to laugh at, weep over, bless and curse. And to laugh and weep with, bless and curse—the world, oneself—with.

The most profound thing I know is to find oneself on the other side of the planet, in a country with which one's own is at war, with someone as uneducated as one is educated, whose culture and religion one does not share or even know, with whom one shares no common tongue—and to find oneself utterly dependent upon that other for one's very life. Three times such a person put his own life at risk to save mine. What it means to find oneself in humanity then gaped open vertiginously before me.

A thinker gains nothing today by traveling to Paris, Berlin, Tokyo, Shanghai. Whether you go for a conference or on sabbatical leave, you will only encounter educated people who think what you think about democracy and market economy, about Christian or Islamic fundamentalism and the Sendero Luminoso, about highbrow conceptual art and middlebrow Madonna, about virtual reality and cellular phones.

The only places worth traveling to, and living in for as many months as one can, are Irian Jaya, Calcutta, Bangladesh, Laos, Honduras, Nigeria, Bhutan. Oh, many more: four-fifths of humanity are outside the archipelago of the technopoles. How supremely important to know the joyous cremation potlatches of Bali and carnaval in Salvador de Bahia, on our planet today where interminable butchery goes on in central Africa and central Europe and the only cause that can unite the industrialized and democratic nations is the control of cheap Middle Eastern petroleum.

It started the night I arrived in Bogotá, when I stepped out of the hotel to get a newspaper, and the woman greeted me not with a smile but with laughter to share. The next morning I bought 100 sheets of typing paper and twenty-five envelopes the day after, and the shopkeeper had to count them over and over again, losing count because doubled up with some joke she remembered or was inventing. Waitresses in greasy spoons tell you a joke they have just heard before they hand you the menu. There is a ragged man who has a tiny newspaper stand around the corner. Every morning I go there at 6:00 A.M. He is singing. He spots me, reaches under the box for the most subversive paper, and dances up to me. I pay him ten centavos and turn back. He calls; I turn around. He asks me if I have heard this joke. I laugh but he knows I didn't get it. While I am laughing, with great skill he tosses a piece of candy into my mouth. Late afternoon, strolling crowds. Every few steps another outburst of laughter in the people I was passing by. You can't imagine what ten days of this does to you. It's worth crossing the seas for. It's more important than any political, economic, or institutional phenomenon in society today on the planet. It's as important as carnaval in Brazil.

The strong, active emotions are excremental, expenditures without return, ever escalating devotions to the unfeasible, the impossible. One loses oneself in them, divests oneself of one's role, function, character, convictions, identity. There is in an inner momentum to this dispossession. No one doubts this when he or she turns to eroticism, the most intense pleasure a human being can know, Freud said, and the force of every exultation. The supreme risk: one is never more vulnerable than when in love, when seized with erotic passion. It is through erotic passion that the other is other—goddess and tigress, god and wolf. Eroticism is the antipode of possessiveness—addiction to expropriation.

The understanding of humanity—the end of that preposterous condition known as self-respect and the joining of humanity—takes place outside the archipelago of the technopoles, in exile, in nomadism, and it commences when finally one night, driven by one's own carnal craving, one abandons oneself to a stranger, destitute in every way as one is destitute spiritually, upon whom one pours all one has of kisses and caresses. It is then that one can begin to join the sensibility, the sensuality, the alien ways of touching and shaping out of which what outside observers and experts call another culture becomes not a booty one brings back in one's souvenirs and snapshots but a force, a hilarity and a despair, a blessing and a curse.

Deep is the world, deeper than day had been aware, and deep its woe, said Zarathustra. But deeper still is joy. Joy is the most comprehensive state, he said; it alone is antimetaphysical, alone able to affirm love and hatred, woe, hell, disgrace, the cripple, world—this world, oh, you know it! Modern philosophy, which called itself antimetaphysical, undercut any possibility of believing what joy reveals of the world; joy is subjective, immanent, an intrapsychic event with but one witness. How rare today are people who are able to believe their joy; they wait for the surge of exultation to pass and make their decisions in prudence. Philosophy today needs the deep thinker who can deconstruct the epistemology of dispassionate objectivity and show that joy is the most comprehensive mind, the most penetrating mind, and that it is in the summits of joy alone that each one will see the path to take. Each important decision must be taken in joy alone.

How strange that there is a "must" in the realm of the rational activity of the mind, and in all the other realms only the prudent calculations of a human life with no other aim than its contentments. No one doubts that an imperative weighs on the rational intellect; as soon as one thinks, one finds oneself bound to conceive things with consistent concepts and to connect them coherently. The epistemology of science admits many forms of rationality, but never doubts the force of the imperative for reason, for consistency and coherence, that weighs upon every thought that arises to think.

This epistemology inherits from Kant the schema that although the force of the imperative for consistency and coherence is laid on the mind, the forms are the mind's own, and outside there is the amorphous content that thought conceptualizes and organizes. Kant was able to conceive the content of thought as without order or ordinance of its own only because of the dogmatic drowsiness of his phenomenology of perception. In this century the phenomenology of perception has been able to construct terminology and identify the patterns of consistency and coherence in the perceived world which command the forms of rationality that prevail in the diverse sectors of the natural sciences. There is a teleology in perceptual life, the phenomenology of perception demonstrated; perception is oriented toward the perception of unequivocal and scrutable things and a layout of compossible things. Perceived things are not given; they are imperatives. They do not appear in coordinates of empty geometrical space but in an ordered layout, a substantial and sequential field, which for its part is not given in perception but is imperative.

But a perceived layout of things along paths is itself suspended not in the void but in the depth of the light, in warmth, in liquid flows, upon the supporting depth of the ground. Light, warmth, flow, the ground are not objects or multiplicities of minute things; they are sensuous elements without boundaries or profiles, elemental depths which support and sustain the perceived and the perceiver. Our relationship with them is conceived only as enjoyment—an involution by which sensuous subjectivity takes form: we enjoy the light and begin to see on our own, we enjoy the support of the earth and move on our own. But the light is not only a means to see, the earth not only a means to support our self-movement to seize hold of, things. The elemental itself summons us imperatively to become luminous, warm, ardent, carnal, terrestrial.

If the phenomenology of perception has shown that things which perception perceives are not givens, but imperatives for perception, that nothingness which is the oncoming of the night is also imperative. A sentient life is not destined for things only, but for the nocturnal. The Enlightenment philosophy that set up human life as destined to know things also invested that life with mastery over things, and divested it of any destiny in the world. But the night that invades and depersonalizes summons every life, summons imperatively.

The Socratic courage, first virtue and transcendental virtue that makes the other virtues—truthfulness, magnanimity, and even wit in conversation—possible, first erected human life as a force that maintains itself of its own forces at the brink of death. The modern philosophy that divested human life of any destiny and made its freedom its supreme value made freedom in the face of death the highest stake. Dostoevski's Kirilov and Heidegger are two projects to interiorize all the force of death itself. But death comes, of itself, summons us: one day we will have to—every day we have to—obey the summons of death.

Vital tasks for philosophy: to recognize the multiple imperatives in the perceived landscape, in the elemental, in the night, in the abysses of death. To set forth the clairvoyance and decisiveness of joy as obedience to an imperative.

## Selected Bibliography

1970 "Intentionality and Corporeity." In *Analecta Husserliana,* vol 2, ed. A.-T. Tymieniecka. Dordrecht: Reidel.

1974 "The Perception of Others." *Philosophical Forum* 5 (3).

1980 "The Imperative to Be Master." *Southwestern Journal of Philosophy* 11 (2): 95–107.

1981 "Sensations." *Philosophy and Phenomenological Research* 42 (2): 60–70.

1982 "Intuition of Freedom, Intuition of Law." *Journal of Philosophy* 79 (10): 558–596.

1983a "The Fatality of Consciousness." *Philosophy Today* 27 (3–4): 247–257.

1983b "Theory and Idealization in Nietzsche." In *The Great Year of Zarathustra (1881–1981),* ed. David Goicoechea. Lanham, Md.: University Press of America.

1984a *Excesses: Eros and Culture.* Albany: State University of New York Press.

1984b "The Signs of Consciousness." *SubStance* 42 (13).

1984c "The Truth Imperative." *Auslegung* 2 (1): 317–339.

1984d "Oedipus Rex: The Oedipus Rule and Its Subversion." *Human Studies* 7.

1984e "The Visible and the Vision." *Journal of the British Society for Phenomenology* 156 (2).

1985 *Libido: The French Existential Theories.* Bloomington: Indiana University Press.

1986a *Phenomenological Explanations.* Dordrecht: Nijhoff.

1986b "Mastery in Eternal Recurrence." In *Analecta Husserliana,* vol. 21, ed. A.-T. Tymieniecka. Dordrecht: Reidel.

1988a "The Din of the Celestial Birds; or, Why I Crave to Become a Woman." In *Psychosis and Sexual Identity,* ed. David Allison et al. Albany: State University of New York Press.

1988b "Substitution." In *Postmodernism and Continental Philosophy*, ed. Hugh J. Silverman and Donn Welton. Albany: State University of New York Press.

1988c "The Elemental Imperative." *Journal of Research and Phenomenology* 18: 3–21.

1989a *Deathbound Subjectivity*. Bloomington: Indiana University Press.

1989b "Painted Faces." *Art & Text* 27: 80–92, special issue, Art Brut.

1991a "Imperatives." In *Merleau-Ponty Vivant*, ed. M. C. Dillon. Albany: State University of New York Press.

1991b "The Irrecuperable." *International Studies in Philosophy* 23 (2): 65–74.

1992a "The Destination." In *Eros and Eris: Contributions to a Hermeneutical Phenomenology Liber Amicorum for Adriaan Peperzak*. Dordrecht: Kluwer.

1992b "The Society of Dismembered Body Parts." In *Deleuze and the Transcendental Unconscious*, ed. Joan Broadhurst. Coventry, England: University of Warwick.

1992c "Phantom Equator." In *Merleau-Ponty, Hermeneutics, and Post-modernism*, ed. Thomas W. Busch and Shaun Gallagher. Albany: State University of New York Press.

1994a *The Community of Those Who Have Nothing in Common*. Bloomington: Indiana University Press.

1994b *Abuses*. Berkeley: University of California Press.

1994c *Foreign Bodies*. New York: Routledge.

1994d "Bodies That Touch Us." *Thesis* 11: 159–167.

1994e "The Society of Dismembered Body Parts." In *Gilles Deleuze and the Theater of Philosophy*, ed. Constantin Bundas and Dorothea Olkowski, pp. 289–303. New York: Routledge.

1995 *Sensation*. Atlantic Highlands, N.J.: Humanities Press.

1996 "Love Song." In *Engendering French Literature and Culture*, ed. Lawrence Schehr and Dominique Fisher. Stanford: Stanford University Press.

1998 *The Imperative*. Bloomington: Indiana University Press.

# THIRTEEN
## Holocaust Child

⊑

# BERND MAGNUS

My research interests have stressed nineteenth- and twentieth-century German philosophy ever since my early undergraduate days, centering first on Heidegger, then on Nietzsche. No noble inspiration was initially at work here; rather, as a Holocaust survivor I was captivated by the zealous notion that there must be something inherent in recent German philosophy that would help to account for the demonic conditions which my family, among millions of others, endured.

Most Holocaust survivors share with rape victims an inability to speak or write about their victimization. The reasons for their silence are similar in both cases. For both sorts of victims the experience cannot be forgotten. One may learn to cope; but one never forgets. And the experiences are so painful and searing that to speak about them is always to relive them, even if only in part. And who would willingly volunteer to be raped again in public?

Until eight years ago, I had never before been able to try to share with an anonymous public what must in the end remain unshareable. Indeed, I was more than thirty years old before I was able to speak as a survivor at all—even to myself. And then, when I was first able to recount the horrors of my childhood, I could do so only among my closest friends.

In order to avoid re-experiencing the traumas, I found myself speaking as if to a stranger even when speaking to myself, describing my psychic violations impersonally, as if someone else's childhood was being described. It seems that I needed to construct a psychological space for myself, a distance between myself and my past, a space which, if breached, always threatened to dissolve me in a cascade of tears. That has never changed. I still cannot, literally *cannot* speak about my childhood without distancing myself from it.

The external circumstances of my childhood are not difficult to recount. I was born on December 28, 1937, in what was then called Danzig, now Gdansk. At the time, Danzig was a *Freistaat*, a free city which belonged to no nation-state, a city under the jurisdiction of the League of Nations. To place my birth date in historical perspective, I was born two years after the infamous Nuremberg Laws were passed, laws which in effect disenfranchised German Jews, depriving them of property rights and legal rights to which their German citizenship would otherwise have entitled them. It was also less than half a year before the *Anschluss,* Germany's annexation of sovereign Austria.

My father was a hide expert, an expert in international leather, and had been assigned to the World Court in The Hague to settle international leather trade disputes. We were in Danzig for most of the late 1930s.

By 1944 the only Magnuses left alive in Germany from my family were my sister, my mother and I—through a succession of miracles and heroic interventions.

In 1983 I learned at Yad Vashem that one great uncle had fled successfully to Argentina before the war. My father, too, survived, having fled Germany in late 1939, I am happy to say. He had survived in the German Jewish community of refugees in Santo Domingo, in the Dominican Republic—one of the three largest Jewish communities to which the persecuted escaped when they were denied admission to the United States. He remained in the Dominican Republic until 1946. All of his initial efforts in 1940 to ransom or smuggle us out of Germany had failed; and the Red Cross listed my father among the dead—mistakenly believing that his transport ship had struck a mine and sunk. We, too, believed that he had perished.

By October 1942 my sister, my mother and I were interred at Bergen-Belsen concentration camp, and my father was informed later that we had perished there, since we were listed as among the Belsen dead. Indeed, one reason for my visit to Yad Vashem in 1983 was to revise and authenticate my family's records, to revise my family's official history.

I shall always remember the uncanny experience of poring over the lists of literally thousands of dead Magnuses—camp by camp by camp—until I could no longer continue when I read the name "David Magnus"—an Auschwitz victim—the name which is also that of my living son. I was limp by the time Ester Aram found the *original* signed 1941 SS deportation orders for my grandparents and my aunt Johanna. They had not been sent to Auschwitz, as I had been told, but were instead sent to their deaths in Lodz and Minsk. In all probability they were clubbed to death by anti-Semitic zealots, or perhaps they starved to death. I shall never know which. At any rate, among the many things that were lost in the confusion of records catalogued at Yad Vashem is the important fact that several Bergen-Belsen inmates had escaped from Belsen between 1943 and 1944, especially during the first Stuka bombing raids. My mother was one such escapee; and she fled clutching her toddler son, me.

My mother, my sister and I survived the balance of the war through cunning, now living underground, now resurfacing. We roamed Poland and Germany with forged documents in constant fear of discovery. The fact that I was circumcised proved a constant danger, which meant that I could not even urinate in a public place for fear of giving away my Jewish identity. We awaited our liberators, the Russian army, in 1945, only to be treated by them as German nationals. The fact that we were Jews was a matter of total indifference to them. The rape, torture, and murders continued. In many ways this period was as gruesome as the Holocaust itself.

Late in 1946, through a miracle too lengthy to recount, my father—who was now in New York City—learned that his wife, daughter, and one son had survived. Within eight months, on August 4, 1947, we were reunited in Ellis Island, N.Y., through the intervention of the Red Cross and Jewish Relief Organizations.

These are the outer circumstances of my early childhood, facts and details which will not be found in my entry in *Who's Who in America*. What also is not to be found there, or anywhere else for that matter, is my memory of women serially raped, mutilated and then dismembered before my very eyes—as if the presence of this seven-year-old child served to heighten the thrill of sadistic perversion. Nor will one find the memory of an illiterate Polish family of four living outside Gedienia who had hidden us and, when discovered, were forced back into their farmhouse at gunpoint while the house and its inhabitants were set ablaze; this I had to witness against the black evening sky from a crawlspace high above the town's school attic perhaps 200 meters away, while my mother held her hand over my mouth to stifle my scream to the point of near asphyxiation. Nor will one find the recorded memory of the starvation, our constant hunger, and the many times I searched graveyards for food (wild pumpkins sometimes grew there!), only to find, in the closing days of the war, dead soldiers—Russians and Germans alike—not yet buried, whose dead bodies were mute testimony transcribing their own fierce mutilation. Nor will one find the recorded memory of this child who, at the age of about eight, took the life of an attacking soldier with that soldier's own pistol.

I mention some of my gruesome memories because it seems to me that it is important to understand that the experience of children who survived the Holocaust as I did can be qualitatively different than that of adult survivors.

I was about eight years old when the war ended. Eight years old was *much too old* ever to forget; but I was also *much too young* even to begin to understand *any* of it. While the Holocaust inscribed itself upon my psyche, I could neither understand it nor contrast it—as adults could do—with what would count as a "normal" life. The boundary which divides madness from normalcy, disease from health, the boundary which marks off the singular, unique, and unspeakable from the common, ordinary, and everyday, that boundary had never been drawn for me, indeed it *could* not have a purchase on the life of a child of the Holocaust. Those who survived the Holocaust as children, as I did, are unprotected by the blissful amnesia of infancy or the adult's power to recall the normal. We are forever deprived of a childhood, not merely in the sense that we are denied a child's normal life and pleasures, but in the deeper sense that we must initially take the bizarre, the evil, the sadistic and perverse as the norm. — While adults and adolescent siblings experienced the horrors and ordeals against the background of an earlier routine life, we the children who survived *as* children knew no distinction between reality and its horrific distortion. In a certain sense each of us has had to construct, for the very first time, the very concept of a normal life against the backdrop of gallows which were our playgrounds, crematoria which were our nurseries. Much later, we alone have had to imagine during our adolescence what it *might* have been like to play cops and robbers, cowboys and Indians, instead of actually being hunted, being captured, actually killing or being killed. And while our adult parents dreamed of the sugarplums they were now denied, we could dream no such dreams since we had never experienced such pleasures.

In my case this meant that I spent my adolescence asking the questions every other thoughtful Jewish youngster was asking: "How could it have happened?," "Why did it happen?," "Why the Jews?," "Why the Germans?" At the same time I rebelled against my own religious tradition and against congregation Ramatorah when I concluded that vice and virtue, good and evil, have little to do with faith or with organized religion.

I could neither love nor believe in a God who allowed the unatoned suffering of innocent children. And what vengeance could ever restore, atone for, or compensate a childhood forever beyond recall? Like Dostoevsky's Ivan Karamazov, I was able to say, "It's not God that I don't accept, it's only that I most respectfully return him the ticket"—if the ticket meant accepting the destruction of the innocent as the price of God's higher purpose. For the Holocaust is surely the most shameful chapter of our inhumanity toward one another, one before which even God would have averted his eyes.

The standard post–World War II answers to some of those questions I mentioned earlier I found deeply unsatisfactory. It was widely believed, for example, that there must be some common measure between the doer and the deed, that crimes against humanity suffered by us—and by no means only by us—required men and women whose evil character and intentions must also be larger than life. Sometimes, of course, this was true. One need only think of the sadistic butcher of Auschwitz, Dr. Mengele, or the many other depraved and sadistic implementors of Adolf Eichmann's Final Solution to the Jewish Question. But the magnitude, the thoroughness, the systematic depravity of the Holocaust contaminated *everything* and virtually *everyone*—sometimes even its victims. And it then became increasingly difficult for me to accept the widely accepted proposition that great crimes require great evil intentions. Moreover, I had begun to notice at the same time that the passion and fervor of the House Un-American Activities Committee and the rise of what we today call McCarthyism often derived their nurture from persons who were well-intentioned, persons who even perceived themselves as combating evil rather than representing it. And I could not forget the twisted and sad irony of a segregated United States armed forces fighting against those in service to a theory of a master race.

In 1960, I began to pursue my doctorate at Columbia University, declining a fellowship at Harvard, in part so that I could study with Hannah Arendt who was a visiting professor at Columbia that year. Nineteen sixty was also the year of Eichmann's capture, the date May 11, 1960, to be precise. In April 1961 the Eichmann trial began. Hannah Arendt was there as a commentator for *The New Yorker* magazine. Her articles were revised and appeared in book form two years later under the title *Eichmann in Jerusalem: A Report on the Banality of Evil.*

Her book caused a sensation despite the fact that her thesis—which has now become a commonplace—is captured in the subtitle of her book: a report on the *banality* of evil.

The notions that evil necessarily requires sinister intentions, that the greater the crime, the more vicious the criminal, and that moral insanity requires personal insanity or demonic power—*those* are the very ideas which Hannah Arendt's book undermined and for which she was initially attacked mercilessly. Moreover, she argued that we shall have understood nothing unless we see the horror *behind* the horror—the horror that quite unextraordinary, average, banal people living what are in many respects quite ordinary lives can commit and set in motion monstrous crimes. Even Eichmann's state-appointed psychiatrists gave him a clean bill of psychic health:

> Half a dozen psychiatrists had certified him as "normal"—"More normal, at any rate, than I am after having examined him," one of them was said to have exclaimed, while another had found that his whole psychological outlook, his attitude toward his wife and children, mother and father, brothers, sisters, and friends, was "not only normal but most desirable"—and finally the minister who had paid regular visits to him in prison after the Supreme Court had finished hearing his appeal reassured everybody by declaring Eichmann to be "a man with

very positive ideas." Behind the comedy of the soul experts lay the hard fact that his was obviously no case of moral let alone legal insanity.

During my late adolescence I had concluded that even if crimes against humanity can be set in motion and committed by ordinary people, surely there must be *something* in the German mentality which accounts for my past. So I studied Nietzsche and Heidegger—who seemed to hear the voice of Being every time I heard the Gestapo knocking at our door.[1] I took comfort from books long since forgotten, books which tried to show that the Holocaust and fascism were logical consequences of Germany's intellectual history. William McGovern wrote a book, *From Luther to Hitler,* which tried to make this claim stick. Karl Popper's *The Open Society and Its Enemies* somewhat more extravagantly argued that Plato as well as Hegel and Marx were the responsible parties. Immanuel Kant was the *only* German philosopher exempted from this casuistry, for it is hard to see how the author of the categorical imperative could be read as a proto-fascist ideologist.

Then to my astonishment and despair I read the following on page 120 of *Eichmann in Jerusalem:*

> The first indication of Eichmann's vague notion that there was more involved in this whole business than the question of the soldier's carrying out orders that are clearly criminal in nature and intent appeared during the police examination, when he suddenly declared with great emphasis that he had lived his whole life according to Kant's moral precepts, and especially according to the Kantian definition of duty. This was outrageous, on the face of it, and also incomprehensible, since Kant's moral philosophy is so closely bound up with man's faculty of judgment, which rules out blind obedience. The examining officer did not press the point, but Judge Raveh, either out of curiosity or out of indignation at Eichmann's having dared to invoke Kant's name in connection with his crimes, decided to question the accused. And, to the surprise of everybody, Eichmann came up with an approximately correct definition of the categorical imperative: "I meant by my remark about Kant that the principle of my will must always be such that it can become the principle of general laws" (which is not the case with theft or murder, for instance, because the thief or the murderer cannot conceivably wish to live under a legal system that would give others the right to rob or murder him). Upon further questioning Eichmann added that he had read Kant's *Critique of Practical Reason.*

If even Kant's name can be invoked in self-justification, then what, if anything, has the experience of the Holocaust taught us about evil?

A question of such gravity requires more space and time than I am permitted on this straitjacketed occasion. What I can say, however, by way of an indirect communication is that what I have learned, among other things, is that my metaphilosophical aversion to moral philosophy—understood as the search for action-guiding principles—is rooted in the experiences I have recounted. For the belief that the correct moral theory will serve as a shield against encroaching madness seems to me to be little more than philosophical arrogance. Ask Schindler. For those with ears to hear, this also helps to explain why I find postmodernism so undaunting, indeed welcome. But all of this is a very long story, one bound to be misunderstood by the few hints given here. Far better, perhaps, to assemble a reminder that even as we act from duty, from a sense of respect for principles, even as we act out of a sense of a moral imperative, in short, the very sense of self-righteousness such behavior can engender could also itself be evil masquerading as good. Cavell helpfully reminds us that "someday, if there is a someday, we will have to learn that evil thinks of itself as good, that it could not have made such progress in the world unless people planned and performed it in all conscience."[2]

## Notes

1. Despite the sensationalism, there is very little that is news to Heidegger scholars in the recent revelations about his politics. Whatever one makes of Heidegger's involvement with the Nazis, especially during his period as Rector of Freiburg, surely his self-serving interview and recounting of his role in the 1966 *Der Spiegel* interview, "Only God Can Save Us Now," was as transparent and as shabby an evasion as could have been imagined. As a Bergen-Belsen survivor, I have been especially on guard against any animus that may unwittingly slip into my reading of Heidegger; and I think I have succeeded consistently in this. But I have resisted no less strenuously the facile inference that Heidegger's politics are connected conceptually to his philosophy—as had Tillich and Marcuse, to take only two examples. Moreover, Heidegger's horrendous personal moral bankruptcy no more allows us to set his thought aside than Frege's virulent anti-Semitism disposes of our obligation to attend to his thought.

I realize that there is something preposterous in treating a topic as complex as this in a brief footnote. And yet I cannot help conveying, in summary fashion, what attitude I think Heidegger's politics do justify: More than thirty years ago, after I had translated one of Heidegger's essays for *The Review of Metaphysics* in a way that had apparently impressed him, I declined his generous invitation to see and talk to him. I rejected his invitation—even as I read and wrote about the author/ philosopher "Heidegger"—because I found the historical person morally repellent and regarded any audience with him as compromising. This is a deeply personal matter, however, and I emphatically did not intend this episode to be action-guiding for others.

2. Stanley Cavell, *Must We Mean What We Say? A Book of Essays* (New York: Scribner's, 1969), p. 136.

## Selected Bibliography

1967 "Who Is Nietzsche's Zarathustra?" Translation of Heidegger in *Review of Metaphysics* 20 (3): 411–432.

1970 *Heidegger's Metahistory of Philosophy: Amor Fati, Being and Truth*. The Hague: Nijhoff.

1971 "Nihilism, Reason, and 'the Good.'" *Review of Metaphysics* 25: 292–311.

1973 "Nietzsche's Eternalistic Countermyth." *Review of Metaphysics* 26 (4): 604–617.

1978 *Nietzsche's Existential Imperative*. Bloomington: Indiana University Press.

1979 "Eternal Recurrence." *Nietzsche-Studien* 8: 362–377.

1981 "Heidegger's Metahistory of Philosophy Revisited." *The Monist* 64: 445–466.

1983 "Perfectibility and Attitude in Nietzsche's Übermensch." *Review of Metaphysics* 36 (3): 633–659.

1985a "Jesus, Christianity, and Superhumanity." In *Nietzsche and the Judaeo-Christian Tradition*, ed. O'Flaherty, Sellner, and Helm. Chapel Hill: University of North Carolina Press.

1985b "Nietzsche and the Project of Bringing Philosophy to an End." In *Nietzsche as Critic and Affirmative Thinker*, ed. Y. Yovel. The Hague: Nijhoff.

1985c "The End of the 'End of Philosophy.'" In *Hermeneutics and Deconstruction*, ed. H. Silverman and D. Idhe. Albany: State University of New York Press.

1987 "Nietzsche." In *Encyclopaedia Britannica*.

1988a "The Deification of the Commonplace: *Twilight of the Idols*." In *Reading Nietzsche*, ed. R. C. Solomon and K. Higgins. Oxford: Oxford University Press.

1988b "The Use and Abuse of *The Will to Power*." In *Reading Nietzsche*, ed. R. C. Solomon and K. Higgins. Oxford: Oxford University Press.

1989a "Nietzsche and Postmodern Criticism." *Nietzsche-Studien* 18: 301–317.

1989b "Self-Consuming Concepts." *International Studies in Philosophy*, Nietzsche Issue, 21 (2): 63–71.

1991 "Deconstruction Site." *Philosophical Topics* 19 (2): 215–243.

1993a *Nietzsche's Case: Philosophy as/and Literature*. With Stanley Stewart and Jean-Pierre Mileur. New York: Routledge.

1993b "Postmodern Philosophy and Politics." In *History of European Ideas* 16 (4–6): 561–569.

1994a *Cambridge Companions to Philosophy: Nietzsche*, ed. with Kathleen Higgins. Cambridge: Cambridge University Press.

1994b "Reading Ascetic Reading: *Toward the Genealogy of Morals* and the Path Back to the World." With Jean-Pierre Mileur and Stanley Stewart. In *Nietzsche, Genealogy, Morality*, ed. Richard Schacht. Berkeley: University of California Press.

1994c Jacques Derrida, *Specters of Marx: The State of the Debt, the Task of Mourning, and the New International*, ed. with Stephen Cullenberg. New York: Routledge.

1994d *Whither Marxism? Global Crises in International Perspective*, ed. with Stephen Cullenberg. New York: Routledge.

1995a "Postmodern." In *The Cambridge Dictionary of Philosophy*, ed. Robert Audi. Cambridge: Cambridge University Press.

1995b "Postmodern Pragmatism." In *Pragmatism: From Progressivism to Post-modernism*, ed. D. Depew and R. Hollinger. New York: Praeger.

1996 "Nietzsche's Works and Their Times." With Kathleen Higgins. In *The Cambridge Companion to Nietzsche*. Cambridge: Cambridge University Press.

1997a "Friedrich Nietzsche's Philosophy: 'Overview' as Ascetic Impulse." In *The Oxford Dictionary of Aesthetics*, ed. Michael Kelly (1998).

1997b "How the 'True Text' Finally Became a Fable." *Nietzscheanna* 6: 1–27.

1997c "Philosophy as a Kind of Writing: *Der Fall Nietzsche*." *REAL: Yearbook of Research in English and American Literature* 13: 125–147.

1997d "The Unexamined Book Is Not Worth Reading." *International Studies in Philosophy* 29 (3): 139–144.

# FOURTEEN
## Reflections

▣

# DAVID M. RASMUSSEN

For most of my philosophical career, apart from fulfilling my duties as professor, I have divided my time between being an author and journal editor. Since my claim to Continental Philosophy is dependent on both roles, for hypothetical purposes allow me to separate them.

### Author

That I was captured by Continental Philosophy as a student perhaps should come as no surprise. As an undergraduate at the University of Minnesota I had studied Kierkegaard along with analytic philosophy. As a graduate student at Chicago I had been inspired by seminars on Hegel, Schleiermacher, Kant, and Husserl. Also, with Mircea Eliade, I studied phenomenology of religion, focusing particularly on his methodology, which had been informed by both the linguistics of Saussure and the phenomenology of Husserl. Thus, when I read by accident Paul Ricoeur's essay, "The Symbol Gives Rise to Thought," although I had been trying to become a Chicago pragmatist, I turned to hermeneutic phenomenology.

Although my original book in Continental Philosophy was on the hermeneutic phenomenology of Paul Ricoeur, whose work continues to influence me, my interests changed—or, one might say, broadened—rather quickly to a philosophical position informed by critique. Eventually, this move away from hermeneutic phenomenology led by a rather circuitous route to Critical Theory. No doubt this transition was fueled by the events of the day, the Vietnam war, the civil rights movement, and the general upheaval experienced by one living in American society in the late sixties. I had already become involved in the civil rights movement while pursuing graduate studies at the University of Chicago. This background, combined with the rather tumultuous days of the early seventies, led me to reexamine my commitment to a certain kind of Continental Philosophy.

In *Mythic-Symbolic Language and Philosophical Anthropology,* I had argued, through a reading of Ricoeur's work, for a hermeneutic orientation to language open to a plurality of interpretations. This, I was to discover, was not enough to answer the increasing demands for a kind of committed philosophical position which could appropriate the needs of society. Already in *Symbol and Interpretation,* I had begun to argue for a kind of political hermeneutic phenomenology, but I became dissatisfied with the resources of phenomenology for critical social analysis. Ultimately it was in my essay *Between Autonomy and Sociality,* which appeared in the first issue of *Cultural Hermeneutics,* that I sought to critique the notion of autonomy, ultimately traceable to Kant, present in both Weberian and phenomenological (Husserl-Schutz) modes of analysis. My critique was based on a form of social philosophy that was informed by Hegel and, of course, Marx. That move, combined with extended study and research in Munich and Frankfurt under the auspices of Fulbright, Mellon, and Boston College, led me eventually, though not immediately, to Critical Theory.

As the series of articles written in the mid-seventies after *Autonomy and Sociality* attest, I became preoccupied with the question of validity in relation to the problem of intersubjectivity. As one originally influenced by the hermeneutic critique of transcendental phenomenology, I was aware of the difficulties associated with establishing a valid foundation for intersubjectivity on a transcendental level. I thought that one could more effectively address the problem by turning to the texts of Hegel and Marx, with the additional advantage of being able to address philosophically the issues of practical life. At that point I was at least momentarily persuaded by Max Horkheimer's formulation of the distinction between traditional and Critical Theory. For a time I attempted to apply elements of that critique to aspects of Husserlian phenomenology.

About that time, I began to read Jürgen Habermas. Habermas's early attempt to rethink the foundations of Critical Theory fascinated me. Although, as my review of his *Legitimation Crisis* in 1976 indicated, I was not entirely satisfied with his attempt to unite the traditions of Marx and Weber, I continued to be interested in his overall project. It was my good fortune to spend time with Habermas in Munich (1981–2), Boston (1984), and Frankfurt (1986 and 1988). This was the period immediately after the publication in German of *Theory of Communicative Action,* the working out of the discourse ethics, and the development of a philosophy of law. The result was my *Reading Habermas,* published in 1990.

Something unexpected happened while I was writing the book on Habermas: my phenomenological past began to haunt me. This is not to say that it became the basis for my critique of Habermas, but rather that Habermas's attempt to rehabilitate Critical Theory at the transcendental level had a familiar ring to it. To one such as myself, who became literate in the nuances of modern German philosophical history, one could not overlook this repetition of the recent philosophical past. This appeared to be something like an attempt to rehabilitate the claims of the first generation of phenomenologists against the second. Of course, important distinctions needed to be made. Habermas's claims were rehabilitated as claims about language and not about consciousness. And, of course, that could make all the difference. Nonetheless, Habermas's project, which for the most part I supported, seemed weak at precisely the point where speech-act theory was used to resolve the traditional problem of intersubjectivity at the level of validity. Indeed, I was left with precisely this problem at the end of *Reading Habermas*.

The next task would be to think through the resources of Critical Theory one more time, a task my most recent essays attempt to do. This is not to reject the Habermasian program, which I regard, in its current incarnation as a philosophy of law in *Facticity and Validity,* as perhaps Habermas's finest achievement and certainly a contribution to the German tradition of philosophy of law that will stand with Hegel and Weber. Rather, it appears to me that the task will be to rethink the linguistic foundations of a Critical Theory beyond the relatively narrow confines of a discourse based solely on an analysis of speech-acts. As I have argued elsewhere, the claims for language are too narrow, while the claims for a theory of rationality are too strong for such an approach.

### Editor

The history of *Philosophy and Social Criticism* began in 1973, when the journal was founded as *Cultural Hermeneutics*. Although that title lasted through only four volumes, we managed to organize and publish a conference, the first of its kind in English, on Hermeneutics and Critical Theory, a special issue on the sociology of knowledge, and early essays on Adorno, Heidegger, Habermas, Foucault, Husserl, Schleiermacher, Dilthey, Rawls, James, Weber, Marx, Hegel, Derrida, Humboldt, Ricoeur, Sartre, Althusser, Mannheim, Gadamer, Schutz, Ortega, and others. The journal also addressed the relationship of philosophy to social science as a theme shaped by the debates over *Geisteswissenschaften* which had been highlighted by Dilthey and effectively brought into twentieth-century discussions of philosophy and social science by phenomenology. Given the spirit of the 1970s, these debates were not without their critical edge. Looking back, it appears that this orientation was intentional, for it was precisely our desire to focus on what we and our contributors thought were the critical issues of the day. The issues of the early seventies, the problem of the relationship between theory and practice, the proper status of the philosophy of action, the conceptualization of the themes of everyday life, were all central to the journal. As the original editorial suggested, we conceived of *Cultural Hermeneutics* as a kind of open forum in which debates over these issues could occur. One can see in retrospect that at least some of those debates did occur. There were, for example, discussions of Critical Theory in its relationship to practice; considerations of the status of hermeneutics in relationship to a philosophy of action; reflections on the concept of justice in political philosophy; critiques of methodologies in the social sciences; the emerging legitimation crisis; critiques of ideology; evaluations of the status of emancipation; analysis of the status of art in relationship to canonical interpretation—even critiques of patriarchal readings of texts found representation in these pages. Imbued with the spirit of a European philosophical tradition which was just beginning to make its mark outside Europe and inside the U.S., the journal attempted to open up a new critical discussion.

The second phase of this story begins with the reincarnation of *Cultural Hermeneutics* as *Philosophy and Social Criticism*. In the four years we had been publishing the journal, we had become increasing skeptical of the word "hermeneutics." The term itself was not entirely to blame. Frankly, when we started publishing the journal, the term was barely known except to that small set of practicing professionals like myself who assumed it to be commonplace. Further, hermeneutics, when it became known to a larger public, tended to convey interpretation only. We discovered that although the journal was hermeneutical, it was doing something more than hermeneutic interpretation. A similar problem related to the term "cultural," which was originally used to convey an interdisciplinary intention. Reluctantly, after some deliberation, the decision was made to drop the term "hermeneutics" altogether. Instead, we decided to tap into that venerable tradition of critical philosophy, which began with the German enlightenment, to which the modern continental philosophical tradition owes its origin. Further, it was that tradition which had taken up again the themes of classical philosophy with a focus on society and public life. Thus was born the title *Philosophy and Social Criticism,* which continues to convey our intention more effectively.

The debates which began in the late seventies and continue today found their way into the pages of the newly named journal. Nuclear war, deconstruction, feminism, ethics and morality, aesthetics, narrative, self-identity, democratization, re-evaluations of Critical Theory, the critical debate over

Heidegger, the final work of Foucault, the emerging debate over rights, the new discourse on politics and law, the debate over the status of the social sciences—all these were in various ways the subjects of essays and special issues, which in the cases of Foucault, ethics and morality, and narrativity became books.

The third phase of the journal is marked by a transition from the role of independent publisher to join forces with an established publisher. I have to acknowledge that the world has changed somewhat from the time when the journal began more than two decades ago. When I began publication, the names of the obscure European thinkers to whom our writers were referring in the early years, or who were in fact contributors themselves, are now commonplace. The terms "hermeneutics," "Critical Theory," and "deconstruction" are now ubiquitous. The boundaries between Anglo-American and continental thought are breaking down. Even the idea of a kind of thinking that can be at the same time theoretical, critical, and public seems to have made some progress in the public mind. My conclusion from this reading is that my journalistic task is not diminished thereby, but enhanced. Finally, I suspect that Continental Philosophy in the present, as opposed to the past, will define itself less in a purely historical and more in an originary fashion. The great names of the continental past will bow to the issues of the present.

## Selected Bibliography

1968 "Mircea Eliade: Structural Hermeneutics and Philosophy." *Philosophy Today* 12: 138–147.

1971 *Mythic-Symbolic Language and Philosophical Anthropology.* The Hague: Nijhoff.

1973a "Between Autonomy and Sociality." *Cultural Hermeneutics* 1: 3–5.

1973–77 *Cultural Hermeneutics.* Dordrecht: Reidel. Editor-in-chief for 400-page annual volume.

1974 *Symbol and Interpretation.* The Hague: Nijhoff. Translated into Japanese.

1975 "The Quest for Valid Knowledge in the Context of Society." *Analecta Husserliana* 5: 165–178.

1976a "Legitimation Crisis: Late Capitalism and Social Theory." *Cultural Hermeneutics* 3 (4): 59–70.

1976b "Capital-Sociality and the Status of the Subject." *Studies in Soviet Thought* 16: 157–173.

1978a "Marx's Attitude toward Religion." *Listening* 13 (1): 27–37.

1978- *Philosophy and Social Criticism.* London: Sage Publications. Editor-in-chief.

1982 "The Enlightenment Project: After Virtue." *Philosophy and Social Criticism* 3 (4): 410–425.

1985a "Communicative Action and the Fate of Modernity." *Theory, Culture and Society.*

1988a "Communication and the Law." *Praxis International* 8 (2): 155–170. Translated into Italian.

1988b *The Final Foucault,* ed. with James Bernauer. Cambridge: MIT Press. Translated into Japanese.

1989a *The Narrative Path: The Later Works of Paul Ricoeur,* ed. with Peter Kemp. Cambridge: MIT Press.

1989b "Introduction: Universalism vs. Communitarianism in Ethics." *Philosophy and Social Criticism* 14 (1): 2–3.

1990a *Reading Habermas.* Oxford: Blackwell. Translated into Italian in 1993; translated into French in 1997.

1990b *Universalism vs. Communitarianism in Ethics.* Cambridge, Mass.: MIT Press.

1991 "On the Necessity of Violence for Any Possibility of Justice." *Cardozo Law Review* 13 (4): 1263–1265.

1993a "Critical Theory: Horkheimer, Adorno, Habermas." In *Routledge Dictionary of the History of Philosophy,* vol. 8, ed. Richard Kearney, pp. 254–289. New York: Routledge.

1993b "Moral Consciousness and Communicative Action." *Philosophical Quarterly* 43 (17): 571–572.

1993c "Social Philosophy in Transition." In *Freedom, Dharma and Rights,* ed. W. Creighton Peden and Yeager Hudson, pp. 3–18. Lewiston, N.Y.: Edwin Mellen.

1993d "Reflections on the 'End of History': Politics, Identity and Civil Society." *Philosophy and Social Criticism* 18 (3/4): 235–250.

1993e "Business Ethics and Postmodernism: A Response." *Business Ethics Quarterly* 3 (3): 271–277.

1994 "How Is Valid Law Possible?" *Philosophy and Social Criticism* 20 (4): 21–44.

1995 "Die Rechtswissenschaft und das Problem der Geltung: Kritische Bemerkungen zu Jürgen Habermas." In *Die Gegenwart der Gerechtigkeit,* ed. Christoph Demmerling and Thomas Rentsch. Berlin: Academie Verlag.

1996a "Jurisprudence and Validity." *Cardozo Law Review* 17 (4–5): 1059–1082.

1996b *The Handbook of Critical Theory.* Oxford: Blackwell.

1996c "Rethinking Subjectivity: Narrative Identity and the Self." In *Ricoeur and the Hermeneutics of Action,* ed. Richard Kearney. London: Sage.

1998 "Narrative, Rights and Legal Practice" (in Russian, Bulgarian, and Yugoslavian). In *Reinterpreting the Political: Continental Philosophy and Political Theory,* ed. Lenore Langsdorf, pp. 155–169. Albany: State University of New York Press.

# FIFTEEN
## An Unpurloined Autobiography

## WILLIAM J. RICHARDSON

I first met Martin Heidegger in the late fall of 1955, when his probing gaze seemed to look through me and beyond me toward some Other that he was sensitive to and I was not. Emboldened by the advice of others whose judgment seemed, at least, to be trustworthy, I took the sign "Office Hours" literally and ventured into the inner sanctum after one of his lectures in the series that constituted the Freiburg University lecture course that term, "The Principle of Reason." His manner was grave, reserved, and professionally indulgent toward this intrepid tyro asking advice from a world-class titan about a doctoral dissertation topic that would explore the titan's thought. I was at that point about to begin graduate studies at the Higher Institute of Philosophy (Louvain) and had been allowed to postpone the beginning of class work precisely in order to be able to follow this course of Heidegger (possibly his last, since he was already "professor emeritus"), in the flesh. I was hoping to decide on a thesis topic early so that it would help to give some specific focus to the work I was about to undertake at Louvain. News of the course had come to me quite by accident while passing through Freiburg the previous summer, and I was eager not to miss whatever advantage the unique opportunity afforded. At any rate, the interview with Heidegger was brief but pointed and, in fact, very helpful. I passed several possible thesis topics by him: no, "The Ontological Difference" would not really be a feasible theme (he had written much more that had not yet been published); yes, "The Nature of Foundational Thinking" would probably be manageable (for the essential had in fact already been said). And so the long journey began.

That initial Freiburg experience was significant in several other ways. Through the purest of accidents I came to share an apartment with a Sicilian Jesuit, Virgilio Fagone, who was one of the few foreigners invited to participate in Heidegger's highly exclusive seminar on Hegel's *Logic* that concluded with Heidegger's own contribution in the form of his essay, "The

Ontotheological Structure of Metaphysics." Fagone would return from these seminar sessions and regale me with stories of what happened there, often reporting Heidegger's remarks concerning his early work in light of the later, especially when the remarks referred to his own interpretation of *Being and Time*. Thus I began to realize vaguely that there was something unique about Heidegger's conception of thinking, and that it was peculiarly stretched between "early" and "late" through what Fagone kept calling the *Kehre*. To be sure, I understood none of this, but Fagone's enthusiasm was so infectious that it was easy to disregard my own incomprehension and nod in agreement with him. Eventually, of course, I did begin to notice differences here and there between what I took to be characteristic of an "earlier" (i.e., pre-*Kehre)* or "later" (post-*Kehre)* style and began to note them in shorthand marginal glosses as "I" and "II" respectively. What began as a convenience became a habit and, without any objection from my subsequent hyper-critical readers (including Heidegger himself at the end), eventually became part of the published version of the work. No one thought to warn me that so innocent an idiosyncrasy might scandalize so many, who took it as an affirmation of a division in Heidegger's development that the entire research disproved. Yet after all these years, I still can't feel any real remorse for that ill-starred orthography. It has always seemed to me that the *Kehre*, with its inevitable "before" ("I") and "after" ("II")—however its nature is understood and whatever its orthography—is by Heidegger's own testimony here to stay and will survive us all. That said, my debt to Fagone is obviously beyond measure.

The semester in Freiburg offered another happy accident. In some mysterious way that I still cannot account for, I fell in with a small group of German students (plus one South American), who were reading *Sein und Zeit* together as only Germans can—word by word, line by line. For whatever reason, they accepted me as a member of their group and taught me how to read Heidegger—and very much more. Coming from different backgrounds, they represented a wide cultural, religious, and political spectrum, but all shared in common the experience of growing up in Nazi Germany, subjected to the ideological excesses of Hitler's Youth Movement. Over many a *Mensa* luncheon ($0.25 per meal at the time) and afternoon coffee and long evening of wining, we clawed over again and again (often with intense disagreement) Heidegger's relation to the Nazi movement—whether personal, political, or philosophical. The result was that when Victor Farias's sensationalist *Heidegger and Nazism* caused such a stir when published in France (1987) and later in America (1989), having been refused by German publishers, we are told, as simply the same old thing, the substance of his "revelations" (if not all of the details) seemed tired, indeed—no longer shocking or surprising or new.

Once settled in Louvain in the spring of 1956, I found that the seductions of Freiburg were quickly forgotten in the pressures of course work. Alphonse De Waelhens, who had previously agreed to direct a dissertation on Heidegger, was appalled at my choice of theme, Heidegger's conception of "essential" thinking ("are you really *serious* about writing on that?"), but with a blind act of faith in Heidegger's own judgment, I managed a squeamish "yes," De Waelhens's skepticism notwithstanding. It is a tribute to his own profound intellectual integrity that he supported my choice of topic, once made, from beginning to end, offering me always a rigorous critical judgment upon everything I brought him or asked about but insisting on no personal position of his own. And this was despite the fact that my eventual reading of the "earlier" Heidegger radically challenged his own (which had long since become classic in the secondary literature), and even though he had profound disdain for the entire drift of the "later" Heidegger, which he considered to be "poetry," not "philosophy" at all. In the best of ways, then, he let my own endeavor "be"; without this liberty of the very best sort, my own work, such as it was, could never have come to pass at all. How could any mentor do more?

Course work was, to be sure, course work, but because of the Heidegger connection I was allowed to sit in on a faculty seminar on still unpublished texts of Husserl organized by the Husserl Archives, and led by its director, Henry Van Breda. This included such participants (in addition to De Waelhens) as Albert Dondeyne, Andre Wylleman, George Van Riet, Jacques Taminiaux, and one other student, Joseph Kockelmans. The level of discussion was quite over my head for a long time, but the experience was enormously enriching.

After finishing course work at Louvain, I returned to Freiburg to begin direct dissertation research. For a year and a half, I lived in quasi-isolation as chaplain to a group of Benedictine nuns in a removed Black Forest cloister built on a place of worship that dated back to Roman times. In this idyllic setting, with a full view of the Vosges, the Rhine, the Alps of Switzerland by (clear) day and the lights of Basel by night, I settled down to work deliberately with no other instruments than the texts of Heidegger himself (all that had been published up to that time), plus the necessary dictionaries. When the work was substantially finished and secondary sources checked, I drew up a scrupulously complete twenty-five page summary of my results in German. Through the good offices of Professor Max Muller, who had become a much valued unofficial mentor on the spot, I sent it to Heidegger, requesting an interview to solicit his criticism. This he granted in February, 1959, and he could not have been more gracious to me personally or more generous with his time. That four-hour *Gespräch* with one of the great philosophical minds of the twentieth century (perhaps of many other centuries, too), remains one of the richest memories of my own intellectual experience. Two days later, Max Muller's assistant stopped me on the street to say that after the visit Heidegger had talked with Muller by phone and told him that he had been favorably impressed by my work. "After so many misreadings, how is it possible," I was told he asked, "that an *American* could get it right?" But this was thirdhand. True or not, it was this alleged seal of approval that, with Max Muller's encouragement, emboldened me to ask Heidegger if he would consider writing a preface for the book when published. When he agreed to do so, I was surprised and, of course, delighted.

But publication was still a long way off. Part of the original research was defended as a doctoral dissertation in 1960. De Waelhens's smiling, sardonic remark at the public defense expressed his own feelings about the entire enterprise: "You seem to have made some sense out of later Heidegger and should do well back in America. You are very lucky, for 'in the realm of the blind, one-eyed men are kings.'" The book itself appeared three years later as: *Heidegger: Through Phenomenology to Thought,* Preface by Martin Heidegger. In 1962, I was invited to defend it publicly as part of the procedure of receiving from the Institute the title of *Maître Agrégé.*

With this kind of background in philosophy in general and Heidegger in particular, what led me subsequently to take an interest in psychoanalysis? After my return to America, I was invited to speak a great deal about Heidegger and to expand the implications of his work in many different directions. One of these directions called itself "existential psychoanalysis," a movement inspired in Europe by Sartre on the one hand and Ludwig Binswanger on the other. In America, it was led chiefly by Rollo May and Leslie Farber, who sought to expand classical psychoanalysis into more contemporary forms without the support of careful, rigorous philosophical conceptuality. I was often asked to explore Heidegger's relevance to such a movement and hence began to think about the application of Heideggerian analyses to specifically anthropological issues. At the same time, I became deeply involved in the counseling of students: problems that were presented as philosophical rapidly become personal. In such matters, I found it all too easy to drift out beyond my depth. This I knew to be dangerous and decided that I should either get some formal training as a counselor or drop this psychotherapeutic direction of the philosophical reflection completely, for it seemed cavalier to discuss the philosophical dimension of psychotherapy without responsible hands-on experience of the real thing.

In 1969 I had the good fortune to receive a grant from the Society for Religion in Higher Education for interdisciplinary study and spent it as a visiting scholar at the Austen Riggs Center in Stockbridge, Massachuetts, a small, not-for-profit institution dealing with the treatment of seriously disturbed mental patients in an open setting. My plan was to explore the relationship between psychoanalysis and philosophy, and this setting gave me the opportunity and the distance to reflect on the direction my own work should take. It was there that I decided to seek formal psychoanalytic training. If I were accepted into a worthwhile program, I would pursue that option; if not, I would abandon that direction completely and pursue one of several other options that were available at the time. As things turned out, I was accepted into a four-year program at the William Alanson White Institute in New York, whose theoretical orientation came from the interpersonal theories of Harry Stack Sullivan. Upon finishing the program, I was invited to join the senior staff at the Austen Riggs Center as Director of Research in 1974.

That same year, another new arrival came aboard as director of education. Formerly director of admissions at Chestnut Lodge, another private, long-term treatment facility, Edward Podvoll was a well-educated, highly gifted, and experienced clinician. One day he observed that there was a lot we could learn from each other and suggested that we read some significant text together. Great idea! My first thought was that *Being and Time* might be too difficult to start with and suggested that we read Paul Ricoeur's study of Freud. For whatever reason, Podvoll was not interested in a philosophical reading of Freud by a non-analyst. My next suggestion was Jacques Lacan's "Function and Field of Speech and Language in Psychoanalysis." To be sure, I had not read much Lacan at that point but had heard his name often during my years in Europe as a "second Freud" who often drew nourishment for his speculation from the likes of Hegel and Heidegger. So together we struggled through this essay. Podvoll was enchanted with it, much more than I. His own spiritual quest had led him into Buddhism, and Lacan's conception of the ego as mirror image as well as of the subject as "without a head" suited his speculative needs perfectly.

The following year, John Muller, a friend and colleague whom I had known from his student days, joined the Riggs staff as research associate. Although Muller, after several years on a Sioux reservation in North Dakota, had come to Riggs with an interest in Jung, and I had long desired to pursue the Heideggerian directions of Medard Boss, Podvoll, who was directing the educational program for the Riggs Fellows and was senior to both of us in terms of clinical experience, wanted to pursue Lacan. Muller and I co-led seminars on Lacan for the staff at Riggs, then for graduate students at Fordham University, and on one occasion for professional psychotherapists at large in a summer institute on Cape Cod sponsored by the Albert Einstein College of Medicine. Although Podvoll soon left Riggs, Muller and I were already caught up in the momentum of a growing interest in Lacan in America and decided to publish the pedagogical materials we used to present the essays of Lacan that had been translated into English (*Lacan and Language: A Reader's Guide to the Écrits*). The methodology proved successful. We then applied it to Lacan's essay on Edgar Allan Poe's "The Purloined Letter." This essay had been taken out of its chronological sequence and made to serve as the introductory essay to Lacan's *Écrits* (1966). There it triggered a celebrated critique by Jacques Derrida. This in turn occasioned a series of essays that circled around Derrida's critique and crystallized many issues that preoccupied deconstructive literary criticism in its relation to psychoanalysis. Starting with our interpretative study of Lacan's original essay, we put all these other essays together into a volume entitled *The Purloined Poe: Poe, Lacan, Derrida.*

I left Riggs in 1979, and after a semester of lecturing at Oxford spent a year in Paris trying to understand Lacan's thought from the inside, so to speak. I began a second didactic analysis, this time in the Lacanian mode, motivated by the same principle that in matters psychoanalytic one ought not write about that of which one has no hands-on experience. When I joined the Philosophy department at Boston College in 1981, I continued at long range the didactic analysis and began a limited psychoanalytic practice along with my teaching responsibilities.

Does all this amount to the abandoning of philosophy in favor of psychoanalysis? I have never thought of it that way. I am profoundly convinced that psychoanalysis in general and Lacan in particular are gravely in need of a philosophical base, and that Heidegger's thinking offers a suggestive paradigm for approaching that task. I do not mean that Lacan's early propaedeutic use of the early Heidegger can be extrapolated into some kind of conflation of the two. That would betray them both. But surely there is some mutual relevance in the fact that each recognizes the primordiality of Language as such. For each, Language speaks human being rather than the reverse, though Lacan's concern is an ontic one while for Heidegger the Being/*Ereignis*/*Kehre* question remains primordial. And there is still Truth for both: Lacan articulates it in terms of Symbolic/Imaginary/Real intertwined in the Borromean knot; Heidegger still speaks of *Aletheia* and the "not" ingredient to *Ereignis*. Is it possible that in the end each might illuminate the other if we let adventive thought have its way with us? Perhaps not, but how will we know if we don't ask? And isn't the asking itself that reaches beyond either a kind of fidelity to both, if only because it is the ultimate exposure to Advent?

## Selected Bibliography

1963 *Heidegger: Through Phenomenology to Thought,* Preface by Martin Heidegger. The Hague: Nijhoff.

1965a "Heidegger and Theology." *Theological Studies* 26: 86–100.

1965b "Heidegger and God—and Professor Jonas." *Thought* 40 (156): 13–40.

1965c "Heideggers Weg durch die Phänomenologie zum Seinsdenken." *Philosophisches Jahrbuch* 62: 385–396.

1965d "The Place of the Unconscious in Heidegger." *Review of Existential Psychology and Psychiatry* 5 (3): 265–290.

1967a "Heidegger and the Quest of Freedom." *Theological Studies* 28: 286–307.

1967b "Kant and the Late Heidegger." In *Phenomenology in America,* ed. J. M. Edie, pp. 125–144. Chicago: Quadrangle.

1968a "Heidegger's Critique of Science." *The New Scholasticism* 42 (4): 511–536.

1968b "The Transcendence of God in the World of Man." *Proceedings of the Catholic Theological Society of America* 23: 201–220.

1971 "Humanism and Existential Psychology." *Existential Humanistic Psychology,* ed. T. C. Greening, pp. 121–133. Belmont, Calif.: Brooks-Cole.

1977a "Heidegger's Way through Phenomenology to the Thinking of Being." *Listening* 12: 21–37.

1977b "Martin Heidegger: In Memoriam." *Commonweal* 106: 16–18. Reprinted in *Man and World* 10 (1): 6–12.

1978 "Religion and Mental Health." In *Encyclopedia of Bioethics,* ed. Center for Bioethics, Kennedy Institute, Georgetown University, Washington, D.C., pp. 1067–1071. New York: Macmillan.

1978–79 "The Mirror Inside: Problem of the Self." *Review of Existential Psychology and Psychiatry* 16 (1/2/3): 95–112.

1980a "Piaget, Lacan, and Language." In *Piaget: Philosophy and the Human Sciences,* ed. H. Silverman, pp. 144–170. Atlantic Highlands, N.J.: Humanities Press.

1980b "Phenomenology and Psychoanalysis." *Journal of Phenomenological Psychology* 11 (2): 1–20.

1982a "Lacan's View of Language and Being." *Psychoanalytic Review* 69 (2): 229–233.

1982b *Lacan and Language: A Reader's Guide to the Écrits.* With J. P. Muller. New York: International Universities Press.

1983a "Lacan and the Subject of Psychoanalysis." In *Interpreting Lacan,* ed. J. H. Smith and W. Kerrigan, pp. 51–74. New Haven: Yale University Press.

1983b "Psychoanalysis and the Being-question." In *Interpreting Lacan,* ed. J. H. Smith and W. Kerrigan. pp. 139–159. New Haven: Yale University Press.

1983c "La psychanalyse et la question de Dieu." *Foi et raison à partir de St. Thomas. Le Discours Psychoanalytique* 8: 17–20.

1985 "Lacanian Theory." In *Models of the Mind: Their Relationships to Clinical Work,* ed. A. Rothstein, pp. 101–117. New York: International Universities Press.

1986a "Psychoanalysis and the God-question." *Thought* 61 (240): 68–83.

1986b "Psychoanalysis and Anti-humanism: Lacan's Legacy." *Krisis* 5–6: 61–80.

1987a "Ethics and Psychoanalysis." *Journal of the American Academy of Psychoanalysis* 40: 196–201.

1987b *Ouvrir les Écrits de Lacan,* adapté par P. Julien. With J. P. Muller. Toulouse: Écrits.

1987c "Meaning in Psychoanalysis." In *Phenomenology-Meaning-Psychotherapy,* the Second Annual Symposium of the Simon Silverman Phenomenology Center. Duquesne University, pp. 89–107. Pittsburgh: Duquesne University, Simon Silverman Phenomenology Center.

1988a "Lacan and the Problem of Psychosis." In *Psychosis and Sexual Identity: Towards a Post-modern View of the Schreber Case,* ed. D. Allison et al., pp. 18–29. Albany: State University of New York Press.

1988b "Lacan and Non-philosophy." In *Philosophy and Non-philosophy since Merleau-Ponty,* pp. 120–135. Continental Philosophy series, vol. 1, ed. Hugh J. Silverman. New York: Routledge.

1988c *The Purloined Poe: Lacan, Derrida, and Psychoanalytic Reading.* With J. P. Muller. Baltimore: Johns Hopkins University Press.

1990a "Coufontaine, Adsum." In *Psychoanalysis and Religion,* ed. J. Smith, pp. 60–73. Baltimore: Johns Hopkins University Press.

1990b "Heidegger's Concept of 'World.'" In *Reconsidering Psychology: Perspectives from Continental Philosophy,* ed. P. Williams and J. Falconer, pp. 198–209. Pittsburgh: Duquesne University Press.

1991a "The Subject of Hermeneutics and the Hermeneutics of the Subject." In *Hermeneutics and the Tradition,* Proceedings of the American Catholic Philosophical Association, 1988, 14 (2)–15 (1).

1991b "La vérité dans la psychanalyse." In *Lacan avec les philosophes,* pp. 191–200. Paris: Albin Michel.

1991c "Law and Right." *Cardozo Law Review* 13 (4): 1339–1342.

1992a "Desire and Its Vicissitudes." In *Phenomenology and Lacanian Psychoanalysis,* Proceedings of Eighth Annual Symposium of the Simon Silverman Phenomenology Center, Duquesne University, pp. 13–36. Pittsburgh: Duquesne University, Simon Silverman Phenomenology Center.

1992b "Heidegger's Truth and Politics." In *Ethics and Danger: Essays on Heidegger and Continental Thought,* ed. A. Dallery and C. Scott, with H. Roberts, pp. 11–24. Albany: State University of New York Press.

1992c "'Like straw': Psychoanalysis and the Question of God." In *Eros and Eris: Liber Smicorum en hommage a Adriaan Peperzak.* The Hague: Kluwer.

1992d "Love and the Beginning." *Contemporary Psychoanalysis* 28 (3): 423–441.

1992e "The Third Generation of Desire." *The Letter: Lacanian Perspectives on Psychoanalysis* 1 (Summer 1994): 117–135.

1993 "Heidegger among the Doctors." In *Reading Heidegger: Commemorations,* ed. John Sallis, pp. 49–63. Bloomington: Indiana University Press.

# SIXTEEN

# Ἀρχή

⌸

# John Sallis

I wish I knew how to begin properly presenting the concerns to which my texts, from *Phenomenology and the Return to Beginnings* on, have been addressed. Then I could at least avoid putting myself in the position of having to begin with a confession that I do not know, of having to put such confession in place of beginning. The difficulty lies, in part, in the impossibility of isolating those concerns, of circumscribing them as though they were pure signifieds outside the texts that address them, of saying them in a way that would leave them intact as they were to have been before being said, serenely independent of this discourse and of all the others addressed to them. The difficulty is one of textuality, of its irreducibility (for which one will not be able to compensate to any great extent even by taking the liberty, as I shall, of inserting several passages, setting them in this text as incisions, thus neither as quotations to be integrated into this text nor as mere documentary asides such as might be consigned to notes). But another, more obtrusive, difficulty is imposed by the way in which these texts bring one back to the beginning, by their circling around to the question of beginning, putting in question not only (the) beginning but also the question as such, its beginning and what would antedate it. To say nothing of the question of presentation and of its propriety, of presence and its limits.

*"It is a circling which sets out from the beginnings so as to return to them. . . . [It] is thus simultaneously a turning towards its own beginnings, toward those beginnings with which the return to beginnings is initiated"* (Phenomenology and the Return to Beginnings, 17).

Yet no confession, no enumeration of the difficulties involved, can quite silence the ancient injunction, the one sounded most decisively in the *Timaeus* (29b): in everything it is most important to begin with the beginning. This injunction and the configuration in which it takes shape are as if borne within us—such is the force of metaphysics, of what has been called metaphysics (the name suspended, appropriately, between singular and plural). Invoking a certain necessity that could not be confirmed in the beginning, one might begin, then, by redoubling the injunction, by beginning with the beginning as it was thought in the beginning, with what Plato and Aristotle called ἀρχή. Especially since this is precisely what determines the beginning of metaphysics, in a sense of beginning that is neither simply historical nor simply structural or configural. For if, as Theaetetus attests, philosophy begins with wonder, its very first move is precisely in the direction of what proves to be the ἀρχή. This move is not so much a second sailing, as one sometimes translates δεύτερος πλοῦς, as rather one of having recourse to the oars when the stillness of the winds has made the sails useless. It is, then, truly a beginning and not just an alteration or recommencement of a movement given by nature. Socrates calls it a turn to λόγοι, and it is this directionality, from φύσις to λόγος, that makes it truly a break, a beginning. It is only in and as λόγος that the ἀρχή can initially announce itself, drawing the soul beyond into its proper extension, which is nothing less than a certain madness; in and through such extension the ἀρχή comes to be manifest, not as merely doubling or imaging what is given by nature but as imposing a reversal that will have been underway from the beginning, a reversal by which the beginning comes to be established as such. In the end the ἀρχή will have proven to be that from which everything comes, the origin. Aristotle calls it—in various regards—the ὅθεν (*Metaphysics* V: 1).

*"Consequently, Socrates tells Cebes, he set out on a 'second voyage' [δεύτερος πλοῦς] in search of causes: 'After this, then, when I had failed in investigating beings [τὰ ὄντα], I decided that I must be careful not to suffer the misfortune which happens to people who look at and study the sun during an eclipse. For some of them ruin their eyesight unless they look at its image [εἰκών] in water or something of the sort. I thought of that danger, and I was afraid my soul would be blinded if I looked at things [τὰ πράγματα] with my eyes and tried to grasp them with any of my senses. So I thought I must have recourse to λόγοι and examine in them the truth of beings [τῶν ὄντων τὴν ἀλήθειαν] ([Phaedo] 99d-e)"* (BEING AND LOGOS, 40F.).

Even today one cannot but begin with this beginning; or rather, one will always already have begun with it, as if it were borne within oneself, bestowed with the very language and conceptuality in which one comes to oneself. It would not be entirely inappropriate to say that one is thrown into it, into the beginning of metaphysics and the metaphysics of beginning.

Yet, in being thrown, in being cast toward the ἀρχή, there is neither the violence nor the abruptness that such a metaphorics might suggest; as one comes to oneself, one has always already been cast in this direction, and if one takes up explicitly this directedness to the ἀρχή, it is always as though one were only resuming deliberately something second nature.

One will almost never succeed in simply breaking with nature, be it first or second nature, and it is almost inevitable that if one undertakes to do so one will pay the price of finding oneself redrawn into the very configuration one would have attempted to escape—or rather, of *not* finding oneself, of submitting oneself to a bond that stubbornly conceals itself while reinforcing the illusion of freedom. Such would be—with rare exception perhaps—the cost of breaking with directedness to the ἀρχή, of cutting oneself loose in the effort, as it were, to contemplate the truth in flesh and blood, utterly apart from the origin to which metaphysics would yoke all things. Not that such a break will cease to be desired or, in that rare exception and at the cost of an unheard-of madness, actually effected:

> To contemplate the truth in flesh and blood, even if one must remain invisible, even if one must plunge forever into the discretion of the most desperate cold and the most radical separation—who hasn't wanted that? But who has had that courage? Only one person, I think. (Maurice Blanchot, *When the Time Comes,* 7)

*"Meaning a drift, meaning adrift—as the very site of self-showing. To be in the world is, then, to mean this drift, to look ahead into it so as to let things show themselves from out of it"* (DELIMITATIONS, 165).

And yet, how can one not cut oneself loose now that the originary ἀρχή has itself been cut loose, set adrift, exposed to currents and winds that are incalculable and uncontrollable? Or, on the contrary, is it not precisely at this moment that it becomes most imperative to bind oneself to the ἀρχή, as to the mast of a ship thrown hopelessly off course by the force of the elements? Not in order merely to resume—or await the resumption of—the course, but rather precisely as a way (is there any other?) of breaking with the metaphysical directedness to origin while also taking up that directedness again, that is, also continuing to think this side of that unheard-of madness. Set adrift, the ἀρχή would become an ark, almost as readily as, with a mere shift of accent, the Greek work transliterated becomes the German *Arche.* Now everything would begin to move, that is, would prove always already to have been in movement, and the double gesture required for thinking, demanded of it today, would be, in turn, doubled everywhere.

*"Everything will be conveyed to this origin, loaded aboard the ark . . ."* (DOUBLE TRUTH).

Of course it would not be a matter of a new theory or presentation of the ἀρχή; for the determination of theory and the demand for presence remain tied to that very ἀρχή that is now released into its redoubling movements. What is required is rather a discourse supplely and intricately woven around this limit. This would be a way of saying what my texts, from *Phenomenology and the Return to Beginnings* on, venture: a thinking set within this open matrix.

Granted its drift, the ἀρχή is not only doubled but pluralized, indeed radically so, as one will say, trying in vain—or in mimicry—to impose determination on a separation that cannot but prove finally abysmal. Such pluralizing, the opening of radical separation in the domain of the ἀρχή—this is precisely what is addressed in the concluding paragraphs of *Phenomenology and the Return to Beginnings*. This text marks the way in which a certain phenomenology shifts the ἀρχή away from its modern locus, identified in this context as the *cogito*. I say *a certain phenomenology*, because what is realized in Merleau-Ponty's work, from the *Phenomenology of Perception* to *The Visible and the Invisible*, represents only one of the essential possibilities of phenomenology. Whereas the *Logical Investigations*, though according a certain priority to perception as compared with memory or phantasy, thematizes perception largely in its capacity to fulfill meaning-intentions, the expressed intent of Merleau-Ponty's work is to delimit what is taken to be purely perceptual experience *as the originary* domain. Not only does this shift tend, in turn, to dislocate—or at least to twist severely— the concept of perception (even in Merleau-Ponty's early work one reads: "A thing is, therefore, not actually *given* in perception, it is internally taken up by us, reconstituted and experienced by us insofar as it is bound up with a world, the basic structures of which we carry with us, and of which it is merely one of many possible concrete forms"); it provokes also the question of another beginning, of an ἀρχή capable of calling forth thought as such. It is to this provocation and this question that the concluding paragraphs of *Phenomenology and the Return to Beginnings* are addressed. In the end, it is a question of two beginnings, of the strife of their difference, and of the power of persisting in that strife, in the expanse of that radical—or rather, abysmal—separation. A name is proposed for that power, a name dislodged from that very locus in German Idealism that gives it its intensity: *imagination.*

*"What is the beginning that calls forth thought . . . ? . . . How does this new beginning call forth thought? . . . With these questions we attempt to ques-*

*tion about questioning. Such self-questioning is what, most of all, is required of philosophy as return to beginnings. For philosophical thought not only has to return while remaining, simultaneously, at a distance, that is, to circle around beginnings; but also it is obliged to let itself be sustained between the two beginnings, in the space, the difference, which separates them"* (PHENOMENOLOGY AND THE RETURN TO BEGINNINGS, 116).

In its most originary breakthroughs phenomenology carries out concretely the inversion and displacement that Heidegger finds sketched in the late work of Nietzsche, the inversion and displacement of such metaphysically founding oppositions as that between intelligible and sensible.

*"But for the slightest twist, Nietzsche would be just the last metaphysician. . . : 'During the time the overturning of Platonism became for Nietzsche a twisting free of it, madness befell him'"* (DELIMITATIONS, 160).

Yet it is not only in this move carried out by phenomenology at the limit of metaphysics that an archaic pluralizing and an abysmal separation are to be marked. On the contrary, a move to the limit can be marked in at least one of those texts through which the very opposition between intelligible and sensible was first established as founding and was bequeathed in decisive form to the history of metaphysics.

*"χῶρα would name that by which the image, from which being as such is withheld, holds nonetheless to being"* ("OF THE χῶρα").

My recent work on Plato undertakes to show that in this text, the *Timaeus*, an abysmal separation is made to open at precisely the point where the opposition between intelligible and sensible first comes to be established, indeed in that very establishing. This separation, the apartness of the χῶρα requires another thinking, a thinking different from that which circulates (metaphysically) within the productional opposition between paradigm and image: Timaeus calls it a kind of bastard reckoning. To this separation there corresponds the pluralizing that is announced from the moment the dialogue begins, in that enigmatic counting that constitutes the first words of the dialogue, Socrates proceeding from *one, two, three* to the question of the missing fourth.

Aside from all pluralizing separation, the archaic is also to be thought and said in its proper movement. This movement is double, and its dyadic character is such as to require, beyond a point, a certain interruption and reconstitution of propriety itself, of the proper, of what one would try to distinguish as the proper *itself,* the proper *as such,* in this duplication (both phrases say merely: the proper proper) displaying the very abysmality that haunts any such distinction. It is toward this double movement that Heidegger thinks in his meditations on truth, especially insofar as he secures the question of truth within his radicalizing of phenomenology, which initially takes the form of a regression from intentionality to disclosedness (*Erschlossenheit*). Whether a way could be laid out leading from the question of truth to this other domain became ever more questionable for Heidegger, and one suspects that in the end every alleged way will prove to be broken, to have required a leap—that one can make one's way toward the ἀρχή and its movement only by making, or somehow being granted, a break with nature in all its powers. One could say accordingly—in truth—the double movement of the ἀρχή as its coming and going, its approach and retreat, its drawing near and its withdrawing.

*"Contributions to Philosophy says . . . : 'The essence of truth is un-truth.' Not only does this saying 'bring nearer the strangeness of the strange essence of truth' but also in saying this strangeness it bespeaks the very interrupting of truth"* (DOUBLE TRUTH).

Another way of saying it is in—as—gathering, as in *The Gathering of Reason,* a virtually tautological title that, while entitling a manifold reading of Kant's critique of metaphysics, broaches also a determination of reason that cannot but expose eventually the abysmality operating within that critique and in a sense subverting it as such, contaminating it, as it were, with what Kant would perhaps still call imagination. *Gathering:* a translation of λέγειν, λόγος, mediated by the text thus entitled by Heidegger, thus transposing that text and what it would say into a foreign (and in some respects richer) metaphorics. Thus still: beginning with the beginning, having recourse to λόγος, the winds filling the sails at the very moment that one also takes to the oars, the ark set upon that "wide and stormy ocean" that Kant, with good reason, could only regard as "the native home of illusion, where many a fog bank and many a swiftly melting iceberg give the deceptive appearance of farther shores" (*Critique of Pure Reason,* A 235f./B 294f.). Even still: one will not have learned, will never have learned, simply to navigate this archaic space, to control the spacing of the ἀρχή and assimilate it to the assurance of presence.

*"The encroachment of imagination upon reason, the installation of radical non-self-presence within the very upsurge of reason, deprives reason, beyond appeal, of its title to serve unquestioningly as its own tribunal"* (THE GATHERING OF REASON, 166).

Nor will the time of the ἀρχή cease to be foreign, even though the ἀρχή intrinsically marks the whence, the ὅθεν, of temporal progression. No longer determinable as eternal—this *no longer* bespeaks interruption of that determination and reaches toward another—the time of the ἀρχή is now even more differentiated from the time in which things run their course and from the inner time, the allegedly pure interiority, of human consciousness. It is not even the time proper to Dasein, ecstatic temporality, from which Heidegger himself, in his initial project, marked it off by differentiating between *die Zeitlichkeit des Daseins* and *die Temporalität des Seins.* It is, in Derrida's phrase, *un autre temps,* reaching toward another tense foreign to its very saying, intensifying all that is questionable in such saying and all that is imperative for it.

*"Originary time will always already (in an order no longer detachable from time) have begun to double itself, will always already have been contaminated by an outside . . ."* (ECHOES, 69).

Even the most classical determination of imagination (as εἰκασία warrants reconstituting its force within the new matrix, letting it name the discursive tracing of the double movement proper to the ἀρχή, as it once named, up to a point at least, the progression through image to origin(al). The name proves still more appropriate if one insists on the indispensability of the image: through the image the origin(al) is revealed, and yet, precisely because it is revealed *only* through the image, it withholds itself, does not show itself as such, is concealed, so that one's vision will arrive at the origin(al) only by also circling back to the image, doubling the movement.

Such doubling movement also defines an essential possibility of phenomenology (this phrase, which I used above, not of course remaining immune to the recoil of this very doubling). On the one hand (here I remain, necessarily, at the most schematic level), phenomenology demands that one bind all that one thinks and says philosophically to the presentation of the things themselves. This demand for presence (regardless of whether *die Sachen* are singular, perceptually presented things or not), is what determines all principles of phenomenology; in Husserl's phrase, it is the principle of all principles, the principle that submits all would-be principles to legitimation by presence.

*"Phenomenology attends to the things themselves as they present themselves. . . . And yet, precisely such explication serves to bring to light certain structures of experience that repel such merely adherent attending to the intuitively present. The most important examples are horizonal structures"* (DELIMITATIONS, 77).

But, on the other hand, through its very adherence to this demand, phenomenology itself brings to light a configuration of horizons that not only structure all coming to presence but also have the effect of withholding things precisely in—as the very condition of—their coming to presence. To say nothing of the horizons themselves, which cannot in the strict sense be presented at all, at least not without ceasing thereby to be horizons.

This essential possibility of phenomenology has not of course gone unnoticed or remained entirely undeveloped. One will recall "The Philosopher and His Shadow," and one will note too the profound affinity with the deconstruction of time, with Derrida's demonstration that the present is produced only in being compounded with the past, presence with absence. Yet it remains for this possibility, for the determinacy, concreteness, and precision—in a word, rigor—that it promises, to be developed within the open matrix of contemporary thought and discourse.

*"It is, then, upon phenomenology that the end of metaphysics opens. Rigorous openness . . ."* (DELIMITATIONS, 163).

## Selected Bibliography

1973 *Phenomenology and the Return to Beginnings.* Pittsburgh: Duquesne University Press.

1975 *Being and Logos: The Way of Platonic Dialogue.* Pittsburgh: Duquesne University Press.

1980a *The Gathering of Reason.* Athens: Ohio University Press. Translated into German as *Die Krisis der Vernunft.* Hamburg: Felix Meiner Verlag.

1980b *Heraclitean Fragments,* ed. with K. Maly. University: University of Alabama Press.

1981a *Merleau-Ponty: Perception, Structure, Language,* ed. Atlantic Highlands, N.J.: Humanities Press.

1981b *Studies in Phenomenology and the Human Sciences,* ed. Atlantic Highlands, N.J.: Humanities Press.

1981c "Into the Clearing." In *Heidegger, the Man and the Thinker,* ed. Thomas Sheehan. Chicago: Precedent Press. Translated into Chinese in *Culture: China and the World* 2 (1988), pp. 352–365.

1982a *Philosophy and Archaic Experience: Essays in Honor of Edward G. Ballard,* ed. Pittsburgh: Duquesne University Press.

1982b "Metaphysical Security and the Play of Imagination: An Archaic Reflection." In *Philosophy and Archaic Experience,* ed. Pittsburgh: Duquesne University Press.

1983a *Continental Philosophy in America,* ed. with H. Silverman and T. Seebohm. Pittsburgh: Duquesne University Press.

1983b *Husserl and Contemporary Thought,* ed. Atlantic Highlands, N.J.: Humanities Press.

1983c "End(s)." *Research in Phenomenology* 13: 85–96. Reprinted in *Heidegger-iana*, ed. G. Moretti. *Itinerari* 25 (1986): 73–85.

1984a "Heidegger/Derrida—Presence." *Journal of Philosophy* 81: 594–601.

1984b "Apollo's Mimesis." *British Journal of Phenomenology* 15: 16–21.

1985 "Meaning Adrift." *Heidegger Studies* 1: 91–100.

1986a *Delimitations: Phenomenology and the End of Metaphysics*. Bloomington: Indiana University Press. Translated into French as *Délimitations: La phénom-énologie et la fin de la métaphysique*. Paris: Aubier.

1986b *Being and Logos: The Way of Platonic Dialogue*. 2nd ed. Atlantic High-lands, N.J.: Humanities Press.

1986c "Imagination and Presentation in Hegel's Philosophy of Spirit." In *Hegel's Philosophy of Spirit*, ed. Peter Stillman. Albany: State University of New York Press.

1987a *Spacings—of Reason and Imagination: In Texts of Kant, Fichte, Hegel*. Chi-cago: University of Chicago Press.

1987b *Deconstruction and Philosophy: The Texts of Jacques Derrida*, ed. Chicago: University of Chicago Press. Paperback, 1988.

1987c "Twisting Free: Being to an Extent Sensible." *Research in Phenomenology* 17: 1–22. Translated into German as "Twisting Free: Das Sein eine Spanne weit sinnlich." In *Twisting Heidegger: Drehversuche parodistische Denkens*, ed. Mi-chael Eldred. Cuxhaven: Junghans Verlag, 1993.

1987d "Echoes: Philosophy and Non-Philosophy after Heidegger." In *Philosophy and Nonphilosophy*. Continental Philosophy series, ed. Hugh J. Silverman, vol. 1. New York: Routledge.

1988a *The Collegium Phaenomenologicum: The First Ten Years*, ed. with J. Tam-iniaux and G. Moneta. Dordrecht: Kluwer.

1988b "Time Out. . . ." In *The Collegium Phaenomenologicum: The First Ten Years*. Co-edited with J. Taminiaux and G. Moneta. Dordrecht: Kluwer.

1988c "Imagination and the Meaning of Being." In *Heidegger et l'idée de la phé-noménologie*, ed. J. Taminiaux, pp. 127–144. The Hague: Nijhoff. Translated into Italian in *Clinamen* 3 (1989): 19–38.

1988d "Dionysus—In Excess of Metaphysics." In *Exceedingly Nietzsche: Aspects of Contemporary Nietzsche Interpretation*, ed. D. F. Krell and D. Wood. Lon-don: Routledge.

1989a "La Mortalité et l'imagination: Heidegger et le nom propre de l'homme." *Cahiers du Collège International de Philosophie* 8 (1989): 51–77. Translated into Chinese in *Philosophy and Man* (1993), pp. 257–279.

1989b "Heidegger's Poetics: The Question of Mimesis." In *Kunst und Technik. Zum 100. Geburtstag Martin Heideggers*, ed. Walter Biemel and F.-W. von Herr-mann. Frankfurt am Main: Vittorio Klostermann.

1989c "Interruptions." In *Dialogue and Deconstruction: The Gadamer–Derrida Encounter*, ed. Richard Palmer and Diane Michelfelder. Albany: State University of New York Press.

1990a *Echoes: After Heidegger*. Bloomington: Indiana University Press.

1990b "Heidegger und Dekonstruktion." In *Zur philosophischen Aktualität Hei-deggers: Symposium der Alexander von Papenfuss und Otto Pöggeler*. Frankfurt am Main: Vittorio Klostermann. Translated into Serbo-Croatian in *Godisnjak Instituta za filozofija* 2 (1989): 205–216.

1990c "Flight of Spirit." *Diacritics* 19: 25–37.

1991a *Crossings: Nietzsche and the Space of Tragedy.* Chicago: University of Chicago Press.

1991b "Monet's Grainstacks: Shades of Time." *Tema Celeste* 30: 56–67. Translated into French as "Ombres de temps: les *Meules* de Monet." *La Part de l'oeil* 7 (1991). Translated into Italian as *Ombre del Tempo: I Covoni di Monet.* Syracusa: Tema Celeste Edizione, 1992.

1991c "Doublings." In *Derrida: A Critical Reader,* ed. David Wood. Oxford: Blackwell. Translated into French as Doublures," *Revue Philosophique* (1990).

1991d "Nature's Song." *Revue Internationale de Philosophie* 45: 3–9.

1992a "Babylonian Captivity." *Research in Phenomenology* 22: 23–31.

1992b "Thresholds of Abstract Art." *Tema Celeste* 35: 42–45.

1993a *Reading Heidegger: Commemorations,* ed. Bloomington: Indiana University Press.

1993b "Spacing Imagination." In *Eris and Eros: Contributions to a Hermeneutical Phenomenology,* ed. P. van Tongeren. Dordrecht: Kluwer. Translated into French as "L'espacement de l'imagination: Husserl et la phénoménologie de l'imagination." In *Husserl,* ed. Eliane Escoubas and Marc Richir. Grenoble: Jérome Millon, 1989.

1993c "Deformatives: Essentially Other Than Truth." In *Reading Heidegger: Commemorations,* ed. Bloomington: Indiana University Press.

1994a *Stone.* Bloomington: Indiana University Press.

1994b *Delimitations: Phenomenology and the End of Metaphysics.* 2nd ed., revised and enlarged. Bloomington: Indiana University Press.

1994c "The Question of Origin." *Southern Journal of Philosophy* 32, Supplement: 89–106.

1994d "De la Chora." In *Le Passage des Frontières: Autour du travail de Jacques Derrida,* ed. Marie-Louise Mallet. Paris: Galilée.

1994e "The Truth That Is Not of Knowledge." In *Reading Heidegger from the Start: Essays in his Earliest Thought,* ed. Theodore Kisiel and John van Buren. Albany: State University of New York Press.

1994f "Mimesis and the End of Art." In *Intersections: Nineteenth-Century Philosophy and Contemporary Theory,* ed. David Clark and Tilottama Rajan. Albany: State University of New York Press.

1995a *Double Truth.* Albany: State University of New York Press.

1995b "Intentionalité et Imagination." In *Intentionalité en Question,* ed. Dominique Janicaud. Paris: J. Vrin.

1995c "Mixed Arts." In *Proceedings of the Eighth International Kant Congress,* ed. Hoke Robinson, vol. 1, pt. 3. Milwaukee: Marquette University Press.

1995d "Timaeus' Discourse on the Χῶρα." In *Proceedings of the Boston Area Colloquium in Ancient Philosophy* 11: 155–169.

1995e ". . . a wonder that one could never aspire to surpass." In *The Path of Archaic Thinking: The Work of John Sallis,* ed. Kenneth Maly. Albany: State University of New York Press.

1996a *Being and Logos: Reading the Platonic Dialogues.* 3d ed. Bloomington: Indiana University Press.

1996b "On Wagner/Artaud." *Review of Contemporary Fiction* 16.

1996c "The Politics of the Χῶρα." In *Ancients and Moderns,* ed. Reginald Lilly. Bloomington: Indiana University Press.

1997a "Rereading the *Timaeus:* The Memorial Power of Discourse." In *The Philosophy of Hans-Georg Gadamer*, ed. Lewis Hahn. La Salle, Ill.: Open Court.

1997b "Platonism at the Limit of Metaphysics." *Graduate Faculty Philosophy Journal* 20: 299–314.

1997c "Uranic Time." In *Time and Nothingness*, ed. Michael Lazarin. Kyoto.

1997d "Bread and Wine." *Philosophy Today.*

1998a "Beyond the Political: Reclaiming the Community of the Earth." In *Phenomenology of Interculturality and Life-World*, ed. E. W. Orth and Chan-Fai Cheung, pp. 192–208. Freiburg/Munich: Karl Alber. Translated into Finnish as "Poliittisen tuolla puolen," *Yearbook of Literary Research Society* 49 (1996).

1998b "Daydream." *Revue Internationale de Philosophie.*

1995c "Levinas and the Elemental." In *Emmanuel Levinas*, ed. Jacques Rolland. Paris: L'Age d'Homme.

1998d *Shades—Of Painting at the Limit.* Bloomington: Indiana University Press.

1998e "A Time of Imagination." In *Interkulturelle Philosophie und Phänomenologie in Japan*, ed. Tadashi Ogawa, Michael Lazarin, and Guido Rappe. Munich: Iudicium.

1999a *Chorology: On Beginning in Plato's Timaeus.* Bloomington: Indiana University Press.

1999b *Interrogating the Tradition: Hermeneutics and the History of Philosophy*, ed. with C. Scott. Albany: State University of New York Press.

1999c *Retracing the Platonic Text*, ed. with J. Russon. Evanston: Northwestern University Press.

# SEVENTEEN

# My Dialogue with Twentieth-Century Continental Philosophy

## CALVIN O. SCHRAG

The request to write about one's relationship to types and trends of thought presents difficulties of rather extensive magnitude. There is first the difficulty of sorting out the defining characteristics of the types and trends of thought at issue, which in the present context have the general designator, "twentieth-century Continental Philosophy." In conjunction with this requirement there is another—that of framing the attitude that the author displays in treating the subject matter. Does the author consider himself to be a native inhabitant of the land that he surveys, or does he behold the terrain from afar? Is he principally a participant in the configurations of thought at issue, or does he function mainly as an observer and critic of the scene?

At the risk of certain violations of grammar, I have decided to define my relationship to the trends and movements at issue as a "dialogue." Insofar as each of these trends and movements involves a multiplicity of authorial participants, the project of carrying on a dialogue with multiple authors is made the more difficult. It requires at the outset a discernment, which is always an interpretation, of the various kinds of philosophical thinking that make up the wider fabric of recent Continental Philosophy. It also would be helpful to inform the reader about the degree of involvement that I have with the particular type of philosophy to be examined.

Happily, there appears to be some general agreement by scholars on the types and trends of philosophical thought that have dominated twentieth-century Europe. Existentialism is a surefire candidate for inclusion. Particularly during the two decades following World War II, Existentialism was very much in vogue, both in the academies and the coffee houses of France and Germany. Prior to this flourishing of Existentialism, however, another philosophical movement had registered its impact not only in France and Germany but also in various philosophical stations across the map of Europe, eventually finding its way across the Atlantic to the shores of the United States. This philosophical movement, "phenomenology," was largely the invention of Edmund Husserl. Although initially separate from Existentialism, in the course of time the two philosophical movements were amalgamated, principally through the efforts of Maurice Merleau-Ponty, yielding what came to be called "existential phenomenology."

Now according to some reports, issued mainly from France, Existentialism died in the spring of 1968 and was ceremoniously observed with a mock funeral for Jean-Paul Sartre, staged by French students from the environs of Paris. That which allegedly replaced Existentialism and existential phenomenology was structuralism, a broadly gauged, multidisciplinary configuration of thought that brought together philosophers, sociologists, linguists, literary theorists, and psychoanalysts. This academically diverse group hoped to solve the "crises of the human sciences" by digging deeper and deeper into the underbellies of the several sciences so as to uncover an infrastructure of invariant linguistic and social relations. However, this fervent hope, shared by the structuralists in the various disciplines, was not long for this world, as it was unable to withstand the anti-structuralist interventions of deconstruction and postmodernism.

While all of this was going on, other modes of philosophizing made their presence felt. Chief among these were hermeneutics and Critical Theory. The principal current representatives of the former are Hans-Georg Gadamer and Paul Ricoeur, while Jürgen Habermas and Karl-Otto Apel are most commonly mentioned in discussions of the latter. Whereas a distinguishing feature of hermeneutical philosophers is their preoccupation with strategies of interpretation, critical theorists are very much concerned about matters of social philosophy and public policy. The lines of demarcation between these two approaches, however, are not all that firmly entrenched. Each has some interest in what the other is doing. Significant communication, although perhaps not agreement, between the two camps does from time to time take place. Also it is not uncommon to find efforts toward mutual understanding undertaken by the believing remnants of Existentialism, phenomenology, structuralism, deconstruction, and postmodernism. Some interdisciplinary commerce between the various types of twentieth-century Continental Philosophy now and then occurs. Thus it needs to be remembered that in any classification of types or forms of thought, one is dealing with open-textured and oft-blurred genres rather than with definitive demarcations.

The story of my philosophical life as it relates to the changing currents of twentieth-century continental thought and their commingling is a story of both participation and observation, involvement and distanciation. It is for this reason that I have chosen to speak of my dealings with the continental tradition as taking the form of a dialogue. A genuine dialogue is a transactional exchange that allows for—indeed requires—the twin doublets of participation/observation and involvement/distanciation. There is much in the continental tradition that has elicited my sympathy and approval; but there is also much that has occasioned dissatisfaction and disavowal on my part. Throughout my career as an interpreter and critic of Continental Philosophy, my attitude toward the subject matter can be summarized as an attitude of *critical engagement*.

This career, and the accompanying attitude, began to crystallize during my graduate studies at Harvard University, where I matriculated for the specific purpose of continuing my undergraduate interest in the philosophy of Whitehead, who had ended his long and illustrious career with an appointment at this prestigious citadel of learning. But this was the fifties, and the Harvard philosophy department was not particularly respectful of the legacy of Whitehead—nor were other philosophy departments in the land. This was very much a decade for neopositivism and analytical philosophy in the American philosophical academy. One senior member of the faculty at Harvard University, John Wild, sought to stem the rising tide of neopositivism by offering courses in existential philosophy, giving particular attention to the philosophy of Martin Heidegger. Wild was later to become one of the principal catalysts in the introduction of recent Continental Philosophy into the American philosophical curriculum.[1]

It was John Wild who suggested that I familiarize myself with Heidegger's *Sein und Zeit* specifically and with existential thought more generally. This suggestion marked a turning point in my program of graduate studies. I spent the following year at Heidelberg University in Germany under the auspices of the Fulbright Commission. At Heidelberg I benefited specifically from the tutelage of Karl Löwith and Hans-Georg Gadamer. Returning to Harvard the following year, I completed and defended my doctoral dissertation, "A Comparative Analysis of Søren Kierkegaard's Dialectical Analysis of the Self and Martin Heidegger's Phenomenological Ontology of Dasein," in the spring of 1956. My central thesis was that Heidegger's ontology of Dasein in *Sein und Zeit* could be read as an ontologization and secularization of Kierkegaard's concrete ethico-religious understanding of the self. My first book, *Existence and Freedom: Towards an Ontology of Human Finitude* (1961), further developed the thesis of my dissertation and broadened the discussion to include the contributions of Sartre, Jaspers, and Marcel on the way to demonstrating that the resources of existential philosophy afforded not another metaphysical system of the classical sort but rather an ontology of finite, human existence.

Clearly, at this stage of my philosophical development there were some deep sympathies with what Heidegger, and the so-called existentialists of the day, were about. Yet this early admiration for and involvement in the existential thinking of the times never blunted my critical assessments. In particular, my immersion in the Heidegger literature prompted critical concerns about Heidegger's approach to the problem of history solely through the lens of a radically historicized *Dasein* and also about his predominantly negative spin on community and communication.[2]

My second major work, *Experience and Being: Prolegomena to a Future Ontology* (1969), was the result of years of teaching and research on the topic of phenomenology. During these years it was specifically the writings of Husserl and Merleau-Ponty that piqued my philosophical interests. Following some of Merleau-Ponty's leads, I sought to secure a rapprochement of the transcendental phenomenology of Husserl and the existential ontology of Heidegger. In *Experience and Being* much is made of Husserl's concept of the *Lebenswelt* and his acknowledgment of the philosophical importance of "experience" (particularly as it is developed in his book *Experience and Judgment*). At the same time I continued my earlier dialogue with Heidegger in an effort to reframe the question about Being from the perspective of a new phenomenology of experience. Remaining sensitive to Heidegger's qualms about the very notion of experience, mainly because of its use as an epistemological foundation of British empiricism, I made an effort to reclaim the ontological commitments in a descriptive elucidation and interpretive analysis of the experienced lifeworld. It is thus that the basic project as illustrated in the title *Experience and Being* needs to be understood: as a splitting of the difference between Husserl's *Experience and Judgment* and Heidegger's *Being and Time*.

The decade of the seventies brought with it new philosophical developments on the European continent. Attention was very much focused on issues having to do with the origin, nature, and goal of the human sciences (*les sciences de l'Homme*). Particularly in France, the developing structuralism called the world's attention to an evident "crisis of the human sciences," in which the several sciences were in profound disagreement over issues of method and purpose, submerged in a vast labyrinth, unable to find their way. The structuralists attempted to lead the sciences out of their predicament by way of the thread of Ariadne, by an analysis that would uncover an infrastructure in which the constitutive elements were held together by a grid of binary relations, at once social and linguistic.

The undergirding argument of my third book, *Radical Reflection and the Origin of the Human Sciences* was that the thread of Ariadne was simply too threadbare to lead us out of the labyrinth. Specifically, I argued that the structuralists could not solve the crisis of the human sciences because they sought their origin and unity in the wrong place. The human sciences find their origin not in an algorithmically structured grid of linguistic and social relations, I argued, but rather in a matrix of originary experience that can be elucidated through a hermeneutic of everyday life.

As structuralism considered itself to be the legitimate successor to Existentialism and phenomenology, so deconstruction appeared on the philosophical scene as the self-anointed successor to structuralism. And the first thing that the deconstructionists deconstructed was the infrastructural and superstructural constructs of structuralism. But the deconstructionists' demolition project had other victims as well. Indeed, pretty much the whole tradition of Western metaphysics and epistemology was dismantled and then followed by an announcement of the "end of philosophy"—a shibboleth that covered many things, chief among which were the "death of the subject" and the displacement of logocentric thought with textuality.

*Communicative Praxis and the Space of Subjectivity* (1986) tells the story of another dialogue—this time with the partisans of deconstruction. One of the interlocutors in this dialogue is Jacques Derrida, the person mainly responsible for the grammar and strategy of deconstructionist polemics. *Communicative Praxis* provided a consolidation of my various dialogic forays into the citadels of deconstructionist theory and practice. Here again my position was one of both involvement and critical distanciation. Sympathetic with the deconstructionist dismantling of speculative metaphysics and foundationalist epistemology, I was able to work out from their terrain, as it were, and forge a new hermeneutics, praxial in nature, whereby to reclaim a subject, decentered and refigured, in the wake of its demise as a metaphysical substrate or epistemological point of origin. This reclaimed and refigured subject no longer functioned as a *foundation for* but rather as an *implicate of* events of speaking and acting within the space of our discursive and non-discursive social practices.

Following my critical engagement with the partisans of deconstruction, the emergence of postmodernism in Continental Philosophy required that I take up another dialogic challenge. To be sure, this dialogue was in some measure a continuation of the previous one, but it also involved the canvassing of some new terrain. Like so many of the other movements and trends in continental thought, postmodernism had wide cultural effects, invading the disciplines of art, literature, history, sociology, philosophy, and even the natural sciences. In philosophy it issued a formidable challenge to the claims of reason. In its celebration of heterogeneity, particularity, and paralogy, it flirted with relativism and nihilism. My work *The Resources of Rationality: A Response to the Postmodern Challenge* (1992) was an effort to address the challenges of the postmodern disparagement of theory, meaning, reference, and value by way of a thought experiment on a new notion of reason, which I came to call *transversal rationality*.

In researching the literature on the postmodern anti-reason posture, I found that the issues at stake were being played out in an ongoing debate between postmodernists (read Jean-François Lyotard) and critical theorists (read Jürgen Habermas). Critical Theory had, of course, been around for some time, going back to the Frankfurt School of the thirties and forties, but it now assumed a new attitude in the person of Jürgen Habermas. The principal issue in this debate had to do with the role of reason in human affairs, private as well as public. While the postmodernists were intent on scuttling the Enlightenment conception of reason (and pretty much all other conceptions!), Habermas engaged in a salvage effort, seeking to rescue and reconstruct the Enlightenment legacy. In *The Resources of Rationality* I began a dialogue with the disputing parties, placing myself "in between," seeking to split the difference with the help of the notion of rationality as transversal. Reason in its transversal dynamics avoids both the snares of claims of universal validity (Habermas) and the pitfalls of particularism and paralogy that appear in the postmodern anti-reason point of view (Lyotard).

My relationship to the various expressions of twentieth-century Continental Philosophy, as expressed in both my published and unpublished works, has been that of a continuing dialogue within and across the changing philosophical scenarios of Existentialism, phenomenology, structuralism, hermeneutics, deconstruction, postmodernism, and Critical Theory. In my engagement with these different philosophical expressions, I have played the role of both participant and critic, responding to the various challenges offered, seeking to keep the philosophical conversation of humankind alive.

## Notes

1. For a discussion of the impact of Continental Philosophy in the United States, and of John Wild's role in it, see James M. Edie, "Phenomenology in the United States," *Journal of the British Society for Phenomenology* 5 (3) (1974).

2. For a more extended discussion of these two concerns and criticisms see Calvin O. Schrag, "Phenomenology, Ontology, and History in the Philosophy of Heidegger," *Revue internationale de Philosophie* 44 (2) (1958).

## Selected Bibliography

1958 "Phenomenology, Ontology and History in the Philosophy of Heidegger." *Revue Internationale de Philosophie* 44 (2): 1–16.

1959a "Existence and History." *Review of Metaphysics* 13 (1): 28–44.

1959b "Kierkegaard's Teleological Suspension of the Ethical." *Ethics* 70 (2): 66–68.

1959c "Whitehead and Heidegger: Process Philosophy and Existential Philosophy." *Dialectica* 13 (1): 42–56.

1961a *Existence and Freedom: Towards an Ontology of Human Finitude.* Evanston: Northwestern University Press.

1961b "Kierkegaard's Existential Reflections on Time." *The Personalist* 42 (2): 149–164.

1961c "Faith, Existence and Culture." *Journal of Religious Thought* 18 (2): 83–91.

1962a "John Wild on Contemporary Philosophy." *Journal of Philosophy and Phenomenological Research* 22 (3): 409–411.

1962b "Ontology and the Possibility of Religious Knowledge." *Journal of Religion* 42 (2): 87–95.

1962c "The Lived Body as a Phenomenological Datum." *The Modern Schoolman* 39 (3): 203–218.

1963a "Towards a Phenomenology of Guilt." *Journal of Existential Psychiatry* 3 (12): 333–342.

1963b "The Meaning of History." *Review of Metaphysics* 17 (4): 703–717.

1963c "The Structure of Moral Experience: A Phenomenological and Existential Analysis." *Ethics* 73 (4): 225–265.

1964 "Existentialism and Democracy." *Pacific Philosophy Forum* 2 (4): 95–100.

1967 "Heidegger and Cassirer on Kant." *Kant-studien* 58 (1): 87–100.

1968a "Re-thinking Metaphysics." In *Heidegger and the Quest for Truth,* ed. M. S. Frings. Chicago: Quadrangle.

1968b "Substance, Subject and *Existenz.*" *Proceedings of the American Catholic Philosophical Association* 42: 175–182.

1969a *Experience and Being: Prolegomena to a Future Ontology.* Evanston: Northwestern University Press.

1969b "Struktur der Erfahrung in der Philosophie von James und Whitehead." *Zeitschrift für Philosophische Forschung* 23 (4): 479–494.

1969c "The Phenomenon of Embodied Speech." *The Philosophy Forum* 7 (4): 3–27.

1970a "Heidegger on Repetition and Historical Understanding." *Philosophy East and West* 20 (3): 287–295.

1970b "Philosophical Anthropology in Contemporary Thought." *Philosophy East and West* 20 (1): 83–89.

1970c "The Life-World and Its Historical Horizon." In *Patterns of the Life World,* ed. with James Edie and Francis Parker. Evanston: Northwestern University Press.

1971 "The Historical as a Feature of Experience." *University of Dayton Review* 8 (1): 7–16.

1972 "Phases of Phenomenological Philosophy in the United States." Translated into Japanese in *Journal of Ideas* (Japanese) 5 (468): 71–78.

1973 "The Transvaluation of Aesthetics and the Work of Art." *Southwestern Journal of Philosophy* 4 (3): 109–124.

1975a "Praxis and Structure: Conflicting Models in the Science of Man." *Journal of the British Society for Phenomenology* 6 (1): 23–31.

1975b "The Crisis of the Human Sciences." *Man and World* 8 (2): 131–135.

1977 "The Topology of Hope." *Humanitas* 13 (3): 269–281.

1979a "A Phenomenological Perspective on Communication." *Resources in Education,* the ERIC index (Nov.) [Microfiche.]

1979b "The Concrete Dialectic of Self-with-Society." In *Experience Forms: Their Cultural and Individual Place and Function,* ed. George G. Haydu. The Hague: Mouton.

1980a "Appendix to Professor Spiegelberg's 'Reflections on the Phenomenological Movement.'" *Journal of the British Society for Phenomenology* 2: 280–281.

1980b "Professor Seigfried on Descriptive Phenomenology and Constructivism." *Philosophy and Phenomenological Research* 40 (3): 411–414.

1980c *Radical Reflection and the Origin of the Human Sciences.* West Lafayette, Ind.: Purdue University Press.

1980d "The Fabric of Fact: Beyond Epistemology." *Eros* 7 (2): 83–97.

1981a "A Response to 'A Response to *Radical Reflection.*'" *Reflections: Essays in Phenomenology* (Winter): 40–45.

1981b "The Texture of Communicative Praxis as New Context for Subjectivity." In *Phenomenology and the Understanding of Human Destiny,* ed. Stephen Skousgaard. Washington, D.C.: University Press of America.

1982a "Being in Pain." In *The Humanity of the Ill: Phenomenological Perspectives,* ed. Victor Kestenbaum. Knoxville: University of Tennessee Press.

1982b "Philosophical Anthropology as an Analytic of Mortality." In *Transparencies: Philosophical Essays in Honor of Jose Ferrater Mora,* ed. P. N. Cohn. Atlantic Highlands, N.J.: Humanities Press.

1982c "The Idea of the University and the Communication of Knowledge in a Technological Age." In *Communication Philosophy and the Technological Age,* ed. Michael J. Hyde. Tuscaloosa: University of Alabama Press.

1983a "A Response to My Critics: Professors O'Neill and Mays." *Journal of the British Society for Phenomenology* 14 (1): 40–49.

1983b "The Challenge of Philosophical Anthropology." In *The Phenomenology of Man and of the Human Condition,* ed. A.-T. Tymieniecka. Dordrecht: Reidel.

1983c "The Question of the Unity of the Human Sciences Revisited." In *The Phenomenology of Man and of the Human Condition,* ed. A.-T. Tymieniecka. Dordrecht: Reidel.

1984 "Decentered Subjectivity and the New Humanism." *Alaska Quarterly Review* 2 (3–4): 115–129.

1985a "Rhetoric Resituated at the End of Philosophy." *Quarterly Journal of Speech* 71 (2): 164–174.

1985b "Subjectivity and Praxis at the End of Philosophy." In *Hermeneutics and Deconstruction,* ed. Don Ihde and Hugh Silverman. Albany: State University of New York Press.

1986a *Communicative Praxis and the Space of Subjectivity.* Bloomington: Indiana University Press.

1986b "On the Hermeneutics of Gadamer and Habermas." Co-authored with Chong-Mun Kim. *Korean Journal of Philosophy* 12–13: 135–148.

1988a "Husserl's Legacy in the Postmodern World." *Phenomenological Inquiry* 12: 125–133.

1988b "Liberal Learning in the Postmodern World." *The Key Reporter* 54 (1): 1–4.

1989a "Authorial Reflections." In *American Phenomenology: Origins and Developments,* ed. Eugene Kaelin and Calvin Schrag. Dordrecht: Kluwer.

1989b *Communicative Rhetoric and the Claims of Reason.* Evanston: Northwestern University, School of Speech.

1989c *Phenomenology in America: Origins and Developments*, ed. with Eugene F. Kaelin. Dordrecht: Kluwer.

1989d "Rationality between Modernity and Postmodernity." In *Life-World and Politics: Essays in Honor of Fred Dallmayr*, ed. Stephen K. White. Notre Dame: University of Notre Dame Press.

1989e *Women Philosophers: A Bio-Critical Source Book*. By Ethel M. Kersey; Calvin O. Schrag, Consulting Editor. Westport, Conn.: Greenwood Press.

1990 "Explanation and Understanding in the Science of Human Behavior." In *Reconsidering Psychology*, ed. James E. Faulconer and Richard H. Williams. Pittsburgh: Duquesne University Press.

1991a "Interpretation, Narrative, and Rationality." *Research in Phenomenology* 21: 98–115.

1991b "Reconstructing Reason in the Aftermath of Deconstruction." *Critical Review* 5 (2): 247–260.

1991c "The Phenomenological Sociology of George Psathas: Appraisal and Critique." *Phenomenology and the Human Sciences* 16 (3): 1–10.

1992a "Communication Studies and Philosophy: Convergence without Coincidence." Co-authored with David D. Miller. In *The Critical Turn: Rhetoric and Philosophy in Postmodern Discourse*, ed. Ian Angus and Lenore Langsdorf. Carbondale: Southern Illinois University Press.

1992b *The Resources of Rationality: A Response to the Postmodern Challenge*. Bloomington: Indiana University Press.

1992c "Traces of Meaning and Reference: Phenomenological and Hermeneutical Explorations." In *Current Advances in Semantic Theory*, ed. Maxim Stamenov. Philadelphia: John Benjamins.

1993 "Phenomenology and the Consequences of Post-modernity." In *Reason, Life, Culture*, ed. A.-T. Tymieniecka. Dordrecht: Kluwer.

1994a *Philosophical Papers: Betwixt and Between*. Albany: State University of New York Press.

1994b "Transversal Rationality." In *The Question of Hermeneutics*, ed. T. J. Stapleton. Dordrecht: Kluwer.

1994c "Method and Phenomenological Research: Humility and Commitment in Interpretation." Co-authored with Ramsey Eric Ramsey. *Human Studies* 17: 131–137.

1995a "The Kierkegaard-Effect in the Shaping of the Contours of Modernity." In *Kierkegaard in Post/Modernity*, ed. Martin J. Matuštík and Merold Westphal. Bloomington: Indiana University Press.

1995b "Ultimacy and the Alterity of the Sublime." In *Being Human and the Ultimate*, ed. Nenos Georgopolous and Michael Heim. Amsterdam: Rodopi.

1995c "Reminiscences on Paul Tillich: The Man and His Works." *North American Paul Tillich Society Newsletter* 21 (1): 3–8.

1996a "The Story of the Human Subject in the Aftermath of Postmodern Critique." *Revue roumaine de philosophie* 1–2.

1996b "Philosophy at the End of the Twentieth Century with a Note on Lucien Blaga." *Romanian Review* 51 (327).

1997a *The Self after Postmodernity*. New Haven: Yale University Press.

1997b "La récupération du sujet phénoménologique." In *Analecta Husserliana*, vol. L. Dordrecht: Kluwer.

# EIGHTEEN

## Thought in the Transformation of 'Transcendence'

## CHARLES E. SCOTT

There are times when I can find what I call 'my' thinking in the way I find continental thought. I think that it is because I often lose my sense of self in the process, and in this loss I find something else that is hard to name.

Contemporary Continental Philosophy has been formed more by processes of critique and transformation than by commitment to established beliefs and truths. But the struggle between critique and transformation on the one hand and upholding the value of traditional truths on the other is also definitive of Continental Philosophy. By intensifying this struggle, we can intensify the transformation of thought and practice, particularly when thought and practice ignore the transformative processes and aporias that define their identities.

The struggle takes place on several planes. On one plane there is the reading of canonized philosophers. Heidegger, for example, finds in Aristotle something that he misses in the Aristotelians: freshness of descriptive perception, originality in addressing the claims of previous philosophers, and the emergence of definitive problems and quandaries for a segment of history whose philosophy combines skepticism and dogmatism. He finds after Aristotle the extremely complex formation of thought that is ready to overcome itself. Other philosophers who are influenced by both Heidegger and Aristotelianism, however, read Heidegger in light of reformulated readings of Aristotle and see in Heidegger a contemporary reformulation of Aristotle's thought, one that maintains Aristotle's importance but rethinks many of his primary thoughts in innovative and yet preserving ways. This approach neither revolutionizes nor fundamentally corrects Aristotle but finds new and imaginative relevance for our time in his work. We might, with Heidegger, wish to intensify this struggle by examining the extent to which reformulations of Aristotle avoid the question of being, the decline of which, according to Heidegger, is found throughout Aristotle's thought as well as throughout the traditions that follow him. Leaving aside the question of the accuracy of Heidegger's descriptive claims, we can say nevertheless that that question—the question of being as Heidegger has given it voice and moment—has been unparalleled in its transformation of twentieth-century thought.

The struggle takes place whenever we pose the question of identity, a question that is also formulated as the question of presence. In my reading of this issue, difference gains, in an irregular manner, priority over identity in Nietzsche's thought. Even this irregular manner is differentiated and not ordered by transcendental or transhistorical agency. Although Nietzsche often refuses a movement of reconciliation as he holds together opposing and contradictory thoughts or values, he also compounds the differences (and hence the irregularity) by suggesting that will to power unites all differences and that will to power is an imaginative construct that cannot be unimaginatively true. In this claim he both reconciles differences and makes the reconciling movement itself arbitrary and differential. It is in such movements as this that the reader experiences the death of God and of Christ in Nietzsche's thought. I believe that one can find the priority of difference over identity in other thinkers, but this clash of differences without reconciliation within Nietzsche's thought has a particular force in the formation of contemporary continental thought. Probably Nietzsche and Husserl are the peaks of difference in the struggle between the values of identity and difference, as Nietzsche's language—beyond his or anyone's intentional direction—both allows differences to appear without a unifying, synthesizing movement that defines appearances, and gives value to difference over identity. Husserl, to the contrary, provides a law of transcendental grounding for the differences among appearances and thereby maintains the priority of transcendental identity. In this struggle people can feel the threat to identity's priority at all levels of experience, and people can also feel the dead weight of sameness in the exhilaration that comes with freeing differences from transcendental order and control.

In the Nietzschean movement, continuing presence loses priority to transformation of thought and social practice. In that movement they benefit from no horizon of transcendence. This is a determination of order and not an elimination of it: orders are forceful arrangements, textures of attraction, repulsion, coercion, and above all, for Nietzsche, domination and submission. Various histories, grammars, and practices variously call for orders. Orders are ways in which people know things and live together. Knowing things and living together join in recognition, and the recognition of something or someone articulates both epistemological and social arrangements

—arrangements of differences, not another kind of identity continuing outside of a lineage in its temporal willing, knowing, or law-giving presence.

Other planes of struggle address thinking: is thinking ecstatic? dialectical? interpretative? Is it beyond knowing and hence not epistemological? Necessarily representative of something other than itself? These planes of struggle address the demise and resurgence of the Enlightenment, critique as deconstructive performance or reflective analysis, and language—can we write or speak in a non-representative performance, saying more than can be known or designated? Other planes of struggle can be added, those of time, space, text, and subjectivity. The metaphor of plane can be dropped. But struggle defines contemporary continental thought, as struggle and the contests of powers within discourses have also characterized other, older philosophical traditions. Our lineages of struggle have given value and definition to truth, beauty, and wisdom, as well as to social roles, racial and gender values, and other important things. The lineages of struggle are a constitutive part of truth, value, and wisdom, and that constitutive role of struggle in our values and truths provides us our reasons for establishing hierarchies and meaning. Our reasons and meanings are born of the struggles and carry the struggles silently within a surface of practice and justification that can seem to be clear and untroubled.

These movements of differential forces also make it reasonable for us to take apart these values and voices by giving accounts of their formation and of their leverage in our perception in order to find out how particular powers and interests have come to regulate and to find a discourse for common practice. We would not be able to undertake such a task were it not for the differences that speak both in and to the controlling truths and values. One approach to these differences, and one that I prefer, is to learn how to think, feel, and speak within different discourses, within, for example, a discourse that is transcendentally ruled, another that is governed by the value of objectivity, and so forth—granting that this approach is motivated by the language of difference. As we learn to think within the jurisdictions of several competing and dominant values, we may find the loss of a dominating voice in our thinking. We may, that is, learn to think in the differences *among* the jurisdictions, as well as in the jurisdictions themselves, and we may in this way find that our thinking is not what thinking was said to be by many of the accepted authorities. We may, especially, depart from those who believe that knowledge and thought are unified, non-differentiated, and independent of the struggles that mark and form them.

To think in this way, to lose belief in a transcendent authority, is to experience a sense of non-belonging. As we think or write in this manner, what enables us to recognize, hope, and value is itself turning through itself, unfixing itself in its unstable weave of conflicts and differences. We belong to our language and culture and to everything that allows us to feel and think in determinate ways. But this is like belonging to no one. No one constant, no one group, no one time and place. Far from leading to nihilism, many continentalists have found freedom from nihilism in this kind of non-belonging, because in it they have been able to form values that are not as anxious in the face of transformation and that do not require dreams of endless meaning at great bodily cost. They have found ways to moderate some of the perceived destructiveness in our lineages of self-sacrifice, disembodied thought, search for deathless meaning, representation, hopelessness in the absence of unity. The claim is not that change is the essence of reality or that we destroy something natural if we attempt to contain change. The claim is rather that our abilities to value and think have been formed in traditions characterized by processes of transformation, overturning definitive values, and enforcement of knowledge, and by traditions that deny their unfixity as part of their self-characterization and authority.

How are we to contest the kind of nihilism that refuses the unfixity of its fixations? Certainly not by turning our backs on these traditions to which we belong. I indicated at the outset that Heidegger reread the canon in a context of struggle and transformation. He showed the emergence, loss, and presence through loss of the question of being. Nietzsche reread the history of both practices and philosophy and revealed the peculiar Western combination of nihilism, power, dominance, and moral judgment. I have emphasized the differential factors with respect to the thought of Nietzsche and Heidegger in contemporary Continental Philosophy. We can reread our traditional philosophers with their refusals and forgetting, or with the ascendancy of non-meaning over meaning in mind. We can reread and rethink our dominant practical and theoretical formulations by emphasizing their own contexts and differences, and not by playing down those contexts in the thought that they inspire. We can follow the forces that constitute these foundations where they lead us—the account of the force of the origin and value of 'good' in *Beyond Good and Evil* was an initiating work by Nietzsche in this area. We can trace the ways in which the priority of identity over difference has produced certain kinds of knowledge and structures of behavior. We can show the ways in which many values, and perhaps even our understanding of normativity, have tended to perpetuate the injuries and destruction that they are seemingly intended to counter. We might look carefully and critically at the desire to be committed to the right causes and to be 'relevant' in our values. In such endeavors we would attempt to produce knowledges that arise from the loss of transcendental beliefs and of intentions to be authoritative. Non-authoritative knowledge? Orders without transcendence?

You can see where I find myself in relation to the values of authoritative knowledge and orders of transcendence—not only negatively, but positively in the sense that the interests of authoritative knowledge and transcendentally founded orders run through the language in which I write and the movements within which I think. The primary strategy that I have suggested for contesting such forces has been one of thinking 'in' the loss of jurisdiction and belonging as one also thinks in the various discursive identities. The 'in' must be elaborated. I am spared that task in this summary, but we can note that 'loss' is correlated with our calling into question the ethics and politics to which we belong. When awareness occurs outside of the patterns that tell us with clarity who we are, that awareness and belonging seem to allow appearances that are difficult to name in our lineages of recognition. It is not something mystical. It is awareness and appearing that take place outside of our accustomed regions of knowledge and conceptualization.

Another concern that motivates these remarks addresses the destructiveness that might become optional by means of a transformation of our dominant languages and thoughts and values. This would be an ethical and political concern, were the meanings and formations of ethics and politics not themselves in question. The issue of destructiveness certainly belongs to ethics and politics, but if ethics and politics are put in question out of ethical and political concern, and in such a way that their structural inevitability becomes optional, we have the following situation: we move toward nonpolitical language and thought, but this movement is itself political. Or, stated another way, our heritage of the polis remains transforming even as ethics and politics fall increasingly into question.

The movement toward nonpolitical language and thought might occur in a turn to the poetical transformation of language, in a critique of politics as such, in a critique of an ethics of commitment, or in reconsideration of the memorial texture of appearance. In such movements, language and thought undergo transformations through and out of a controlling sense of presence and identity, transformations that do not obliterate identity, but rather issue in experiences and affections that are not empowered primarily by identity and presence. Within identity-controlled perspectives, such experiences seem like radical mortality or a victory for nothing. But these transformations in language and thought are movements away from identity-controlled experience and knowledge, which are ruled by will, subjectivity, and the accompanying sense that appearances require some absolute stabilizing presence. I believe that claims for the primacy of this kind of identity-driven schema aim in the wrong direction, and that one of the edges of contemporary continental thought has crossed the boundaries defined by this approach into a region of differentiation, where words and their combinations can emerge with a new life, one that parts ways with the traditional lineages to which we primarily belong.

This boundary crossing has the effect, among other things, of eroding political clarity and calling into question the value of politics as we often experience it. It replaces political certainty with uncertainty. And it embodies a redirection of the political toward connections that are not primarily articulations of acts of will and principles of identity. Perhaps that is a direction toward non-tribal relations. It is toward very different experiences and values in associations among individuals when compared with many of our images of community and political purposes. It suggests a subtle decline in the force of symbols and metaphors, of unified force and superior meaning, and of the language that supports them: the language of charisma, of the hero, of sacrality, of metaphors of hierarchical height or of surpassing depth. This boundary crossing involves a movement toward values and meanings that transform the basis for political experience, as patterns of recognition and value change beyond our ability to predict them by traditional manners of recognition and establishing normative practices.

I have been concerned with awareness and appearances that take place outside of our accustomed regions of knowledge and conceptualization, with emphasis on connections that are not articulations of acts of will and principles of identity. Thinking in the emergence of these appearances and connections, as well as thinking in the losses that accompany them, provide a mentation that is considerably different from the mentation that has been called reason and thought. It is in the performance of this difference that our philosophical struggle finds its highest pitch of feeling and disagreement. Thought in this difference is where an edge is forming, where who we are is changing slightly, and where the power of a sense of both presence and self slips in its intensity, opening the way for thinking that embodies both the opening and the loss and, with them, neither the overman nor a new god, perhaps not a new tribe, but something else that is not now within the reach of our names.

## Selected Bibliography

1964 "Heidegger's Question about Thought." *Southern Journal of Philosophy* 2 (4).

1966 "Heidegger Reconsidered: A Response to Professor Jonas." *Harvard Theological Review* 59 (2).

1972 "Consciousness and the Conditions of Consciousness." *Review of Metaphysics* 25 (4).

1973a "Existence and Consciousness." *Explorations in Phenomenology*, ed. D. Carr and E. Casey. The Hague: Nijhoff.

1973b "Heidegger, Madness, and Well-Being." *Southwestern Journal of Philosophy*, special Heidegger edition (Fall).

1973c *Martin Heidegger: In Europe and America.* Co-edited with E. Ballard. The Hague: Nijhoff.

1975 "Daseinsanalysis: An Interpretation." *Philosophy Today.*

1980a "Freedom with Darkness and Light: A Study of a Myth." In *New Directions in Psychotherapy,* ed. Gerald Epstein. *Studies of Non-Deterministic Psychology,* vol. 5. New York: Human Sciences Press.

1980b "Psychotherapy: Being One and Being Many." *Journal for Existential Psychiatry and Psychology* 16 (1/2/3).

1981a "The Role of Ontology in Sartre and Heidegger." In *The Philosophy of Jean-Paul Sartre,* ed. P. Schilpp. La Salle, Ill.: Open Court.

1981b "Utter Darkness and Aether: The Element of Hades and the Element of Zeus." In *Philosophy and Archaic Experiences,* ed. John Sallis. Pittsburgh: Duquesne University Press.

1982a *Boundaries in Mind: A Study of Immediate Awareness Based in Psychotherapy.* Chico, Calif., and Chicago: Scholars Press and Crossroads Press.

1982b "History and Truth." *Man and World.*

1983 *Dreaming: An Encounter with Medard Boss,* ed. Chico, Calif.: Scholars Press.

1984a "Foucault's Practice of Thinking." *Research in Phenomenology* 14.

1984b "Speech and the Unspeakable in the Place of the Unconscious." *Human Studies: A Journal for Philosophy and the Human Sciences* (Summer).

1986 "The Pathology of the Father's Rule." *Thought* (Spring).

1987a "On the Unity of Heidegger's Thought." *Research in Phenomenology* 17.

1987b "Postmodern Language." In *Postmodernism—Philosophy and the Arts,* ed. Hugh J. Silverman. Continental Philosophy series, vol. 3. New York: Routledge.

1987c *The Language of Difference.* Atlantic Highlands, N.J.: Humanities Press.

1988a "Heidegger and the Question of Ethics." *Research in Phenomenology* (Winter).

1988b "Psychotherapy: Being One and Being Many." *Review of Existential Psychology and Psychiatry.*

1988c "The De-struction of Being and Time in *Being and Time.*" *Man and World* 21.

1988d "The Middle Voice in *Being and Time.*" In *The Collegium Phaenomenologicum,* ed. Guiseppina Moneta, John Sallis, and Jacques Tamineaux. Dordrecht: Kluwer.

1989a "Assimilating Continental Thought in the Range of American Philosophy." *Soundings* 71 (4).

1989b "The Middle Voice of Metaphysics." *Review of Metaphysics* 42 (4).

1989c *The Question of the Other,* ed. with Arleen Dallery. Albany: State University of New York Press.

1990a "Genealogy and *Differance.*" *Research In Phenomenology.*

1990b *The Question of Ethics: Nietzsche, Foucault, Heidegger.* Bloomington: Indiana University Press.

1991a "Beginning with Belonging and Nonbelonging in Derrida's Thought: A Therapeutic Reflection." *Soundings* 74 (3/4).

1991b "Heidegger's Rectorial Address and the Question of Ethics." *Graduate Faculty Research Journal* (New School for Social Research).

1991c "Nietzsche's Masks." In *Nietzsche and Post-modernism,* ed. Clayton Koelb. Albany: State University of New York Press.

1992a "*Adikia* and Catastrophe: Heidegger's Anaximander Fragment." *Heidegger Studies.*

1992b "Responsibility and Danger." In *Ethics and Responsibility in the Phenom-*

*enological Tradition.* Pittsburgh: Duquesne University, Simon Silverman Phenomenology Center.

1992c "The Pleasure of Therapy." *ellipsis* 1 (2).

1992d "The Question of Ethics in Foucault's Thought." *British Journal of Phenomenology.*

1992e "The Question of the Question in *The Language of Difference* and *The Question of Ethics.*" *Research in Phenomenology.*

1993a "Authenticity/Nonbelonging." In *Reading Heidegger: Commemorations,* ed. John Sallis. Bloomington: Indiana University Press.

1993b "Did Nietzsche Overcome Himself?" *Lonergan Review* 2.

1993c "Thinking Non-Interpretively: Heidegger on Technology and Heraclitus." *Epoché: A Journal for the History of Philosophy.*

1994 "The Pleasure of Therapy." In *Speculations after Freud: Psychoanalysis, Philosophy, and Culture,* ed. Michael Munchow and Sonu Shamdasani. New York: Routledge.

1996 *On the Advantages and Disadvantages of Ethics and Politics.* Bloomington: Indiana University Press.

1998a "Appearances." *Graduate Faculty Philosophy Journal* (New School for Social Research) 10 (2).

1999a "Appearing to Remember Heraclitus." In *The Presocratics after Heidegger,* ed. David Jacobs. Albany: State University of New York Press, forthcoming.

1999b *Interrogating the Tradition,* ed. with John Sallis. Albany: State University of New York Press.

1999c *The Time of Memory.* Albany: State University of New York Press.

1999d "Heroes in Twilight." *The Journal of Southern Philosophy,* forthcoming.

1999e "Nietzsche, Feeling, Transmission, *Phusis.*" *The Journal of Nietzsche Studies,* forthcoming.

1999f "Memory of Time in the Light of Flesh." *Continental Philosophy Review,* forthcoming.

# NINETEEN

## Continental Philosophy on the American Scene
### *An Autobiographical Statement*

▣

# HUGH J. SILVERMAN

The dates do not trace a chronology . . . epistemological markers of events and discursive developments . . . persons, programs, publications, and places constitute elements of an itinerary . . .

## 1966

This was a watershed year. Michel Foucault published *Les Mots et les choses*, which he concluded by announcing the disappearance of the modern subject as a figure of the contemporary episteme. Jacques Lacan published his much-celebrated *Écrits*, in which the self is understood through a chain of signifiers. Roland Barthes produced *Critique et verité*. Jacques Derrida presented his "Structure, Sign, and Play in the Discourse of the Human Sciences" at the Johns Hopkins "Criticism and the Sciences of Man" conference. And I entered graduate school at the age of twenty-one.

That same year, I attended the annual conference of the Society for Phenomenology and Existential Philosophy (SPEP) at Penn State University for the first of more than twenty times. Before entering college, I had read Sartre and Camus and was fascinated by Pascal and Descartes; as an undergraduate, I studied some analytic philosophy of language and James's pragmatism. But as a graduate student, I encountered Husserl and Merleau-Ponty. Phenomenology struck me as a philosophy that made sense. And SPEP made it especially vivid for me. I heard lectures by living phenomenological philosophers—Paul Ricoeur on Husserl and Wittgenstein, William Richardson on Heidegger—and a translation of Derrida's "The Copula Supplement: Philosophy before Linguistics" was circulated to all participants. I met the white-haired John Wild and many other figures who would become legends or friends, colleagues or counterparts. Little did I know that fourteen years later I would become co-director of that very same Society.

In the mid-1960s, the only labels available for these European-derived philosophies were "phenomenology," "Existentialism," "phenomenological existentialism," and "existential phenomenology." Existential psychology and even existential psychiatry were on the rise. "Continental Philosophy" did not yet exist.

Although I had already spent two summers (1963 and 1965) studying in Paris, in 1966 the names of Foucault, Barthes, Lacan, and Derrida were completely new to me. But a year later, after completing a master's thesis on "Merleau-Ponty's Phenomenology of Perception and Robbe-Grillet's Novels," I began six years of doctoral study at Stanford University. In the summer of 1968, I went to Paris on a small scholarship, arriving just in the middle of the May–June revolts. It was a tumultuous but exciting time. Paris was in turmoil. Workers and students had joined together to launch a full-scale attack on the miserable state of the economy and the educational system. The Rue St. Jacques was completely torn up as cobblestones became ready-to-hand weapons. The Sorbonne was effectively closed; in July, classes were held in the Lycée Louis le Grand behind the Pantheon.

## 1971–72

By the time I returned to Paris for the academic year 1971–72 as a *boursier du gouvernement francais,* the French educational system had been radically transformed. At the University of Paris-X (Nanterre) philosophy department, where Mikel Dufrenne received me in his doctoral seminar, Jean-François Lyotard, Louis Marin, Gilbert Lascault, and many others came to lecture. Dufrenne himself was developing his account of "expressivity" in aesthetic experience. Levinas was lecturing on Heidegger's *Introduction to Metaphysics,* which I followed carefully while trying to read Heidegger in the German (with the help of a year's study at the Paris Goethe Institut). Dufrenne sent me to see Paul Ricoeur, who included me in his research seminar on "Metaphor" at the Centre de Recherches Phenomenologiques. And Roland Barthes invited me to attend his seminar on the recent history of semiology at the Ecole Pratique des Hautes Etudes. Barthes had not yet been elected to the Collège de France, but Foucault and Lévi-Strauss had, and I attended their lectures regularly.

I had traveled to Paris with the support of my Stanford dissertation advisor, the former dean of Humanities and Sciences, Philip Rhinelander. My purpose was to write on the concept of "ambiguity"—what I called "existential ambiguity" to distinguish it from linguistic and perceptual ambiguities and then to develop this notion through the thought of Heidegger, Sartre, and Merleau-Ponty. Dagfinn Føllesdal had taught me to read Husserl carefully and systematically. Rhinelander showed me how to think about philosophical problems not only in the broad history of ideas, but also in that they signify in human, educational, and social terms; he insisted they should not become what Whitehead called "inert ideas." John Goheen, who had established Stanford's philosophy department and served as chair for many years, made philosophy and its history come alive for me. We had the idea to compile an anthology on "theories of the self." I wrote short introductions to many of the major twentieth-century theories. Although the project was never completed, it was invaluable when I began to teach philosophical psychology several years later.

I went to Paris as a budding phenomenologist. Everywhere friends and peers in France told me that phenomenology was *passé,* that I would need to learn about structuralism and especially what was forcing itself to be called "poststructuralism." I had read Dufrenne's *Pour l'homme* (1968), in which he shows (from his existential phenomenological perspective) the limitations of Heidegger, Lévi-Strauss, Althusser, Foucault, Derrida, et al. while also offering his own conception of the human subject. But many claimed that these were precisely the figures one needed to read and study, that Dufrenne's phenomenology, so ably developed in his 1952 *Phenomenology of Aesthetic Experience* and in subsequent books, could not stand up to new developments in structuralism, semiology, and poststructuralism. I took as my task to determine whether this was right or not.

Before I left for Paris, James Edie had offered me the project of translating Merleau-Ponty's *Consciousness and the Acquisition of Language* for his Northwestern University Press series. I learned that Merleau-Ponty, while lecturing at the Sorbonne as professor of child psychology and pedagogy in the late 1940s, had already discovered intimate connections between his own phenomenology of perception and the semiology of de Saussure. This gave me the confidence to pursue the connection further. It also helped me to work out the theory of "ambiguity" for my 1973 doctoral thesis on Heidegger, Sartre, and Merleau-Ponty.

What I did not count on during my year in Paris was the role that Jacques Derrida would come to play in my own thought. Indeed, I knew little of Derrida when I was invited to a weekend seminar in June 1972 in which he held forth for more than six hours each of three days in a small seminar room at the Ecole Normale Superieure (rue d'Ulm). Although these lectures occurred near the end of my stay, they marked my subsequent philosophical development.

## 1974–79

In 1974, I accepted an appointment as assistant professor of philosophy and comparative literature at the State University of New York at Stony Brook. What intrigued me about Stony Brook were the few phenomenologically oriented philosophers who were already there, but also that I would be expected to teach both in the philosophy department and in the new comparative literature program.

After a year, I was asked to run the philosophy department colloquium, which I did for the next seven years. I sought to establish a broad-based dialogue among philosophers of different colors, but also (with a grant from the Matchette Foundation) to establish a continuing lecture series by philosophers from Europe. There were weekly Friday colloquia, and at least once each year we organized a conference on campus: "Leonardo and Philosophy" (spring 1976); "Aesthetics and the Public" (supported by the New York Council for the Humanities for the fall of 1976); "Linguistics and Literature" (fall 1976); "Piaget, Philosophy and the Human Sciences" (spring 1977); "The Post-Structuralist Enterprise" (fall 1977; Richard Rand and I put together the first conference on Derrida's thought with Derrida himself present); "History, Critique and Text" (spring 1979); and the fourth annual Merleau-Ponty Circle conference (fall 1979).

At the same time that it was important to provide a dynamic and exciting intellectual environment on campus, I was also glad to accept speaking invitations elsewhere. I thought that this would help to enhance the role of what was soon to become Continental Philosophy, as well as the reputation of the departments and university to which I was committed. I participated in the first conference of the International Association for Philosophy and Literature (IAPL), which was held at Harvard Divinity School with a small group of thirty people in 1976 (at which time I was elected to the IAPL executive committee, on which I have served for almost two decades); and I participated in the first Merleau-Ponty Circle conference in the fall of 1976 (where I offered my rereading of Merleau-Ponty's last course lectures, which I had translated as "Philosophy and Non-Philosophy since Hegel"). For the past nineteen years, the Merleau-Ponty Circle has been held in September at a different university; I have attended all but one.

During this five-year period, I read several dozen papers at a variety of conferences and universities on topics related to the work of Dufrenne, Sartre, Beckett, Merleau-Ponty, Foucault, Heidegger, Piaget, and Barthes, as well as on the differences between Sartre's phenomenology and different forms of structuralism. I was also developing some theoretical accounts of the self, of literature, of language, of communication, and of culture in connection with what I then called a "hermeneutic semiology."

When I began teaching at Stony Brook in 1974, no one used the term "Continental Philosophy." In February 1978, the University of Chicago (under the genius of Michael Sukale) organized a conference on "Continental Philosophy" where I presented my first reading of Derrida, entitled "Self-Decentering in Derrida." The term "Continental Philosophy" was already in the air, curiously at one of the least likely places—the philosophy department at the University of Chicago.

That June, I was invited to teach a three-week graduate seminar at Duquesne University. I entitled it "Sartre/Barthes/Foucault"; at the time, Barthes and Foucault were practically never taught in a philosophy department. The students in the seminar numbered fewer than ten, but they included Stephen Watson, Dorothea Olkowski, Fred Evans, Dan Tate, Peg Birmingham, all now familiar names on the contemporary scene. That summer I also met Wilhelm Wurzer, who had just joined the Duquesne faculty and with whom I would, more than ten years later, organize the International Philosophical Seminar in the South Tyrol each summer.

From Duquesne, I flew to my first Warwick Continental Philosophy Workshop, organized by David Wood. It was an incredible concatenation of personalities and interests all coinciding in this one place for several days in England. The topic was "Heidegger and Language" and—for me—this was the birth of Continental Philosophy! I knew none of the participants beforehand—I would not be who I am now without them: David Wood himself, whose paper on Heidegger and Derrida mirrored my own; David Krell, then teaching Americanistics at Mannheim in Germany; Robert Bernasconi from Essex; Tony O'Connor from Cork, Ireland, who later came to spend a year with us at Stony Brook; Alfons Grieder, who maintained the hermeneutic tradition at the City University, London; and if memory serves, John Llewelyn from Edinburgh, Wolfe Mays from Manchester, and John Heaton from London were there too. Like the 1966 SPEP meeting at Penn State, this 1978 Warwick Workshop marked a turning point for me, for I discovered that European philosophy had a place in Britain. From Warwick, I continued on to a psychology conference in Munich, where I developed further my "hermeneutic semiology of the self," which I had first presented at the Williams College Conference on Hermeneutics the previous year. Then in Perugia, Italy for my first Collegium Phaenomenologicum, I participated in three of the five weeks organized by Thomas Sheehan on Heidegger's *Sein und Zeit*. Perugia was only a year or two old at the time, but I would go on to contribute to the Collegium seven different summers between 1978 and 1988, twice giving a week-long course. The summer was not yet over; I then flew from Nice to Uppsala, Sweden, for the World Congress of Sociology, where I presented my account of heterotopias as arising out of the conjuncture of utopias and dystopias. And at the end of August,

I spoke at an American Psychological Association session in Toronto on the status of philosophical psychology. That fall, I returned twice to Duquesne, for the Merleau-Ponty Circle and for my eighth SPEP conference, where I gave an invited lecture on Sartre and Barthes. In retrospect, I do not quite know how I made it through the year, but since I had just turned thirty-three during the summer, I suppose I was still young and agile enough to traverse the path. In any case, they granted me tenure at Stony Brook that academic year, but I hardly noticed, because in the spring of 1979 I was invited to teach at New York University the first of four semesters, three as graduate seminars, on the "Philosophical Essay" in comparative literature.

Near the end of the 1970s, the self-definition of the strongest element of the Stony Brook philosophy department—its phenomenological-existential tradition—was transformed into a Continental Philosophy contribution to the doctoral program. The difference was not insignificant. The introduction of the term "Continental Philosophy" became critical to the reshaping of the Stony Brook program, and later to the self-definition of many other graduate programs in philosophy. More than twelve years after the ground-breaking 1966 Johns Hopkins Humanities Center conference, philosophy departments began to take on the rightful responsibility of teaching Continental Philosophy. And Stony Brook was at the lead in this respect.

## Of Inscriptions and Textualities

It has now been just twenty years since I joined the Stony Brook department. In the first decade, I set as my task to work through the philosophical dilemma with which I was presented when I went to Paris: the phenomenological basis that I had brought with me, and the structuralist alternative that I encountered there. I wanted to write the differences between phenomenology and structuralism while also developing a position which I came to call a hermeneutic semiology.

In *Inscriptions: Between Phenomenology and Structuralism* (1987), I demonstrate how a hermeneutic semiology operates between the phenomenological tradition, in which meaning is given in an act of experience, and the semiological tradition, in which significations are proliferated along chains of sign relations. *Inscriptions* focuses particularly on the relations between the theory of the self and the role of language in human experience. Can there be a theory of the self apart from a theory of language, or must the self be already inscribed in the production of signs and signifying practices? In order to address this question, I begin with the founder of phenomenology—Edmund Husserl and his theory of the self. Heidegger's reformulation of phenomenology into a hermeneutic of the Being of beings is later turned into an account of language speaking and the speaking in the place of language. But it was Sartre's strong opposition to structuralism in all its phases that also marks the place between. With elements of the Husserlian theory of the constitutive self de-transcendentalized, Sartre also incorporates elements of the Heideggerian commitment to an existentialized and differential theory of the self. But what Sartre rejects (though only partially) is the role of language in the constitution of the self. Merleau-Ponty, by contrast, provides the link and articulates the place between as the "speaking subject" ("speaking speech" and "spoken speech"). Furthermore, Merleau-Ponty's notions of the ambiguity of experience, of the incorporated subject, of indirect language, articulate and describe this place between the phenomenological and structuralist alternatives. While only suggested in *Inscriptions,* Foucault's concept of epistemological practices in accounting for the disappearance of the human subject in the contemporary discourses of the human sciences, and Derrida's *différance* as an operation of self-decentering, provide reformulations and attempts to go beyond the "place between." In short, archaeology of knowledge and deconstruction signal a transformation and a further inscription of ambiguity now as hermeneutic semiology, which is neither semiological structuralism nor phenomenological hermeneutics.

In my second decade at Stony Brook, which culminated in *Textualities: Between Hermeneutics and Deconstruction* (1994), my task was to articulate further this "between place" as a theory of difference. Through readings of philosophical, literary, artistic, anthropological, autobiographical, and political texts, I sought to elaborate an understanding of the textuality of texts rather than to give a theory of the text. A textuality occurs when a text constitutes or determines itself in terms of specifiable meaning structures, or when inscriptions mark the interstices of a number of texts. For instance, in certain philosophical texts there is often an inscription of the self as written, though the attention may be on an abstract conceptual formulation. By contrast, in many autobiographical texts, the writer is typically known as something entirely other than a writer of autobiographies, e.g., Thoreau, Nietzsche, Sartre, and Lévi-Strauss. Autobiographical textuality operates in both cases. Autobiographical textuality is an especially rich node in which the link between the self and language is textually inscribed.

But also scriptive, visual, and institutional textualities, to take some examples which I explore at length in *Textualities,* provide access to the reading of paintings, poems and novels, philosophical theories, films, and universities as textualized institutions. In order to examine these textualities in some detail, I wanted to carefully articulate something like a theory of textuality. To do so, I looked at the texture of current continental theory it-self—in particular, hermeneutics, semiology, interrogation, and deconstruc-tion. The passage from hermeneutics to deconstruction through Saussurian and Barthesian semiology and Merleau-Pontean interrogation demonstrates how the poverty of sign systems can be overcome in juxtaposition with the severe limitations of a hermeneutic theory based purely on interpretation. Interrogating the places of difference, the moments of juxtaposition, the margins of inscriptions, has opened up the frame for studies of the textu-alization of texts. This is not a fetishism of texts as some have claimed, for the interest is not in the texts themselves. And texts are not limited only to written inscriptions. Ultimately the readings—how the texts are inscribed in culture, experience, and institutions—operate to mark what is given im-portance, what is seen, what is heard, and what underlies who we are, how we are, and what we know.

## 1980–86

The 1980s marked the flowering of Continental Philosophy on the Ameri-can scene. At first, those who had come to accept the term "Continental Philosophy" actually understood it as a synonym for "European Philoso-phy." They mistook it for a geographical alternative to British analytic phi-losophy expanded to include recent developments in American linguistic philosophy. Some thought of it as just a new name for what used to be called "Phenomenology and Existentialism," which had occupied the space of no more than one course in a largely analytic philosophy curriculum. Still others were worried that this term somehow obliterated the prevailing phenomenological method which they, as phenomenologists in the Hus-serlian tradition, wanted to apply in a wide range of human science disci-plines.

In the winter of 1980, I was invited to spend a term at the University of Warwick as visiting senior lecturer. During my several months in Britain, I had an opportunity to give (and to benefit from reactions to) preliminary versions of what would later become *Inscriptions* throughout England, Ire-land, the Netherlands, and Belgium. Teaching with David Wood in the "Re-cent Continental Philosophy" course and with Martin Warner in the phi-losophy-literature Degree seminar was a fascinating experience. I learned firsthand how the British higher educational system works. Discussions with David Wood were often oriented toward an understanding of what "Conti-nental Philosophy" could mean and how we could develop new directions for contemporary philosophy with it. From his point of view, "Continental

Philosophy" was still a representation in Britain of what was going on in France and Germany, and since we were both interested in deconstruction and poststructuralism this was the focus of our attention.

I was looking for new ways to talk about this growing philosophy that was spreading like wildfire in the United States. As Continental Philosophy proliferated, and with it the term itself, it became clear that it was a mode of philosophizing all of its own, one that drew upon European philosophical traditions but was adapted particularly for an English-language context and type of thinking. Largely interpretive, evaluative, textual, and cultural-aesthetic-political, Continental Philosophy took on a rather unique style and brand of theoretical practice. The writings of Hegel, Marx, Nietzsche, Kierkegaard, Husserl, Heidegger, Sartre, de Beauvoir, Merleau-Ponty, Benjamin, Adorno, Saussure, Barthes, Lacan, Foucault, Derrida, Kristeva, Irigaray, and Lyotard, among others, constituted what I have elsewhere called "reference texts." The field was broadening to include not only transcendental phenomenologists, existential phenomenologists, and hermeneutic phenomenologists, but also structuralists, semiologists, hermeneutic semiologists, critical theorists, Freudian psychoanalysts, French feminists, poststructuralists, deconstructionists, and postmodernists. Many new topics, concerns, and perspectives not even treated by European philosophers would become important for English-language continental philosophizing.

Having returned to the U.S. in April 1980 for some additional lectures, I went back to Europe in July for a conference in Manchester on the Phenomenology of the Body. I then gave a lecture series in French to advanced (non-French) students on "l'esthetique de Merleau-Ponty" for the Centre International d'Etudes Françaises at the Université de Nice, an assignment I would repeat the following summer on the topic of "l'autobiographie en France." Other than the Cerisy conference on Sartre the year before, it was the first time that I had been invited to lecture in France.

In the fall of 1980, I was elected co-director (with Don Ihde) of the Society for Phenomenology and Existential Philosophy. One of our first tasks was to rethink the meaning of the society and its purpose. There were significant tensions at work: some wanted SPEP to remain committed to the presentation of the major texts and practices of the phenomenological tradition. Interpretations of Husserl texts would be of principal interest, to be followed by studies of Sartre and Merleau-Ponty. For devoted Husserlians, Heidegger was outside the frame. For those committed to the human sciences, applications to psychology and sociology were the passion. For some, structuralism and semiology had been too long excluded. For others, poststructualism and deconstruction were the new wave. For still others, French feminism had to be included. And another group felt that Critical Theory and the Frankfurt School needed a place. The task was to create a forum for all these different commitments in the contemporary philosophical context. One of the earliest debates in the executive committee from 1980 on was the question as to whether even the name of the society was obsolete, whether "Continental Philosophy" should not be somehow included in the title.

We decided to keep the paleonymn but to transform the annual SPEP programs to address contemporary concerns in Continental Philosophy. Gradually the society grew from a modest group of about 300 adherents to some 1,200 by the time I completed my second term as co-director in 1986. No longer were the fall conferences filled mostly with white-haired old men; by 1986, participants included a large contingent of students and young faculty members, both male and female. We introduced "Current Research Sessions" where recent books would be discussed by other philosophers familiar with the field, with a response from the author. With the enormous growth of Continental Philosophy publications in the 1980s, there were many more new books available for these sessions than there were places on the program.

As an executive director of SPEP, I was expected to edit or co-edit five volumes of essays resulting from the six annual conferences between 1980 and 1986. Perhaps the most successful was the one entitled *Hermeneutics and Deconstruction* (1985) which even struck the fancy of columnist William Safire, who devoted one of his syndicated articles to the terms "hermeneutics" and "deconstruction." Friends sent me a copy of the article from Paris, where it appeared in the *International Herald Tribune. Postmodernism and Continental Philosophy* (1987) also marked a new direction (an interest in the articulation of postmodernism) that SPEP had already undertaken. The final volume, *Writing the Politics of Difference* (1988), as its title suggests, confronts the multiple philosophical and political differences that had come to mark SPEP.

In 1983, with Thomas Seebohm (for the Husserl Circle), John Sallis (for the Heidegger Conference), and myself (representing the Merleau-Ponty Circle), Duquesne University Press published *Continental Philosophy in America*. A small committee from each society had selected the four best essays presented at the annual conferences from 1975 to 1980. We produced a second volume with Algis Mickunas (for the Husserl Circle), Ted Kisiel (for the Heidegger Conference), and Al Lingis (for the Merleau-Ponty Circle) for the years 1980 to 1985 under the title *The Horizons of Continental Philosophy* (1988).

In the mid-1980s, while completing *Inscriptions*, my British editor at Routledge asked if I would be interested in developing a journal in Continental Philosophy. A small group of Stony Brook graduate students (Jim Hatley, Brian Seitz, J. Barry, later joined by James Clarke) expressed a similar interest on the other side of the Atlantic. We decided to create something rather unique and special—what would be neither a journal nor a book series but something in between. Articles would be solicited according to a special theme (alternating between a figure/movement and a current topic), but contributed essays would also be considered. In order to maintain the highest quality, every essay would be reviewed by at least two members of the staff and by at least one outside reader. To date, the Routledge *Continental Philosophy* series has published seven volumes.

## 1987–94

In the spring of 1987, having served on the executive committee and having participated in the organization of every conference since its inception in 1976, I became executive director of the International Association for Philosophy and Literature (IAPL). In light of this new position, SUNY Press agreed to an arrangement with the IAPL (similar to the one we had established in SPEP) for the publication of volumes resulting from annual conferences. The first, which I edited with Gary Aylesworth, appeared under the title *The Textual Sublime: Deconstruction and its Differences* (1990). Since then, Gary Shapiro's *After the Future* and Thomas R. Flynn and Dalia Judovitz's *Dialectic and Narrative* have appeared in the series published by Northwestern University Press.

An increasing number of avenues for publication in Continental Philosophy had began to take shape. Among them, the Humanities Press *Contemporary Studies in Philosophy and the Human Sciences* book series was born in 1979. We published some of the most prestigious translations and original contributions in the field. In 1989, Keith Ashfield, the new publisher, decided to reform Humanities Press's editorial direction and asked me to edit the *Contemporary Studies* series with Graeme Nicholson. This was the beginning of a whole new life for the series, including *inter alia* translations of works by Maurice Merleau-Ponty, Otto Pöggeler, Carlo Sini, Gianni Vattimo, Maurizio Ferraris, Sarah Kofman, Hermann Lang, and Dominique Janicaud. The press also asked me to form another series entitled *Philosophy and Literary Theory*, which would blaze new trails at the juncture between Continental Philosophy and poetic/literary/aesthetic theory with books by Wilhelm Wurzer, Véronique Fóti, Jean-François Lyotard, Stephen Barker, Robert Bernasconi, Richard Kearney, Michael Naas, Gianni Vattimo, and Jean-Luc Nancy.

In the next six years, when not carrying out my regular duties at Stony Brook, I would serve as visiting professor in England, Italy, Austria, and France. In the spring of 1988, I went to the University of Leeds in England as visiting professor of philosophy (while David Holdcroft taught in my place at Stony Brook). The Leeds students had a passion for Continental Philosophy. George Ross MacDonald taught Nietzsche texts the first term and I followed with Nietzsche interpretations by Heidegger, Derrida, and Deleuze. That spring, I was again invited to give a number of papers up and down England, Scotland, Wales, and Ireland. Everywhere I went I learned about the dire conditions British academics were experiencing at that time. A visiting professorship in the fall of 1989 at the Univeristá di Torino, Italy on "Art and Truth" provided me with the opportunity to develop further what would become *Textualities*. The occasion to teach, discuss, and explore new ideas with Italian colleagues and students in Torino helped to enhance my growing interest in contemporary Italian philosophy.

In the summer semester of 1993 as Gastprofessor at the University of Vienna's Philosophisches Institut, I lectured on "Ästhetische Theorie und Postmodernes Denken" and "Dekonstruktion als Philosophie," and the following January, as Professeur invité for the Faculté des lettres at the Université de Nice, I took up the topic "Derrida Lecteur de Husserl." In each of these cases, my sense of European philosophers and students, their interests, their commitments, their philosophical concerns, has helped to enhance my sense of where Italian, French, and German philosophy is moving in the present decade. Perhaps not as ironic as it may seem, the interest in Continental Philosophy as practiced in the U.S. has now begun to be appreciated in Europe. That French, Italian, and Austrian philosophers (as in Britain already a decade ago) want to know more from American continental philosophers —that they now recognize American philosophy as hardly just analytic or even post-analytic philosophy—has opened up the field of discussion and understanding much more broadly.

These recent invitations and teaching experiences have also provided a context for directions I want to take in my own thought dealing with the question of postmodern philosophy and aesthetic theory. Since the completion of *Textualities,* I have been attempting to explore how the textualization and juxtaposition of events, experiences, ideas, institutions, and texts constitute the postmodern frames of the modern; how the postmodern textualizes itself in modernity; and how quoted, repeated, recognized, and culturally imbedded inscriptions mark postmodern theories, films, buildings, and literature. The role of Continental Philosophy in the articulation of postmodernism for contemporary cultural theory and textual practice continues to open up a rich domain of inquiry for my future work.

Recently, I have had the opportunity to develop my current ongoing research on postmodern textuality as visiting professor at the University of Helsinki (January 1997) and as Gastprofessor again at the University of Vienna (June 1997). In many respects the students and colleagues at these institutions as well as those at SUNY–Stony Brook in the departments of philosophy and comparative studies have provided exciting contexts and multiple frames for this ongoing research.

## Selected Bibliography

1973 Maurice Merleau-Ponty, *Consciousness and the Acquisition Of Language*, trans. and preface. Evanston: Northwestern University Press.

1974 "Artistic Creation and Human Action." *Mosaic: Literature and Ideas* 8 (1).

1976a "Dufrenne's Phenomenology of Poetry." *Philosophy Today* 20 (4).

1976b "The Self in Husserl's Crisis." *Journal of the British Society for Phenomenology* 7 (1).

1978a "A Cross-Cultural Approach to the De-Ontological Self Paradigm." With David A. Dilworth. *The Monist* 61 (1).

1978a "Heidegger and Merleau-Ponty: Interpreting Hegel." In *Radical Phenomenology: Essays in Memory of Martin Heidegger,* ed. John Sallis. Atlantic Highlands, N.J.: Humanities Press.

1978c "Sartre versus Foucault on Civilizational Study." *Philosophy and Social Criticism* 5 (3).

1978d "Self-Decentering: Derrida Incorporated." *Research in Phenomenology* 8.

1979a "Biographical Situations, Cognitive Structures and Human Development: Confronting Sartre and Piaget." *Journal of Phenomenological Psychology* 10 (2).

1979b "For a Hermeneutic Semiology of the Self." *Philosophy Today* 23 (2).

1979c "Merleau-Ponty's Human Ambiguity." *Journal of the British Society for Phenomenology* 9 (1).

1980a "From Utopia/Dystopia to Heterotopia: An Interpretive Topology." *Philosophy and Social Criticism* 78 (2).

1980b *Jean-Paul Sartre: Contemporary Approaches to His Philosophy,* ed. with Fredrick A. Elliston. Pittsburgh: Duquesne University Press.

1980c *Piaget, Philosophy and the Human Sciences,* ed. Atlantic Highlands, N.J.: Humanities Press. Translated into Spanish as *Piaget, la Filosofía y las Ciencias Humanas.* Mexico: Fondo de Cultura Económica, 1989.

1980d "Phenomenology." *Social Research* 47 (4). Special issue "Philosophy: An Assessment," ed. Peter Caws.

1980e "Un Egale Deux ou l'espace autobiographique et ses limites." *Le Deux (Revue d'esthétique),* ed. M. Le Bot, pp. 10–18.

1981a "Merleau-Ponty and the Interrogation of Language." In *Merleau-Ponty: Perception, Structure, Language,* ed. John Sallis. Atlantic Highlands, N.J.: Humanities Press.

1981b "The Limits of Logocentrism (On the Way to Grammatology)." In *Heidegger and Language,* ed. David Wood. Coventry, England: Parousia Press. Reprinted in *Phenomenology and the Human Sciences,* ed. J. N. Mohanty. The Hague: Nijhoff, 1985.

1982a "Autobiographical Textuality: The Case of Thoreau's *Walden.*" *Semiotica* 41 (1–4).

1982b "Beckett, Philosophy and the Self." In *The Philosophical Reflection of Man in Literature,* ed. A.-T. Tymieniecka. *Analecta Husserliana* 12. Dordrecht: Reidel.

1982c "Cézanne's Mirror Stage." *Journal of Aesthetics and Art Criticism* 40 (4). Reprinted in *The Merleau-Ponty Aesthetics Reader: Philosophy and Painting,* ed. Galen A. Johnson. Evanston: Northwestern University Press, 1994.

1982d "Communicability." In *Interpersonal Communication: Essays in Phenomenology and Hermeneutics,* ed. Joseph J. Pilotta. Washington, D.C.: University Press of America.

1982e "The Philosopher's Body and the Body of the Photograph." *Journal of the British Society for Phenomenology* 13 (3).

1983a *Continental Philosophy in America,* ed. with John Sallis and Thomas Seebohm. Pittsburgh: Duquesne University Press.

1983b "The Continental Face of Philosophy in America." *Philosophy Today* 27 (4). Translated into Dutch by Adriaan Th. Peperzak as "Orientatie: Continentale filosofie in Amerika," *Wijsgerig Perspectief op Maatschappij en Wetenschap* 25 (4) (1984/85).

1983c "Writing (on Deconstruction) at the Edge of Metaphysics." *Research in Phenomenology* 13.

1984 "The Self in Question." In *Phenomenology in Practice and Theory,* ed. William S. Hamrick. The Hague: Nijhoff.

1985a *Hermeneutics and Deconstruction.* Ed. with Don Ihde. Albany: State University of New York Press.

1985b "Merleau-Ponty's New Beginning: Preface to *The Experience of Others.*" Co-translated with Fred Evans. *Review of Existential Psychology and Psychiatry* 18 (1–3).

1985c "Textuality and the University." *Boundary 2* 13 (2–3).

1985d "The Autobiographical Textuality of Nietzsche's *Ecce Homo.*" In *Why Nietzsche Now?,* ed. Daniel O'Hara. Bloomington: Indiana University Press.

1986a "Interrogation and Deconstruction." *Phänomenologische Forschungen.* Band 18, "Studien für neueren französischen Phänomenologie." Freiburg: Karl Alber.

1986b "Le Lieu de l'histoire: Sartre et Foucault." *Etudes Sartriennes* 2–3. Special number of *Cahiers de sémiotique textuelle* 5–6, Université de Paris X.

1986c "Postmodernism, Language, and Textuality" [Part I]. *Phenomenology and Pedagogy* 4 (1). "What Is Textuality?" [Part II]. *Phenomenology and Pedagogy* 4 (2).

1986d "Who Signs This Poem? On the Institution of Poetry." *Rivista di estetica* 26 (22). Special number on "Filosofia e Poesia."

1987 *Inscriptions: Between Phenomenology and Structuralism.* New York: Routledge.

1988a *Philosophy and Non-Philosophy since Merleau-Ponty.* With a translation of Merleau-Ponty's "Philosophy and Non-Philosophy since Hegel." Continental Philosophy Series, ed., vol. 1. New York: Routledge.

1988b *Postmodernism and Continental Philosophy,* ed. with Donn Welton. Albany: State University of New York Press.

1988c *The Horizons of Continental Philosophy: Essays on Husserl, Heidegger and Merleau-Ponty,* ed. with Algis Mickunas, Theodore Kisiel, and Alphonso Lingis. Dordrecht: Kluwer.

1989a *Derrida and Deconstruction.* Continental Philosophy Series, ed., vol. 2. New York and London: Routledge.

1989b "Philosophical Passages: An Essay in Self-Presentation." In *American Phenomenology: Origins and Developments,* ed. Eugene Kaelin and Calvin O. Schrag. Dordrecht: Kluwer.

1990a "Merleau-Ponty and Derrida: Writing on Writing." In *Ontology and Alterity in Merleau-Ponty,* ed. Galen Johnson and Michael B. Smith. Evanston: Northwestern University Press.

1990b *Postmodernism—Philosophy and the Arts,* ed. Continental Philosophy Series, ed., vol. 3. New York: Routledge. Translated into Korean in the Koreaone Academy of Literature series. Seoul: Koreaone Press, 1992.

1990c *The Textual Sublime: Deconstruction and Its Differences,* ed. with Gary E. Aylesworth. Contemporary Studies in Philosophy and Literature, vol. 1. Albany: State University of New York Press.

1991a *Gadamer and Hermeneutics,* ed. Continental Philosophy Series, ed., vol. 4. New York: Routledge.

1991b "The Text of the Speaking Subject: From Merleau-Ponty to Kristeva." In *Merleau-Ponty Vivant,* ed. M. C. Dillon. Albany: State University of New York Press.

1991c *Writing the Politics of Difference,* ed. Albany: State University of New York Press.

1992a "Merleau-Ponty and Postmodernism." In *Merleau-Ponty: Hermeneutics and Postmodernism,* ed. Thomas Busch and Shaun Gallagher. Albany: State University of New York Press.

1992b *Merleau-Ponty: Texts and Dialogues.* Ed. with James Barry, Jr. Atlantic Highlands, N.J.: Humanities Press.

1992c "The Inscription of the Moment: Zarathustra's Gate." *International Philosophical Studies* 24 (2).

1993a "Foucault/Derrida: Ursprünge der Geschichte," trans. Erik Vogt, *Österreichische Zeitschrift für Geschichtswissenschaften,* Klios Texte 3.

1993b *Questioning Foundations: Truth/Subjectivity/Culture,* ed. Continental Philosophy Series, ed., vol. 5. New York: Routledge.

1993c "Visibilität und Textualität: . . . ein nahezu vollkommener Chiasmus. . . ," trans. Anke Müller. *Fragmente—Schriftenreihe zur Psychoanalyse* 41 (Kassel). Also published in *Der Entzug der Bilder: Visuelle Realitäten,* ed. Michael Wetzel and Herta Wolf. Munich: Fink.

1994a "French Structuralism and After." In *Twentieth-Century Continental Philosophy,* ed. Richard Kearney. Routledge History of Philosophy Series, vol. 8. New York: Routledge.

1994b "Postmodernism and Contemporary Italian Philosophy." *Man and World* 27: 343–348.

1994c *Textualität der Philosophie—Philosophie und Literatur,* ed. with Ludwig Nagl. Wiener Reihe, Themen der Philosophie. Band 7. Vienna and Munich: Oldenburg.

1994d "Textualität der Postmoderne: Lyotard, Ereignis, Erhabenes," trans. Erik Vogt. In *Textualität der Philosophie: Philosophie und Literatur,* ed. with Ludwig

Nagl. Wiener Reihe, Themen der Philosophie. Band 7. Vienna and Munich: Oldenbourg.

1994e *Textualities: Between Hermeneutics and Deconstruction.* New York: Routledge.

1994f "Traces du sublime: La Visibilité, l'expressivité et l'inconscient," trans. Carol Richards. *"Esthétiques en chantier:" Revue d'esthétique* 22: 83–92.

1995a "Lyotard en het postmoderne sublime." In *Lyotard Lezen: Ethiek, Onmenselijkheid en Sensibiliteit,* ed. Richard Brons and Harry Kunneman, pp. 80–88. Amsterdam: Boom.

1995b "The Child's New Logic (Derridean Choreographies)." *Zarathustra's Joyful Annunciations—Joyful Wisdom: Studies in Postmodern Ethics* 4: 86–101.

1995c "The Mark of Postmodernism: Reading *Roger Rabbit.*" *Cinémas: Revue d'études cinematographiques/Journal of Film Studies* 5 (3): 151–164.

1996a "Modernism and Postmodernism." In *Encyclopedia of Philosophy.* Supplement. New York: Macmillan.

1996b "Traces of the Sublime: Visibility, Expressivity, and the Unconscious." In *Merleau-Ponty: Difference, Materiality, Painting,* ed. Véronique Fóti, pp. 128–136. Atlantic Highlands, N.J.: Humanities Press.

1996c "'Wenn ich Fremder bin, gibt es keine Fremden': Reflexionen über postmoderne Fremde," trans. Daniel Weidner. *Psychoanalyse und Philosophie, Mitteilung des Instituts für Wissenschaft und Kunst* 51 (1): 10–16.

1997a *Inscriptions: After Phenomenology and Structuralism.* Paperback ed. Evanston: Northwestern University Press.

1997b "Nietzsche's Italics: Chaiasmatic Inscriptions—Between the Sheets" and "Nietzches Cors(iv)o: Chiasmatische Inschriften/Ein-schreibungen—Zwischen den Tafeln." In *Nietzsche in Italien: Text—Bild—Signatur,* by Maria Theresia Litschauer. Vienna.

1997c *Piaget, Philosophy and the Human Sciences,* ed. Evanston: Northwestern University Press.

1997d *Philosophy and Non-Philosophy since Merleau-Ponty,* ed. with a translation of Merleau-Ponty's "Philosophy and Non-Philosophy since Hegel." Evanston: Northwestern University Press.

1997e "Postmodern Interruptions: Between Merleau-Ponty and Derrida." In *Écart and Différance: On Seeing and Reading in Merleau-Ponty and Derrida,* ed. M. C. Dillon, pp. 208–219. Atlantic Highlands, N.J.: Humanities Press.

1997f *Textualitäten: Zwischen Hermeneutik und Dekonkrution,* German translation of *Textualities: Between Hermeneutics and Deconstruction* by Erik Michael Vogt. Vienna: Turia und Kant.

1998a *Cultural Semiosis: Tracing The Signifier,* ed. Continental Philosophy Series, ed., vol. 6. New York: Routledge.

1998b "Maurice Merleau-Ponty." *Blackwell Encyclopedia of Philosophers.* Oxford: Blackwell, forthcoming.

1999 *Philosophy and Desire,* ed. Continental Philosophy Series, ed., vol. 7. New York and London: Routledge.

2000 *Painting and Truth: Derrida/Heidegger/Kant,* ed. with Wilhelm S. Wurzer. Atlantic Highlands, N.J.: Humanities Press, forthcoming.

# TWENTY

# Andenken and Compassion

# JOAN STAMBAUGH

With regard to my own efforts and where I think philosophy, continental and interdisciplinary, may be able to go in the United States, I would like to discuss briefly Heidegger and Eastern thought. Let me just preface this by saying that I think Michel Foucault's intra/extra-philosophical excursions were the beginning of postmodern thinking in France. Of all the French thinkers I have read, I find Foucault's writings, particularly *Madness and Civilization,* the most fascinating and lucid. Foucault fascinates not because he beguiles but because he is dealing with truly intriguing material in an innovative philosophical way.

Although I studied in Freiburg im Breisgau for nine years, except for a brief introduction on the street I never met Heidegger personally during this period. The cult of foreign students, many of them American, around him was repellent to me. I was content to have heard his last lecture course ("Der Satz vom Grunde") and to study his works. Two years later, after I returned to this country to teach, I thought "Well, why not meet him?" I wrote, identifying myself as best I could, and in August 1966 I went to see him. It was not long after this that Heidegger, through Glenn Gray, requested that I attempt a translation of *Identität und Differenz.* Thereafter, I went to see and work with him every summer until his death in 1976.

I hardly think that Heidegger can be called a pure phenomenologist. Even in *Being and Time,* phenomenology remains for him a method, a how and not a what. The "what," the subject matter in *Being and Time,* is "existential." Death, guilt, Angst and authenticity-inauthenticity hardly belong to pure phenomenology. Unlike his teacher Husserl, Heidegger never bracketed the world and constantly polemicized against a "worldless subject." Later, world, poetically thought as the Fourfold, came to virtually displace the term "being," which was simply too heavily weighted with tradition to be capable of much further fruitful development.

We may have yet to critically assess Heidegger's thought, not only in the later, often cryptic writings (e.g., the *Beiträge*), but even the early ones, including and preceding *Being and Time*. Heidegger ventured out a long way, and even if he did not "succeed" in doing precisely what he set out to do in the exact way he envisioned it, he opened up a vast philosophical terrain. I believe it was Otto Pöggeler who said that Heidegger spent too much time unbuilding or deconstructing the history of philosophy to the neglect of developing his own thinking. Perhaps this is true, but one person can only do so much in a lifetime. What is needed now, however, is not slavish textual exegeses of certain sacred philosophical texts. We have had enough of that. I believe we need to think critically about the texts and teach students to think critically about them.

It is difficult for me to say what there is in Heidegger, particularly in the later Heidegger, that American continental thinkers can pick up on. In my opinion, *Being and Time* got rid of the Cartesian subject-object split and also got rid of the related, equally Cartesian concept of objective presence (*Vorhandenheit*). I do believe that Heidegger got out of, not overcame, metaphysics without selling out to literary criticism. What he called for at the end of philosophy was a new and different kind of thinking: instead of *vorstellen*, representational, calculative, objectifying, reifying substantializing thinking, he practiced *Andenken* and *Besinnung*, a kind of poetic, pondering thinking that does not distort its object, that does not *have* an object at all, but themes, like musical themes. These are unobjectifiable. This kind of thinking has been called in English "meditative thinking." While I do not believe this translation is downright false, it can be misleading. The only sense in which Heidegger comes within shouting distance of the word "meditation"—a term admittedly vague, unspecific, and fraught with its own host of problems—is that he does not think *about*, for example, the thing; he thinks the thing. In other words, the thing presences in his thinking. As Bergson said about his conception of metaphysics, it is "a science that enters into its object as opposed to moving around it." Thinking for Heidegger was essentially *experience*, not in the sense of *Erlebnis* or a kind of thrill-seeking which he abhorred, but in the sense of *Erfahrung*, of literally going through something. He would not call his thinking "meditation," but a specific and rigorous kind of practice. The thinking that he sought to cultivate was *experiential*, not conceptual.

I turn now to the possible significance of Eastern thought for American continental thinkers. As far as I know, up to now any serious treatment of Eastern thought has taken place primarily in the area of religious studies. For instance, there is considerable dialogue taking place between Christian and Buddhist thinkers. A leading figure in this dialogue and a Buddhist scholar, Masao Abe, has devoted a chapter of his book, *A Study of Dogen*, to the problem of time in Heidegger and Dogen. Dogen, a Japanese contemporary of St. Thomas, was, in the opinion of many, the greatest thinker Japan ever produced.

Let me hasten to add that I did not acquire an interest in Eastern thought through Heidegger, Nietzsche, or Schopenhauer. I had access to The Sacred Books of the East as a teenager and, although I am sure that my understanding of these texts was at best minimal, I was irresistibly drawn to them.

As a graduate student in Germany I began the arduous task of trying to learn Sanskrit. After several semesters in Freiburg reading and translating stories and myths about every sort of creature imaginable—birds, insects, all animals, and occasionally a human being—I went to my professor and announced that the time remaining to me in Europe was extremely limited and this particular creature-vocabulary was not exactly what I needed for Indian philosophy. My professor admitted that he had never been able to understand philosophy and that the best person for that was Erich Frauwallner in Vienna. Off I trekked to Vienna for the six months left to me of my scholarship. Professor Frauwallner allowed me to attend all of his courses, which he held in his home, and even tailored a course to my interest in Buddhism. The participants were a couple of assistants and myself.

To return to the question of a possible dialogue between East and West, the point of a dialogue as opposed to an argument is that both sides can learn from each other. For example, the East can learn from the West an emphasis on historical thinking. What can we learn from the East?

At the very least, some kind of unsentimental, unembarrassed "spirituality," for the lack of a better word. From Buddhism, and not only from Buddhism, we can learn something about soteriology, the liberating of human and sentient beings from suffering. Some of the solutions or at least responses to existentialist and psychotherapeutical problems such as *Angst* (Kierkegaard, Heidegger), despair (Kierkegaard, Tillich), the courage to be (Tillich), ontological insecurity (R. D. Laing), to name only a few, can be found in the study and, above all, the practice of Buddhist thinking, attitudes, and ethics. The study alone is not sufficient; these attitudes and modes of existence have to be lived and practiced.

From Buddhism the West could also learn compassion, an attitude advocated in any religion but grossly ignored in most other areas of life, for example, on Wall Street and in law and medicine. Of course there are exceptions, but one has to search long and hard for them. From Taoism we could learn *wu wei*, non-interference, allowing things to be as they are, ceasing to manipulate people and situations.

However, it is not the case that the West has nothing "theoretical" or philosophical to learn from the East. The Buddhists, especially the Yogacara or Mind-only school, have subtle and intricate analyses of consciousness. In his book *The Zen Doctrine of No-Mind,* D. T. Suzuki gives a diagram of the Buddhist scheme of the Unconscious consisting of levels A, B, C, and D. He goes on to say: "In this the Unconscious A, B, and C belong to the transcendental order, and are essentially of one and same nature, whereas the unconscious D is of the empirical mind which is the subject of psychology." He might perhaps have added "of philosophy" with reference to Schopenhauer, Eduard von Hartmann, and the later Sartre who, after initially rejecting any unconscious mind in *Being and Nothingness,* reinstated it in *L'Idiot de la Familie.*

## Selected Bibliography

1959 *Untersuchungen zum Problem der Zeit bei Nietzsche.* The Hague: Nijhoff.

1962 "Thornton Wilder." *Praxis.*

1964a "Das Gleiche in Nietzsches Gedanken der Ewigen Wiederkunft des Gleichen." *Revue internationale de Philosophie* (Brussels).

1964b "Music as a Temporal Form." *Journal of Philosophy.*

1968a "Der Begriff der Vergänglichkeit im Buddhismus." *Acts of the XIV International Congress for Philosophy* (Vienna).

1968b "Geist und Welt." *Acts of the XIV International Congress for Philosophy* (Vienna).

1970 "Commentary on Heidegger and Buddhism." *Philosophy East and West* (July).

1972 *Nietzsche's Thought of Eternal Return.* Baltimore: Johns Hopkins University Press.

1980 "On the Meaning of Ambivalence. *Philosophy Today.*

1983 "The Greatest and Most Extreme Evil." *Philosophy Today* (Fall).

1984 "Emptiness and the Identity of Samsara and Nirvana." *Journal of Buddhist Philosophy* 2.

1986 *The Real Is Not the Rational.* Albany: State University of New York Press.

1987 *The Problem of Time in Nietzsche.* English translation by J. F. Humphrey. Lewisburg, Pa.: Bucknell University Press.

1988 "The Use and Abuse of *The Will to Power.*" In *Reading Nietzsche,* ed. R. C. Solomon and K. Higgins. Oxford: Oxford University Press.

1990 *Impermanence Is Buddha-nature.* Honolulu: University of Hawaii Press.

1991a "The Other Nietzsche." In *Nietzsche and Asian Thought,* ed. Graham Parkes. Chicago: University of Chicago Press.

1991b *Thoughts on Heidegger.* Washington D.C.: University Press of America.

1992 *The Finitude of Being.* Albany: State University of New York Press.

1994a "Philosophy—An Overview." In *The Encyclopedia of Religion,* ed. Mircea Eliade. New York: Macmillan.

1994b *The Other Nietzsche.* Albany: State University of New York Press.

1995 "The Turn." In *Festschrift for William Richardson,* ed. Babette Babich.

1996 *Being and Time.* English translation of *Sein und Zeit* by Martin Heidegger. Albany: State University of New York Press.

1999 *The Formless Self.* Albany: State University of New York Press.

# TWENTY-ONE

## From Seceda to Captiva and More . . .[1]

▉

## WILHELM S. WURZER

In a filmic tour of one's *Lebenswelt,* it is not unusual to interface cities and thoughts, landscape and reflection.

Born in Linz, Austria in 1948, I was drawn to silence early in my childhood because of the immense noise of the reconstruction era that followed World War II. In the early fifties, I was glad to move to Sterzing, Südtirol. For the South Tyroleans, Südtirol—formerly Austrian, now Italian—means paradise on earth. For the UN, it is probably a dissident *promesse du bonheur.* For myself, it was to some extent then, and surely now, a kind of *Heimat,* a peculiar constellation of freedom, wine, and Hexen within the limits of Italianization. Beyond the joyful creativity of its people, beyond quality leather shoes, wines, schnapps, and Leberknödel, alongside South Tyrolian ham, sausage, and bread, there are the Dolomites with their dangerous peaks. Lured to this wide, wild landscape, visitors are astonished by the endless hiking routes, the sublime slopes of forests, the challenging knife-edged cliffs for climbing, the exhilarating possibilities for skiing. *Gemütlichkeit* names not merely the mood of South Tyroleans, but also a distinct feeling of being on the way to the mountains, to the gushing brooks, the cool forests and the heart (*Gemüt*) that appreciates the narrow lanes of arcades, the patrician homes, and the Gothic architecture of such old medieval towns as Brixen.

Upon returning to Upper Austria in the early fifties, I became a student at the old boarding school, Stift Wilhering, indicative of discipline, Latin, music theory, and soccer which was played very near the mighty Danube. I was only there for two years, but I am grateful to its teachers for urging me "to live voluntarily among ice and high mountains—seeking out everything strange and questionable in existence," as Nietzsche says.[2] As a child, I did not appreciate the austere Austrian manner of teaching. Now I have mostly fond memories of Stift Wilhering. In particular, I recall listening to the radio for about fifteen minutes per week. Each Sunday night at 7:45, the director of the school would turn on the radio, and as we lay in bed between wakefulness and sleep, we were permitted to hear murder mysteries. This was indeed an Austrian gesture of freedom, one moment in the destiny of a *homines optimi* education. A decision by my parents to move to Canada ended my experiences at Wilhering. It also marked an unwanted divergence from the German language.

I found Toronto both exciting and challenging. Suddenly, the terrain became technologically more refined. I had to learn another foreign language. English was more difficult to grasp than Italian, which I had learned in South Tyrol. English signified a new beginning, the spectacle of a different world, a certain absence of *das Naturschöne* but nonetheless very ravishing. I met a young Hungarian and together we were amused to observe the frequent blue skies above the waves of Lake Ontario.

When I attended high school in Milwaukee, Wisconsin, in the early sixties, my childhood feelings for South Tyrol vanished. The benign conformism of mainstream American culture overwhelmed me. Some days I escaped into Virgil's *Aeneid* and Aristotle's *Metaphysics;* other days I found comfort in composing folk songs. I was constantly struggling to raise the curtain which kept me from a certain *Heimat.* This curtain was public education, an addiction to the superfluous, to the stupor of suburban consciousness. This unpleasant educational experience made it difficult to remember the rhythmic dance of childhood. While studying at Marquette University, I took Nietzsche's advice to break the windows and leap into freedom. In 1968, I arrived at the University of Freiburg, Germany, hoping to liberate myself from the disenchanting ideologies of the American Midwest.

A different journey begins in Freiburg—the light of new textualities: Plato, Plotinus, Spinoza, and Nietzsche—the genealogy of the art of *Denken,* indebted to Heidegger, to Fink, and, no doubt, to the beauty of the landscape. Freiburg, Heidegger, Nietzsche, and the erotic narratives of Black Forest nights. So much mind, so much body, irresistibly drawn into a magical renaissance, a rigorous source for poetic *Augenschein.* Can one ever forget Freiburg?

My hope of teaching became a reality in the well-known philosophy department at Duquesne University, Pittsburgh. Its graduate program in philosophy bears a strange resemblance to the one at the University of Freiburg. I was fortunate to begin my career in a department steeped in the phenomenological tradition. Surrounded by stimulating colleagues and bright graduate students, it was and still is a pleasure to teach in this unique department and to participate in the flowering of this international university. Duquesne is a community of students, faculty, and administrators from many corners of the world. Here, I have seen the other face of America, the one that looks beyond conformism and the average to a sincere promotion of an international vision of global needs and responsibilities for peace, justice, and freedom. In this kind of atmosphere, I have enjoyed directing more than twenty dissertations on the philosophies of Spinoza, Kant, Nietzsche, Heidegger, and Derrida by such familiar young scholars as Peg Birmingham, Dorothea Olkowski, Vanessa Howle, and James Quick.

In 1990, together with Hugh J. Silverman, I founded the International Philosophical Seminar (IPS). Each summer the IPS brings together a group of highly distinguished scholars in philosophy and literary theory in the pleasant alpine atmosphere of Südtirol. The seminar provides a framework for regarding *Heimat* differently. Beyond ideological residues, it signifies a free environment for *Denken* with a view toward an intensely rigorous "temporalizing," a wide spectrum of voices and thoughts. Südtirol marks *"una piccola terra"* in the typography of diverse philosophers, who are always ready to perform most appropriately by coming-towards (*Zu-kunft*) the "truth" by means of a necessary turn to *Ausflug,* into the open, *im Walde, i monti.* For the IPS, the *Ausflug* is inevitable; it belongs to the philosophical text.

My life too has always belonged to a kind of *Ausflug,* a celebration of concrete displacements, a moving from Linz, Austria to Sterzing, Italy, to Stift Wilhering, Austria, to Toronto, Canada, to Milwaukee, Wisconsin, to Freiburg, Germany, to Pittsburgh, Pennsylvania. Beyond my extended stays in these places, my favorite brief visits have been to Captiva, Florida and Deer Valley, Utah in the winter and St. Ulrich, Südtirol in the summer. A filmic tour, my life is a joining (*Gefüge*) of cities, towns, beaches, mountains, streams, and postmodern moods.

In addition to my professional commitment to philosophy and the liberal arts, I am also dedicated to certain hobbies such as listening to Bruckner and the later Beethoven, reading the *Wall Street Journal,* rereading Baudelaire's *Les Fleurs du Mal,* Rilke's *Migration des Forces,* Wharton's *The Muse's Tragedy and Other Stories* (not necessarily in this order), investing in stocks, hiking in the Dolomites between Seceda and Col Raiser, walking in Sewickley, and, most importantly, skiing. These diversions are closer to *Denken* than one might think. No doubt a striking affinity between "re-creation" and "creation" lies in the unknown outcome of one's activities—the losses and gains, the fallings, some surprising smooth runs, in short, the challenge—quite simply, the spontaneous movements which reveal a fusion of the kinetic and contemplative.

Another allegiance, namely to my parents, Prisca and Stefan Wurzer, has surely affected my life. They have always given freely; they are paragons of patience, kindness, and arduous work. My sisters Jolanda and Helga, too, are very dear to me. And surely, Elizabeth Santos, my wife, an attorney/philosopher, has marked my itineraries, always evoking "truth in travel."

Her intelligence, beauty, and love are a constant inspiration. In addition, my dog Daisy, a boxer, who livens up the day, really does have an eye that sleeps and wakes. And what would life be without my young daughter, Cristiana.

In effect, an alliance of manifold textual voices within and beyond specific textualities shows itself in my work after *Nietzsche und Spinoza,*[3] in a kind of post-Kantian reading of Nietzsche, Heidegger, Foucault, and Adorno. A leading question surfaces, in large measure a coming-together of philosophy and a certain *phainesthai,* which I name "filming." *Filming and Judgment,* therefore, advances an unprecedented reading of judgment as post-phenomenological de-shining.[4] This de-shining ultimately lets capital be seen differently. Let out into a "Rilkean" open, capital emerges as a sublime fissuring beyond Kant's free play of *Einbildungskraft,* indeed beyond "filming" as phantom of a metaphysical coating indicative of Western thought.

There is no anticipation of being, truth, or *telos* in filming. Indeed, it signifies the obliteration of metaphysical anticipations. A concise phenomenology of *Ur-teil* beyond the rhetoric of the visual, in a *logos* that lets Adorno and Heidegger be seen in a purely non-imaginal film, unfolds the intimacy of Critical Theory and deconstruction. This intimacy points back to Kant's *Beurteilung,* not in order to reveal reflective judgment again, but rather to show how the reflective judging that "has been" (transcendental-aesthetic) now arises from how thinking will be as it comes-toward (*Zukunft*) capital.

Accordingly, filming is not the name for producing films but rather a post-aesthetic marking of how thinking may "function." Without anchoring philosophy, filming points to a non-Cartesian eye within the ready-to-hand constellations of imagination, *phainesthai,* and capital. It delights in imaging off images on the way to a new worldhood of judging (*Ur-teil*). To that end, filming begins to think what metaphysics leaves unthought—judgment's *Ab-grund* in relation to a displaced imagination. Consonant with a manner of judging which differs from a dialectical, technical determination of judgment (*Urteilskraft*), filming signifies a poetic rupturing of *Ur-teil.* This brings to view the open strife of imagination as pure work of art, dislodging *Ur* from *teil* in order to unfold a nonimaginal route to such postmodern scenes as the "anti-art" of capital.

*Filming and Judgment* explores a double unfolding of filming in Western culture by illustrating both the illusions of representation from the standpoint of "capital" and the unlimited narrative possibilities of another presentation of capital. Quite simply, it indicates that filming is neither an authentic nor an inauthentic judging. More pointedly, filming exceeds the cinematic displacement of representation in transgressing the boundaries of a free imagination without abandoning a tectonic of judging. Thus it promotes a site in which mimesis is fractured and the old universal concept of capital withdraws from its current particular "infrastructural" content.

*Filming and Judgment* has been reviewed in numerous interdisciplinary journals. On the one hand, it has been characterized as "a remarkable text, fundamentally, deliberately unsettling"; "an original attempt at drawing together postmodernist theory and film"; "a gerund endowed with verbal force, comparable to *writing* (Derrida's *ecriture*)"; "intertextual in a postmodern mode"; "[containing] some extremely profound insights, as in the readings of Kant and Fassbinder"; "an opposition to Baudrillard's aesthetics of excess." On the other hand, it has been described as "somehow symptomatic of the current use and abuse of 'Continental Philosophy'"; "arousing feelings akin to the Terminator . . ."; "this intense study philosophizes with a chain saw"; "the level of discussion tends toward the stratospheric, the kind of poststructuralist star wars that leaves many breathless." In short, the reviews provide a collision of views, evidence at least of the provocative nature of this project. While *Filming and Judgment* was written mostly for philosophers, it appears to be read and reviewed more frequently by literary theorists. I hope that the work's apparent inscription of a new film language does not prevent philosophers from reading it more thoughtfully. While it may be regarded as an interdisciplinary text, its primary concern is to focus more clearly on rewriting the foundations of hermeneutics in relation to post-Heideggerian phenomenology.

In *A Critique of Ethical Indifference (From Kant to Heidegger)*, a work recently completed, I explore the sovereignty of listening, which Heidegger names *sigetics* in *Beiträge zur Philosophie*. What matters here is Heidegger's surprising and unsettling claim that the point of philosophy is not to *question* but to *listen*. Its task is to turn from a dialectic of grasping/controlling the order of words to a bold, provocative way of listening. Paradoxically, this innovative way with language is finally linked to listening to the silent steps of the last god, thereby deepening the poetic experience with language within a dimension of the last (*Ereignis*).

I examine not only the cogency of Heidegger's argument regarding sigetics, but also that of earlier thinkers and poets such as Kant, Hölderlin, Nietzsche, and Rilke, who have thought about sigetics without specifically naming it. I examine these thinkers' departures from Heidegger's position, their reluctance to allow the sigetic dimension to be characterized outside a socio-historical context. In tracing the genealogy of sigetics, I enumerate its importance in relation to contemporary philosophy and literary theory.

This work also addresses the issue of a certain dissatisfaction with Heideggerian phenomenology, namely, what it means to prefer the pure, the authentic, the great, and whether it is legitimate to align these preferences with the philosophical enterprise. After Auschwitz, we cannot afford to ignore the demonic character of purity and the fatal aesthetic seduction of a Heideggerian "stillness" transposed onto an ideology of the best and the greatest. Contrary to what Heidegger might have believed, sigetics can be viewed as resistance against habitual thinking without engaging in a highly exclusive and sometime even perilous treatment of language. Hölderlin, in fact, as this study documents, links the poetic power of the word with ahistorical freedom for all of humankind. Similarly, Kant, Fichte, and even Nietzsche regard language as art without trampling on humanity. Heidegger's poetic styles of thought, on the other hand, turn in part toward the voice of an exclusive *Volk,* a confluence of associations for which he must be held responsible.

This project also highlights sigetics as a prelude to a philosophy of the future. Its importance, both before and after Heidegger, is shown to arise out of a sensitive poetic concern for the textuality of silence. So, from the outset, sigetics concerns "making silence," a distinctive form of yielding to language. Thus beyond hermeneutics, the "quiet problem" of sigetics, which is shown to be more than another linguistic phenomenon, lingers as a question of the meaning of the earth, its concealed voice, its distinctive power of being (*Übermacht*).

Studying the texts of Derrida, Lyotard, and Lacoue-Labarthe quite rigorously and observing the intense events of our infrastructure for the last two decades, I am increasingly motivated by the question, "And what do we want of philosophy?" I believe it must be more than pure textual surging, the eternal return of interpreting the same. With the emergence of modern history in the form of commodity exchange, there appears nothing that the maddening presence of capital cannot re-present. Thus, as Adorno put it, "it might be better to stop talking about the sublime all together."[5] Losing its aesthetic textuality, the transcendental game ends and, paradoxically, as the sublime fades into capital, a new figurability for *Denken* turns out to be more powerful and chilling than Being (*Sein*).

One of philosophy's indispensable tasks, then, is to rewrite Marx by rewriting Derrida under another heading, perhaps that of a certain textual dwelling. Quite plainly, for Derrida, philosophy's responsibility is to think "about the necessity for a new culture, one that would invent another way of reading and analyzing *Capital,* both Marx's book and capital in general; a new way of taking capital into account . . ."[6] This is something I have articulated thematically in *Filming and Judgment,* prior to the appearance of *The Other Heading.*

Now I begin an new alliance with my earlier work, tentatively entitled *Wild Alliances: Timecapital and the New Machine.* I re-examine Heidegger's intriguing concept of *Zuhandenheit* (readiness-to-hand) from the standpoint of a capitalizing temporality—more precisely, from the standpoint of a (wild) transformation of being into capital. This orientation could not have been pursued by Heidegger (even if he had wanted to) precisely because he confined Dasein's most proper ontological performance, namely time, more accurately temporalization (*Zeitigung*), to a transcendental ecstasis. Linking temporality to capital, however, makes it possible to retain an ecstatically open understanding of temporalization without falling into the fascinations of a phenomenological *Sackgasse*.

More pointedly, *Wild Alliances* addresses the issue of transcultural readings of capital, in which wild being is shown to be the free play of unlimited possibilities, not only with regard to a post-aesthetic convergence of satellites, television, fax, cellular telephones, and global computer networks, but also with regard to letting this convergence yield to "critique." A new mood sets in motion the collision of these diverse electronic operations. Its discourse echoes a baffling economy swaying ever so openly from "book to screen," from text to filming, from capitalism to the self-apparition of wild being. More concretely, and in sum, capital signifies for the most part the twilight of its former old and new *Dublette*. Now a peculiar *Zeig-Zeug,* it indicates neither the other nor the self. Nor does it signify a triumph of privatization. As heir of Prometheus, capital may be regarded as the revolution of (dis)continuous alliances, as *disappropriation,* always properly private, yet often properly disclosing problematic electronic convergences.

## Notes

1. Seceda is a pleasant mountain in Gröden, Südtirol. Captiva is familiar to those who prefer "the other Florida" in Florida, a tropical island off the coast of Fort Meyers. I'm captivated by both and separated from them most of the year.
2. *On the Genealogy of Morals; Ecce Homo,* trans. Walter Kaufmann (New York: Vintage Books, 1969), p. 218.
3. (Meisenheim am Glan: Verlag Anton Hain, 1975).
4. *Filming and Judgment: Between Adorno and Heidegger* (Atlantic Highlands, N.J.: Humanities Press, 1990).
5. *Aesthetic Theory,* trans. C. Lenhardt (London: Routledge and Kegan Paul, 1984), p. 283.
6. *The Other Heading,* trans. Pascale-Anne Brault and M. B. Naas (Bloomington: Indiana University Press, 1992), p. 71.

## Selected Bibliography

1975a *Nietzsche und Spinoza*. Meisenheim am Glan: Anton Hain.
1975b "Nietzsche's Dialectic of Intellectual Integrity." *Southern Journal of Philosophy* 13 (2): 235–245.

1977 "Between Idealism and *Dasein:* Friedrich H. Jacobi." *Dialogos* 11 (29–30): 123–136.

1978 "Nietzsche's Return to an Aesthetic Beginning." *Man and World* 11 (1–2): 59–75.

1981 "'Mens et Corpus' in Spinoza and Nietzsche: A Propaedeutic Comparison." *Dialogos* 16 (38): 81–91.

1982 "Crisis in Philosophy." *Journal of Evolutionary Psychology* 7: 34–42.

1983 "Nietzsche's Theory of Hermeneutics." *British Journal* of *Phenomenology* 14 (3): 258–270.

1988a "On the Occlusion of the Subject: Heidegger and Lacan." In *The Horizons of Continental Philosophy*, ed. H. J. Silverman and A. Lingis. Dordrecht: Kluwer Academic Publishers.

1988b "On the Occlusion of the Subject: Heidegger and Lacan." In *Horizons of Continental Philosophy: Essays on Husserl, Heidegger, and Merleau-Ponty*, ed. Algis Mickunas, Theodore Kisiel, and Alphonso Lingis, pp. 168–189. Dordrecht: Nijhoff.

1988c "Postmodernism's Short Letter, Philosophy's Long Farewell." In *Postmodernism and Continental Philosophy*, ed. D. Welton and Hugh J. Silverman, pp. 243–250. Albany: State University of New York Press.

1990a "The Critical Difference: Adorno's Aesthetic Alternative." In *The Textual Sublime*, ed. H. J. Silverman and G. E. Aylesworth. Albany, N.Y.: SUNY Press.

1990b "Filming—Inscriptions of *Denken.*" In *Postmodernism—Philosophy and the Arts*, ed. Hugh J. Silverman, pp. 173–186. Continental Philosophy Series, vol. 3. New York: Routledge.

1990c *Filming and Judgment: Between Heidegger and Adorno.* Atlantic Highlands, N.J.: Humanities Press.

1990d "The Critical Difference: Adorno's Aesthetic Alternative." In *The Textual Sublime*, ed. Hugh J. Silverman and Gary E. Aylesworth, pp. 213–221. Albany: State University of New York Press.

1992 "Nietzsche and the Problem of Ground." In *Antifoundationalism, Old and New*, ed. Beth Singer and Tom Rockmore, pp. 127–142. Philadelphia: Temple University Press.

1993 "History and the End of Politics: Heidegger's Sigetic Venture." In *Politics at the End of History*, ed. F. B. Dasilva and M. Kanjirathinkal. pp. 75–100. New York: Peter Lang.

1994a "Fichte's Parergonal Visibility." In *Fichte, Historical Contexts/Contemporary Controversies*, ed. Daniel Breazeale and T. Rockmore, pp. 211–219. Atlantic Highlands, N.J.: Humanities Press.

1994b "Heidegger und die Enden der Textualität." In *Philosophie und Textualität*, ed. Ludwig Nagl, pp. 139–160. Vienna: Wiener Reihe.

1996 "Heidegger's Silent Inhumanity: To Think the Nobility of Being." In *Martin Heidegger and the Holocaust*, ed. Alan Milchman and Alan Rosenberg. Atlantic Highlands, N.J.: Humanities Press.

1997a "And What Do We Want of Philosophy?" In *Lyotard: Aesthetics and Politics*, ed. Hugh J. Silverman. New York: Routledge.

1997b "Kantian Snapshot of Adorno: Modernity Standing Still." In *The Actuality of Adorno: Critical Essays On Adorno and the Postmodern*, ed. Max Pensky. Albany: State University of New York Press.

1997c ". . . wild being/écart/capital . . ." In *Écart and Différance: Merleau-Ponty and Derrida on Seeing and Writing,* ed. M. C. Dillon. Atlantic Highlands, N.J.: Humanities Press.

1999a "Beyond a Western Aesthetic: Hitchcock's *Vertigo.*" In *Filmästhetik,* ed. Ludwig Nagl. Vol. 10, Wiener Reihe. Vienna: Oldenbourg Verlag.

1999b *Filmen, Kapital und Urteil: Zwischen Heidegger und Adorno,* trans. Erik Vogt. Vienna: Turia + Kant, forthcoming.

2000a *Painting and Truth,* ed. with Hugh J. Silverman. Atlantic Highlands, N.J.: Prometheus Press, forthcoming.

2000b *Visibility and Expressivity,* ed. Evanston: Northwestern University Press, forthcoming.

# TWENTY-TWO

## Between Phenomenology and the Negative's Power

## EDITH WYSCHOGROD

Think for a moment of the Hegelian Absolute not as an ontological and logical vacuum that sucks into itself all that is but rather as the obverse or contesting of a negation, a negation that refers to the non-existence of the totality of the world and to a maximum intensity of disvalue that can be attributed to the world. Imagine the Absolute in a struggle before an abyss best described ontologically as "the weariness of all things" and axiologically as "a striving after wind." I think of my work as inhabiting the discursive space between the two, between the *Phenomenology's* struggle against this non-existence—its efforts at "looking the negative in the face and tarrying with it," as Hegel says—and *Ecclesiastes'* attempt to articulate the extent and power of the negative. I see the task of a postmodern (a)philosophy as deconstructing or disseminating this totalizing Absolute and as the articulation of the abyssal *Urgrund* that the Absolute strives ceaselessly and vainly to overcome. An exposure of the failure of totalizing thought requires turning not to death, or to the difference between Being and beings as Martin Heidegger would have it, for these already are presupposed in the weariness of the world in its worldliness, but to a negation that is ethical.

I have in much of my thinking tried to configure this unstable conceptual situation in four moments of negation: the first as actual nihilatory power, the power to destroy the world's inhabitants through recourse to the twentieth century's techniques of mass extermination, this in conversation with Hegel, Heidegger, and Emmanuel Levinas; the second as an ethical capacity canceling egoity, a breaking into the plenitude of self by another that overrides the self's interests and renders it hostage to the other, this in dialogue with Levinas, Jean-François Lyotard, Maurice Blanchot, and Jean-Luc Marion; the third as the passion and ardor of desire, less as an erotics of present-day sexuality than as the concealed/revealed *dynamis* of certain classical philosophical texts, this in discussion with Jean-Paul Sartre, Jacques Lacan, Gilles Deleuze, Julia Kristeva, Michel de Certeau, Jacques Derrida, and Levinas; and the fourth and most recent as a reconfiguring of the past as a rift that both opens and discloses temporal existence in history and memory, this in exchanges with Edmund Husserl, Heidegger, Levinas, Michel Foucault, and Lyotard.

The first moment in the articulation of negation, man-made mass death as I describe it in *Spirit in Ashes,* begins with the twentieth century's invention of nuclear, biological, and chemical warfare and death and concentration camps. I call the state of affairs in which the effort is made to compress the annihilation of the largest number of persons within the briefest possible time frame, together with the social, political and cultural disruptions this nihilatory process introduces, the death event. In the concentration camps immediate qualitative experience is demythologized into relations of utility and mathematized constructs or numbers so that its inhabitants are treated as commodities, while at the same time the very same inhabitants are re-mythologized as the demonic others. Under the pressure of the confrontation with man-made mass death, Heidegger's ontic/ontological distinction with respect to the encounter with finitude collapses, for what is to count as ontic clue, what as ontological "ground," in the context of Auschwitz?

The logic of the death event is based on the formal structures and abstractions of the Western philosophical imagination now implemented in the sphere of actual world affairs. Thus the negation of a fully immanentized Hegelian Absolute is not simply an abstraction, an exercise in the history of thought, but displays itself in concrete existence, in the earthquakes and upheavals that Nietzsche predicted, manifests itself cognitively as silence and existentially in the death event itself. In Blanchot's depiction of what he calls the disaster, this inexhaustible desolation "does not have the ultimate for a limit but bears the ultimate away."

Against the backdrop of a devastation that Heidegger rightly shows as continuing to grow in our time and that Jean Baudrillard, Mark C. Taylor, and others have exposed as giving rise to the ontology of simulation and hyperreality (images of images), a second order of negation breaches the first in a movement of denegation, or the affirmation of this negation. Such an affirmation does not signal approval of an ontology born with the death of modernity but acquiescence to an inevitability.

In *Saints and Postmodernism,* I develop the second or ethical moment of negation in consonance with Levinas's description of the Other as commanding self-abandonment and as demanding that I become hostage to the Other. But in the light of the postmodernity I have sketched and in contradistinction to Levinas, I am coming less and less to regard the self as a figure of satisfied plenitude, as an egoity, a Cartesian subject. Rather the self is always already fragmented by the trenchant critiques of selfhood beginning in Hume and Nietzsche and continuing in recent French thought and by the death event itself. Efforts to engorge the self by the superstars of world politics and entertainment must be seen against the backdrop of a disseminated *cogito* and the shards of a culture that precludes reassembly. The generosity spurred by the advent of the Other cannot be read as the gift of one's unitary self to the "widow and the orphan," to the vulnerable Other, but as a gift that emanates from an always already broken subject.

I suggested too in *Saints and Postmodernism* that ethics must look not to moral theory nor to a theory of justice but rather to narratives, stories of saints' lives that as yet bear no scars of this new brokenness. These martyred lives will manifest the imprint of earlier hagiographic virtues: generosity, compassion, self-immolation. But the backdrop of the postmodern world— corporeal sufferings endlessly churned out in televised hyperreal simulated appeals—will always contest such compassion. Is this compassion "real"? Is it sufficient unto the need it addresses? Is it honest in the Nietzschean sense or does it conceal the bitterness of *ressentiment*? The fiction of Jean Genet, and in quite different ways the Japanese writers Yukio Mishima and Shisaku Endo, depict both saintly magnanimity and the antinomian fracturing of this saintly generosity by portraying what I call saints of depravity, those who practice unconstrained desire but in whom altruistic impulse remains a driving force. But these writers could not yet have depicted the skin of images diffused across the surface of the globe.

Driven by the problems saintliness raises and still in the context of the ethical moment of negation, I have begun to think and write about the corporeality of asceticism as it might be configured in the framework of a Levinas-like ethics. With Foucault's analyses of sexuality in the classical world in mind, I analyze the Greek view of the body as bound up with a renunciation that arises both in the context of the Platonic and Aristotelian elaborations of *dike* (justice) and in Platonic and neo-Platonic accounts of *eros.* Medieval asceticism, I think, takes up both *dike* and *eros,* and interprets the body's mortification as a preliminary to its becoming a conduit for transcendence. Are the ascetic innovations of medieval religiosity—the practices of the athlete of piety, as St. Simeon is called by Theodoret of Cyrrhus—pre-figurements of a contemporary erotics as depicted by Foucault, Deleuze and Guattari, Baudrillard and others? Or are they the castrati of Nietzsche's *Twilight of the Idols?* Is the self-mortification of a St. Mary the Egyptian or a St. Anthony closer to the desire for alterity than modernity's endless nattering about the erotic that Foucault excoriates? And, if so, how can this be configured in a post-Nietzschean, post-Freudian world without trying (as some have done) to return by way of a postmodernism *pretendu* to a bygone world?

These questions are implicit in the third moment of negation, the negation that is desire, the driving force in much Western philosophical reflection. By attributing a linguistic and textual character to the unconscious, Lacan has created strategies for interpreting ontological and theological texts in a non-reductive, post-Freudian psychological idiom. Texts can then be thought of in an odd way as "having wishes" or "displaying resistances" so that hermeneutical acts become an exposure of the truth of a text's desire.

The ever provocative ontological argument can be treated as a case in point. I have analyzed Anselm's proof as a coming to consciousness of desire, the yearning to know a God who is named at the outset but whose name resists interpretation, a resistance expressed by the voices of the others dredged up from a Lacanian unconscious, the fool, the monk Gaunilon, both of whom frustrate Anselm's yearnings. Anselm must restore each fragment of language they present to the chain of meanings from which it has slipped so that objections can be surmounted and his desire come to expression. Proof grasped in this fashion is not only logical demonstration but a *rite de passage,* the echo of a passion undergone. Anselm must first envisage the possibility that God is not, a kind of agony in the garden that throws him into despair. What if God is only an imaginary object? What if God can never be released into the chain of signifiers as a being having actual existence? What if the being whose existence one ultimately proves is not God, for is not the unconscious the place of discourse of the unattainable Other? Is Anselm not the captive of a never-to-be-resolved difference that will continue to oscillate in the proof: the difference between a highest being and a being such that a greater cannot be conceived? The formal elegance of the proof gives way to its pathos, denial of direct access to the transcendent Other, the source of jouissance. The anguish of Western texts from Plato to the British empiricists and Kant can be exposed by appealing to the not— not possible, not existing, not true—that is intrinsic to the formal structures themselves.

In my most recent thinking I return to the problem of man-made mass death with this question: if the various accounts of truth offered by Western thought are deconstructed, then how is the importunity by the indigent other that her suffering be witnessed in its *Leibhaftigkeit* to be expressed? How is the demand of a Levinasian Ethic of ethics to be met if history cannot be written or memory trusted? And how is one to get around Nietzsche's attack upon memory as the ball and chain of *Nachträglichkeit*?

If, as some would argue, the historical object is indeterminable and history only a philosophy of history, then historians' claims are nothing but the facades of concealed interests. (This is I believe the dilemma that drives Lyotard's herculean efforts to engender justice without universality and makes him a premier thinker of this question). These worries lead directly to the fourth mode of negation, configuring the negation that is the past as the never.

A difficulty intrinsic to the everyday view of history as a record of the past is its underlying assumption that events, memory, and story are, first, distinguishable, and second, sufficiently homologous so that the historian can tell it, the event, as it was, because she (or someone) can remember it. Numerous attacks and not only those that are postmodern in provenance, have undermined the view of truth that sustains this picture. But a difficulty in the commonsense view of history that has gone unnoticed is the interpretation of time as most primordially future time. Heidegger's ecstatic view of time is in accord with this perspective in that he sees the past primarily in future terms. It is as if one were to say: "Even then, in the past, what was of importance was that one always looked ahead, for even then one was always already thrown over the abyss of one's own future nonexistence."

I want to show that the primacy of the past in configuring temporality has been covered up. What has gone by can never be brought back materially: no not, never. Without this negation there can be no sense of passage. "It was" is as an unsurpassable negation that breaks into the materiality of the world. That which opens up through this negation appears to be entitative, the past, but it can only return in word or image. The past as the no, not, never is not one of time's ecstases; it *is* time as the breach opened up by the world between itself and itself in the manner of "It was before but cannot be again." This irrecuperability, this never, can perhaps be lived as a charge the Other places upon me, the imperative of her history that both defies writing and still demands to be written.

I do not yet know how I shall pursue the lure of this question.

## Selected Bibliography

1970 *Emmanuel Levinas: The Problem of Ethical Metaphysics.* The Hague: Nijhoff. Second edition with new introduction, Fordham University Press, forthcoming.

1972 "Emmanuel Levinas and the Problem of Religious Language." *The Thomist* 26 (1): 1–38.

1973a "Death, Sport and the Elemental." In *The Phenomenon of Death: Faces of Mortality,* ed., pp. 166–198. New York: Harper and Row.

1973b *The Phenomenon of Death: Faces of Mortality,* ed. New York: Harper and Row.

1975a "Reply to Approaches to Existence." *Philosophy East and West* 25 (3): 773–778.

1975b "The Concept of the World in Samkara: A Reply to Milton K. Munitz." *Philosophy East and West* 25 (3): 301–308.

1977 "Romantic Consciousness and Biblical Theology." In *Auschwitz: The Beginning of a New Era?*, ed. Eva Fleischner, pp. 331–342. New York: Ktav.

1978a "Death and Some Philosophies of Language." *Philosophy Today* 22 (4): 255–265.

1978b "Sons without Fathers: A Study in Identity and Culture." *Journal of the American Academy of Psychoanalysis* 6 (2): 249–262.

1980a "Concentration Camps and the End of the Life-World." *Centerpoint: A Journal of Interdisciplinary Studies* 4 (1): 32–41. Reprinted in *The Holocaust: Its Impact on Philosophy*, ed. Alan Rosenberg and Gerald Meyers. Philadelphia: Temple University Press, 1987; and in *Thinking through Death*, ed. Scott Kramer and Kuang-Ming Wu. Melbourne, Fla.: Krieger, 1989.

1980b "Doing before Hearing: On the Primacy of Touch." In *Textes Pour Emmanuel Levinas*, ed. FranHois Laruelle, pp. 179–203. Paris: Jean Laplace.

1980c "Martin Buber and the No-Self Perspective in Nietzsche and Buddhism." In *History, Religion and Spiritual Democracy: Essays in Honor of Joseph T. Blau*, ed. Maurice Wohlgelernter, pp. 130–135. New York: Columbia University Press.

1980d "The Moral Self: Emmanuel Levinas and Hermann Cohen." *Daat: A Journal of Jewish Philosophy* 4: 35–58.

1981a "Empathy and Sympathy as Tactile Encounter." *Journal of Medicine and Philosophy* 6 (1): 23–41.

1981b "Is Man Infinite? A Phenomenological Perspective." In *Proceedings of the American Catholic Philosophical Association* 55: 99–107.

1981c "The Civilizational Perspective in Comparative Studies of Transcendence." In *Transcendence and the Sacred: Proceedings of the Boston University Colloquium on Philosophy and Religion*, pp. 58–79. Notre Dame: Notre Dame University Press.

1981d "The Logic of Artifactual Existents: John Dewey and Claude Levi-Strauss." *Man and World* 14 (3): 235–250.

1982 "God and 'Being's Move' in the Philosophy of Emmanuel Levinas." *Journal of Religion* 62 (2): 145–155.

1983a "From Being to Meaning: Toward a Phenomenological Hermeneutic," a review of Paul Ricoeur, *Hermeneutics and the Human Sciences: Essays on Language, Action and Interpretation*, ed. John B. Thompson. Cambridge: Cambridge University Press, 1981, *Semiotica* 44 (3–4): 371–382.

1983b "Time and Non-Being in Derrida and Quine." *Journal of the British Society for Phenomenology* 14 (May): 112–126.

1985a "Plato and Some Surrogates in a Jain Theory of Knowledge." In *Civilizations East and West: A Memorial Volume for Benjamin Nelson*, ed. E. V. Walter, pp. 73–89. Atlantic Highlands, N.J.: Humanities Press.

1985b *Spirit in Ashes: Hegel, Heidegger and Man-Made Mass Death*. New Haven: Yale University Press. Paperback ed., 1989.

1986a "Exemplary Individuals: Towards a Phenomenological Ethics." *Philosophy and Theology: Marquette University Quarterly* 1 (1) (Fall): 9–31.

1986b "On Deconstructing Theology: A Symposium on *Erring: A Post-modern A/Theology* by Mark C. Taylor," ed. with a response, "Crossover Dreams." *Journal of the American Academy of Religion* 54 (3): 523–524, 543–547.

1988a "From the Disaster to the Other: Tracing the Name of God in Levinas." In *Phenomenology and the Numinous: The Fifth Annual Symposium of the Simon*

*Silverman Phenomenology Center*, pp. 67–86. Pittsburgh: Duquesne University Press.

1988b Review essay of Mark C. Taylor, *Altarity*. *Journal of the American Academy of Religion* 56 (1) (Spring): 115–130.

1989a "Derrida, Levinas and Violence." In *Derrida and Deconstruction*, pp. 182–200. Continental Philosophy Series, ed. Hugh J. Silverman, vol. 2. New York: Routledge.

1989b *Lacan and Theological Discourse*. Ed. with David Crownfield and Carl Raschke. Albany: State University of New York Press.

1989c "Man-Made Mass Death and Changing Concepts of Selfhood." In *Freedom*, ed. Alan M. Olson, Vol. 5, Boston University Series in Philosophy and Religion, pp. 180–197. Notre Dame: University of Note Dame Press.

1989d "Man-Made Mass Death: Shifting Concepts of Community." *Journal of the American Academy of Religion* 58 (2): 165–176. (Text of plenary address, American Academy of Religion, November 1989.)

1989e "Recontextualizing the Ontological Argument." In *Lacan and Theological Discourse*, ed. with David Crownfield and Carl Raschke, pp. 97–118. Albany: State University of New York Press.

1990a *Saints and Postmodernism: Revisioning Moral Philosophy*. Chicago: University of Chicago Press.

1990b "Works That 'Faith'": The Grammar of Ethics in Judaism." *Cross Currents: Religion and Intellectual Life* 40 (2): 176–193.

1991 Review Essay on Robert C. Neville, *Recovery of the Measure*. In *Journal of Speculative Philosophy* 5 (3): 212–218.

1992a "Does Continental Ethics Have a Future?" In *Ethics and Danger: Essays on Heidegger and Continental Thought*, ed. Arleen B. Dallery et al., pp. 229–242. Albany: State University of New York Press.

1992b "How to Say No in French: The Lineage of Negative Theology in Derrida." In *Negation and Theology*, ed. Robert C. Scharlemann, pp. 39–55; response to queries, pp. 131–136. Charlottesville: University Press of Virginia.

1993a "From Ethics to Language: The Imperative of the Other." Review essay of *Re-Reading Levinas*, ed. Robert Bernasconi and Simon Critchley, *Semiotica* 97 (1/2): 163–176.

1993b Introduction and afterword for symposium, "Trends in Postmodern Jewish Thought." *Soundings* 76 (1) (Spring): 129–137; 191–196.

1993c "Killing the Cat: Beauty and Sacrifice in the Novels of Genet and Mishima." *Theology and Literature* 25 (2): 105–119.

1993d "Mind of the Critical Moralist: George Steiner as Jew." *New England Review* 15 (2): 168–88. Reprinted in *Reading George Steiner*, ed. Nathan A. Scott, Jr., and Ronald A. Sharp, pp. 151–179. Baltimore: Johns Hopkins University Press, 1994.

1994a "Facts, Fiction, Ficciones: Truth in the Study of Religion." American Academy of Religion 1993, Presidential Address. *Journal of the American Academy of Religion* 62 (1): 1–16.

1994b "History, Memory, Revelation: Writing the Dead Other." *Archivio di Filosofia*, proceedings of conference of Instituto di Studi Filosofici "Enrico Castelli," Rome, Italy, 62, no. 1–3: 113–126.

1994c "Tainted Greatness: Depravity and Sacrifice in Genet." In *Tainted Greatness*, ed. Nancy Harrowitz, pp. 253–276. Philadelphia: Temple University Press.

1995a "The Howl of Oedipus, the Cry of Heloise: From Asceticism to Postmodern

Ethics." In *Asceticism,* ed. Vincent L. Wimbush and Richard Valantasis. Oxford: Oxford University Press.

1995b "Taking the Low Road: Postmodernism and Interreligious Conversation." A symposium on Robert Neville's theology. *American Journal of Theology and Philosophy* 16 (2): 189–198.

1995c "The Art in Ethics: Aesthetics, Objectivity and Alterity in the Philosophy of Emmanuel Levinas." In *Ethics as First Philosophy,* ed. Adriaan Peperzak, pp. 137–148. New York: Routledge.

1996a "Hellenism, Hasidism, Holocaust: A Postmodern View." In *Interpreting Judaism in a Postmodern Age,* ed. Steven Kepnes, pp. 301–324. New York: New York University Press.

1996b "Towards a Postmodern Ethics: Corporeality and Alterity." In *Ethics and Aesthetics: The Moral Turn in Postmodernism,* ed. G. Hoffman and A. Hornung. Heidelberg: Winter.

1996c "The Demise of the Aufhebung and the Rise of the Between: From Ethics to Philosophy of Religion in Martin Buber." Proceedings of conference of Instituto di Studi Filosofici "Enrico Castelli," Rome, Italy, 63, no. 1–3: 727–746.

1998 *The Ethics of Remembering: History, Heterology and the Nameless Others.* Chicago: University of Chicago Press.

# CONTRIBUTORS

DEBRA BERGOFFEN is Professor of Philosophy and Director of the Women's Research and Resource Center at George Mason University.

ROBERT BERNASCONI is Moss Professor of Philosophy at the University of Memphis.

JOHN D. CAPUTO is the David R. Cook Chair of Philosophy at Villanova University.

EDWARD S. CASEY is Professor and Chair of Philosophy at the State University of New York, Stony Brook.

BERNARD FLYNN is Professor of Philosophy at Empire State College.

THOMAS R. FLYNN is Samuel Candler Dobbs Professor of Philosophy at Emory University.

PATRICK A. HEELAN is the William A. Gaston Professor of Philosophy at Georgetown University.

DOUGLAS KELLNER is Professor of Philosophy at the University of Texas at Austin.

JOSEPH J. KOCKELMANS is Emeritus Professor of Philosophy at Pennsylvania State University.

DAVID FARRELL KRELL is Professor of Philosophy and Director of the Humanities Center at DePaul University.

DAVID MICHAEL LEVIN is Professor of Philosophy at Northwestern University.

ALPHONSO LINGIS is Professor of Philosophy at Pennsylvania State University.

BERND MAGNUS is Professor of Philosophy at the University of California, Riverside.

DAVID RASMUSSEN is Professor of Philosophy at Boston College.

WILLIAM J. RICHARDSON is Professor of Philosophy at Boston College.

JOHN SALLIS is Liberal Arts Professor of Philosophy at Pennsylvania State University.

CALVIN O. SCHRAG is the George Ade Distinguished Professor of Philosophy at Purdue University.

CHARLES E. SCOTT holds the Edwin Erle Sparks Chair in Philosophy at Pennsylvania State University.

HUGH J. SILVERMAN is Professor of Philosophy and Comparative Literature at the State University of New York, Stony Brook.

JOAN STAMBAUGH is Professor of Philosophy at Hunter College of the City of New York.

WILHELM S. WURZER is Professor and Chair of Philosophy at Duquesne University.

EDITH WYSCHOGROD is J. Newton Razor Professor of Philosophy and Religion at Rice University.

JAMES R. WATSON is Professor of Philosophy at Loyola University, New Orleans. He is coeditor (with Alan Rosenberg) of *Contemporary Portrayals of Auschwitz and Genocide: Philosophical Challenges.*